BRITISH CINEMA

Studio head and star: Michael Balcon with Jessie Matthews

BRITISH CINEMA

THE LIGHTS THAT FAILED

JAMES PARK

B.T. Batsford Ltd, London

*This book is dedicated to the memory
of my father, John Gavin Park*

By good movies I do not mean movies that meet some esoteric standards, but those presenting situations and ideas that induce the spectator to re-examine his life and its purposes. Out of the experience, he may arrive at spontaneous new decisions about himself and his way of life, decisions that awaken in him, or encourage him to persist in, the elusive search for meaning and the widening of his consciousness of freedom.

Bruno Bettelheim

One's favourite films are one's unlived lives, one's hopes, fears, libido. They constitute a magic mirror, their shadowy forms are woven from one's shadowy selves, one's limbo loves.

Raymond Durgnat

© James Park 1990
First published 1990

All rights reserved. No part of this publication may be reproduced, in any form or by any means, without permission from the publishers.

ISBN 0 7134 6698 7

Typeset by
Lasertext, Stretford, Manchester

Printed in Great Britain by
Courier International, Tiptree, Essex
for the publishers
B.T. Batsford Ltd
4 Fitzhardinge Street
London W1H 0AH

Cover illustrations (*clockwise from top left*): criminal action in George Pearson's *Ultus* (1915); Alec Guinness in *Kind Hearts and Coronets* (1949); Micha Bergese in *The Company of Wolves* (1984); courtesy of BFI Stills, Posters andDesigns.

Contents

List of Abbreviations   6

Acknowledgements   7

Preface   8

Introduction: Brief Moments   12

1 Beginning Behind   18

2 Transition   26

3 Reaching England   41

4 Dark Conflicts   66

5 Indian Summer   88

6 Dirty Words and Pop   106

7 Descending Spiral   128

8 The Light Brigade   143

9 The Goldcrest Films   159

Conclusion   168

Appendix: Dance with a Stranger   174

Notes   185

Bibliography   187

Index   188

List of Abbreviations

ABPC   Associated British Picture Corporation

ACC   Associated Communications Corporation

ACT   Association of Cinematograph Technicians

ACTT   Association of Cinematograph, Television and Allied Technicians

AFD   Associated Film Distributors

AFM   Allied Filmmakers

AIP   Association of Independent Producers

ATP   Associated Talking Pictures

BBFC   British Board of Film Censors

BFI   British Film Institute

BIP   British International Pictures

CFC   Cinematograph Films Council

FBI   Federation of British Industries

GFD   General Film Distributors

MOI   Ministry of Information

MPPC   Motion Picture Patents Company

NFFC   National Film Finance Corporation

NFS   National Film School

NFTS   National Film and Television School

TESE   Thorn EMI Screen Entertainment

Acknowledgements

The argument of this book draws heavily on the work of many film historians. I am particularly indebted to the following for the stimulation their writings provided: Robert Murphy, Charles Barr, Jeffrey Richards, Raymond Durgnat, Tony Aldgate and the late Rachael Low. I would also like to thank Susan Boyd-Bowman for putting up with my ravings during a BFI Summer School, and those people with whom I have discussed the contemporary realities of British filmmaking over the past ten years, particularly David Puttnam, Stephen Woolley, Don Boyd, Peter Greenaway, Alan Parker, Michael Radford, Roland Joffé, Julien Temple, Paul Mayersberg, Peter Sainsbury, Al Clark, Roger Randall-Cutler, Michael Newell, Neil Jordan, Jake Eberts, James Lee, Sandy Lieberson and Bill Gavin.

This book would not have been written without the help and encouragement of my flat-mate, Ondine Upton.

I would also like to express my gratitude to the staff of the BFI Library. Film stills appear by courtesy of the Stills Division of the National Film Archive.

Some of the illustrations in this book come from stills issued to publicize films made or distributed by the following companies: Anglo-Amalgamated, The Archers, Associated British, Atlantic Film Distributors, The Boultings, BFI Distribution, British Lion, CCW, CEW, Central Television, Channel Four Productions, Columbia, Crawford Films, Ealing, EMI, Exclusive, Gainsborough, Gaumont British, General Film Distributors, Goldcrest, Hammer Films, HandMade Films, Harma, Independent Artists, ITC Productions, Indo-British, London Films, Palace Pictures, Pathé, Rank, Twentieth Century Fox, Two Arts, UIP, Umbrella Films, United Artists, Universal, Virgin, Warner Brothers.

Although every attempt has been made to trace the present copyright holders of photographs, the author and publishers apologize in advance for any unintentional omission or neglect and will be pleased to insert the appropriate acknowledgement to the companies concerned in any subsequent edition of this book.

Preface

It was in the winter of 1985 that I had my first experience of a full-blown British film crisis. During six years as a film reporter I had heard a lot about previous traumatic periods in the industry's history: Black November when not a single film went before the cameras; the financial panic of 1938 that toppled the flamboyant Hungarian-born producer Alexander Korda from control of his own studio; the disastrous consequences of a botch-up in communication between the industry and government some three years after the end of the Second World War, and the day the Americans packed up and went home at the end of the 1960s. Nevertheless, I was totally unprepared to look on as the company I had seen grow out of small beginnings reeled from the consequences of having spent too much money on movies that really weren't very good, and a British corporation with over 50 years of filmmaking activity to its credit was asset-stripped by two producers from Israel.

Watching the scavengers pick over the wreckage of these two companies, Goldcrest and Thorn-EMI Screen, was a particularly gloomy experience, especially as there were other reasons for being downhearted. Only a couple of years earlier I had written a book, *Learning to Dream: The New British Cinema*, in which I expressed considerable optimism about the likely achievements of a new generation of film directors, people such as Neil Jordan, Michael Radford and Roland Joffé. While the companies were collapsing in ruins, these directors seemed to be having considerable difficulty living up to the expectations created by their first films.

Reflecting on what had gone wrong, I became increasingly disturbed by indications of fatalism in the remarks of many involved in the recent events. A comment made by the producer David Puttnam to the journalist Sue Summers was typical:

> Maybe we lied to ourselves, because it helped, at a particular moment, to believe that what was happening was really significant, and that it had the potential to last, rather than being an ephemeral moment like all the others. But it's just an echo of the history of the British film business. It's never been a real industry, just the story of a few individuals.[1]

Puttnam had every reason to be depressed. He had traded on his public image as the producer who got the British film industry moving with his 1981 film *Chariots of Fire*, and now the whole thing was coming apart. He was not only

Hugh Hudson sizes up Brad Davis, the American runner in
Chariots of Fire **(1981)**

a board member at Goldcrest, the company that was going under, but also coproducer of one of the films whose escalating budgets had given Goldcrest its terminal headache. Arguably, he was also in a position to have a deeper knowledge than I did of what had actually happened. Nevertheless, I just couldn't see it his way, not at all.

If Goldcrest had landed itself in trouble, it was through making a series of silly mistakes, culminating in the commitment to make three films from unsatisfactory scripts on inflated budgets. While one could argue that these errors flowed from the frustrations experienced by any British company entering into competition with the American majors, it seemed to me nonsense to declare that the latest film industry crisis was inevitable, and unfair to explain away the mistakes made by the managements of either Goldcrest or TESE by reference to the earlier misadventures of Cecil Hepworth, Alexander Korda, J. Arthur Rank, Michael Balcon or Bryan Forbes.

For Puttnam and others, the appeal to history was an excuse for not thinking too deeply about what had gone wrong, and why. That refusal was universal among British filmmakers, and the reasons for it lie deep in their psyches. Because of the external pressures operating on the British film industry, filmmakers look at its problems as something they can do little about. They will happily lament Hollywood's domination over the nation's screens, the greater resources available to the American majors, the power of Britain's exhibition duopoly or unfair competition from television, and they'll ask government to sort out the mess. What they won't do is apply their minds to the question of what filmmakers could do to improve the situation.

This lack of positive thinking was very evident after the Goldcrest débâcle. Another producer, Otto Plaschkes, remarked:

> We should cover the cricket pitch for the time when rain stops and play can recommence. When the government changes, we can seek some serious finance. If you believe in film as a popular art and a wonderful way of showing the flag, it is possible to believe that a different government will support it.[2]

Plaschkes was not to know at the time just how long it would be before 'play' could indeed recommence – it wasn't until mid-1990 that the Prime Minister discovered how sick the film industry had become; she invited a group of leading producers and directors to come for a chat. But one does have to ask whether filmmakers waiting for the government to change are going to be adventurous in exploring the opportunities that do exist and any new openings that appear. It's possible to admire the enormous contribution state funding has made to Britain's theatre and opera, even to wish for an enlarged area of state-funded production in the UK, but also feel it's the whingeing of film producers that has so often given the industry its lame-duck appearance. 'The way people bleated,' remarked film financier John Reiss in 1985, 'one would think the film industry was dead.'[3]

Crisis is an endemic condition in any film industry. Production companies have to invest considerable sums of money in untried products, then pitch them at a public whose tastes are constantly shifting. What is particular about the British film industry is not the frequency of its crises so much as the lack of resolution with which they are greeted. People will lament the film industry's sorry condition, but they won't look to see if they can learn anything from what has happened about how to ensure economic survival and creative vitality in the future.

Puttnam may see the history of British filmmaking as 'just the story of a few individuals', but what has sometimes made it possible for a group of directors, producers and writers to achieve creative heights are shifts in the structure of the industry or general cultural attitudes. My purpose in researching this book was to explain those brief moments when British filmmaking flourished, and why they came to so abrupt an end. Why, for example, did a group of directors who concurrently produced a series of striking films go on and, only a few years later, turn out a string of duds? What was the relationship between the development of a few ambitious companies and the flowering of creative talent? What factors encouraged bold, exciting commercial filmmaking, and what led to the sort of films that dragged the companies which made them into oblivion?

British Cinema: The Lights that Failed will have achieved its goal if it stimulates the sort of debate among filmmakers that ensures the outcome 'next time' is very different from what happened 'last time', or even the 'time before'.

Introduction:
Brief Moments

The national character is often blamed for the mediocrity of British movies. Either it's argued that British life doesn't show up well in front of a film camera, or that British filmmakers aren't capable of using that camera to probe behind the surface of things. In either case, the problem with British movies is seen as British inhibition. The nation's filmmakers, like its people, can't express emotion; they lack drive and passion, they're tame and repressed. As a result, the British can write novels and plays, even produce an occasional world-class painter but, when it comes to cinema, they might as well forget it.

Much British cinema does lack emotional punch, and many screen Englishmen conceal their feelings so effectively beneath a stiff upper lip that it's fair to ask whether they're really human at all. Nevertheless, there are many films that undermine this argument, suggesting that British character won't do as an explanation of poor filmmaking. Cinema may come more naturally to driven Americans, bustling Italians or even philosophically-minded Frenchmen but, when British filmmakers actually confront their national inhibitions, amazing things do happen. Films as varied as *The 39 Steps*, *The Wicked Lady*, *Brief Encounter*, *The Red Shoes*, *The Fallen Idol*, *The Spanish Gardener*, *Accident*, *The Draughtsman's Contract*, *Another Time, Another Place* and *A Fish Called Wanda* are exciting precisely because they work to expose the social and cultural constraints to the expression of emotion, showing up the tension between the bland exterior and the seething interior. Inhibition has been seen as the insoluble problem of British movies: it could be represented as the source of their great potential.

The great British films all tap into a problem, the gap between what is felt and what can be expressed, that is universal but gains a particular inflection from being seen in the British context. While these pictures articulate the vision of directors like Alfred Hitchcock, Carol Reed, Michael Powell and David Lean, or writers like Noël Coward, Graham Greene, Emeric Pressburger and Harold Pinter, the films were made possible by production contexts that encouraged these talented individuals to engage with questions that others simply skated over. British films are too rarely good, not because of national character, but because of a production system that is inadequate to the task of generating a regular output of full-blooded films.

Filmmaking is such an enormously complex process that it's almost impossible for the outsider to apportion blame for the success or failure of a particular project. Unless you were there, you can't know whether a film's failings should be attributed to the writer's incompetence or the director simply misunderstanding the script. Perhaps the producer hurried the film prematurely into production, or the director didn't carry out the necessary preparation. The lighting cameraman may have been going through a bad patch, or simply been driven crazy by the sort of director who can't make up their mind about anything. It may have been that the editor didn't know how to cut a scene, or that the financiers called in a hack to re-edit the picture. Critics are free to express opinions on such matters, but most of what you hear is pure speculation.

What one knows is that, when a film works, it's because writer, director and producer were working in harmony and could inspire everybody else on the project with their joint vision. So when one producer or studio is responsible for a string of hits, it's only necessary to find out what distinguishes its operation from that of other, less successful, operations, or what has changed when the same producer or studio hit a bum run, to discover what makes for successful film production.

People have always needed to believe that individuals make films. Otherwise, how would producers know what to buy, PR people what to sell, or critics whom to idolize. If one believes that the director did it, then giving credit, or distributing blame, is a reasonably simple matter. Just pluck the name from a film's credits, and forget the rest of the list. The result is that there isn't really a model which describes filmmaking in its full complexity. Most accounts assume it's a director's medium, in which the writer merely provides raw material and the producer a certain amount of logistical backup, enabling directors to put their vision on the screen. Alternatively, filmmaking is seen as a sort of relay race in which each member of the creative team has control of certain moments – the producer handing over to the writer, who hands over to the director, who hands over to the lighting cameraman and so on until everything comes back to the producer again. The assumption here is that the more quality names you have in the race, the more likely the product is to be of high calibre.

In reality, no concatenation of highly talented individuals ever made a great film. More important than the qualifications of the artists and technicians working on the film is the creative environment in which they operate, and the way it organizes their collaborations. Filmmaking is really a group activity. It works when those involved play well off each other, helping individuals to realize their strengths. Bad films emerge from creative anarchy which brings out the weaknesses of those involved.

Precisely because relationships are so fragile, it's in the planning stages, when a bundle of ideas and concepts are hammered out into a script, that the battle for a film is won or lost. Long before the director first calls 'Action', or anybody has to worry about time, money, the weather or an irritable starlet, the producer, director and writer can sort out the lineaments of the project by focusing on what the film is trying to do, and how it can be made to work. From a good script will emerge a film in which every scene carries an emotional charge, involving the audience in the experience of the characters on the screen while also moving the film forward. A badly-planned script, by contrast, necessarily leads to a badly-organized film, and the only reason anyone thinks otherwise is because so much seems to be going on during the shooting stage – money is spent, crowds of extras run in front of the cameras, tempers become heated and everybody becomes very tired – that the person trying to control this chaos appears to the casual observer as the only significant creative force.

The original *auteur* theory sought to explain how a director could make a distinctive body of work within a filmmaking system, the Hollywood studios, whose factory-like production processes seemed designed to crush out individuality. But the same evidence could have led to a theory celebrating the system which, by laying down norms, establishing disciplines and, most important of all, providing scripts that, while not always particularly imaginative, were at least a sound basis to work from, *enabled* these directors to realize their individual vision. When the studio system collapsed, many of the directors who had flourished within it found themselves unable to impose themselves on a process that too easily slipped out of their control.

There were British studios, like Rank's Independent Producers or Ealing in the 1940s, that, for a time at least, produced a similarly productive working environment, providing constraints for directors and writers to work against, and dedicated script departments which produced competent material for them to work from. In each case the studios were able to produce a steady supply of good, sometimes amazing, films. Too often, however, producers have not even got to first base, because the requirements for evolving strong scripts have been so poorly understood.

Writing, it's true, isn't thought of as one of the problems of British cinema. It's the one thing the nation that produced Shakespeare (albeit 400 years ago!) thinks it can do rather well. But writing *screenplays* is something the British do very badly indeed. Outside the script departments of a few studios, too many producers have taken lazy routes to their scripts. They have relied upon the ideas of novelists and playwrights with no deep interest in cinema, or the work of second-raters who might have produced something good if they had worked within a more stimulating environment, but never had the chance. Or worse, they have simply transposed plays and novels to the screen, producing work at so many removes from the original stimulus to creation that the prospect of the finished film having any appeal to a contemporary audience was almost non-existent.

One could argue that British inhibition has played a part in the poverty of British scripts. Perhaps the gentlemanly tradition that prevailed at some British studios was less stimulating than the rebarbative climate created by Hollywood moguls. Or producers have not been sufficiently provocative and challenging in their discussions with screenwriters, failing to generate the levels of energy required to maximize a script's possibilities. Perhaps the undramatic cosiness so often depicted on the screen is only a symptom of an unproductive cosiness in British film production.

But the poor organization of British production is a direct consequence of the way British filmmakers have felt their inferiority to both the American film industry and American cinema. This inferiority problem is shared with most film cultures, but the British felt it particularly hard because the two nations' cultural and economic histories were so closely entwined. From early on, Hollywood used British stories and lured British actors, later also directors and technicians, across the Atlantic, while making a mint out of British cinemagoers and developing strategies to drive the local product off the nation's screens. Since the early 1920s, therefore, it has been impossible to talk about any aspect of British cinema without drawing unfavourable comparisons with Hollywood. The thrusting, dynamic and optimistic Americans made the nostalgic and pessimistic British feel rather sorry for themselves.

Instead of seeing Hollywood as a powerful rival to be confronted and challenged, British producers have too often looked upon the US film industry as a much-wooed lady who will one day fall into their arms. After all, because of a shared language, no barrier need prevent British films from having the same universal appeal as Hollywood products. Don't we have a kinship with the Americans, the 'Transatlantic branch' of our race? Wouldn't American distributors welcome the opportunity to diversify their product range with some little English films? Such thinking has generally been wrong on every count. At least two-thirds of Americans have never had any reason to think of the British as their Anglo-Saxon cousins; the East European émigrés who ran the studios were no more likely than their successors to look upon British producers as partners, and nobody would queue to see a film just because it was British.

So strong was the filmmakers' infatuation with Hollywood that they were unable to work from an understanding of the situation that faced them, and develop British cinema according to its own economic and cultural realities. For the most part, Hollywood has set the agenda. Not so much in the earliest days, when US producers had not yet sufficiently geared themselves up to satisfy the demands of their market, so that British exports to the States were largely unproblematic. But, as soon as American distributors no longer needed British films, and the local producers had started to make longer films, the quality of British filmmaking nosedived. UK filmmakers abandoned their innovations with film narrative, producing instead dull, static recordings of theatrical productions in order to secure pictures of the required length. The new generation of producers that subsequently emerged came to believe it was possible for the British film industry to 'take on' the Americans, although this grand ambition had more to do with a desire to efface their inferiority complex than any serious resolve to face reality. Meanwhile, the aspiration further skewed the industry. Open field sites in the vicinity of London were taken over for the construction of studios in the belief that it was heaps of brick and iron rather than organizational flair that explained the success of Louis B. Mayer or Samuel Goldwyn. And the production of numerous low-budget pictures stimulated by the Cinematograph Act of 1927 – passed to get the film industry moving again – was treated, for the most part, not as an opportunity to experiment with new styles and cultivate new talent, but as an occasion for allowing mediocrities to make low-budget versions of Hollywood pictures.

British cinema increasingly became a bargain-basement imitation of Hollywood. Instead of five large companies dominating production, distribution and exhibition, as in the US, it had two, Rank and ABPC. Producers were so busy fighting their own corner, and so mesmerized by the success of Hollywood, that they didn't have the strength to argue that keeping the industry fragmented and flexible, learning from Hollywood's example without simply imitating its outward forms, might be a better way of catering for a market the size of Britain than heading up the road of monopoly. Even today, when the tottering of a Goldcrest or TESE is taken as a sign that the film industry is going under, it's assumed that big companies are the key to surviving in the film business, because that's the way they do things in LA.

The American connection has also disfigured the debate about what sort of films British producers should be making. When, in the late 1920s, a critical backlash developed against films that made themselves vacuous in an attempt to match Hollywood styles, the only way people could think of doing it was to define British cinema as the *opposite* of Hollywood – abandoning melodrama and flamboyance for realism, restraint and understatement. British filmmakers have been struggling ever since with the conflicts created by this critical manoeuvre. Should they be making low-budget films pitched largely at the local market and emphasizing their Britishness, as the critics demand, or big films on the Hollywood model for the world? Does being true to oneself, and not selling out to Hollywood, really mean abandoning melodrama for realism, showmanship for seriousness, spectacle for solemn emotion, tight scripts for improvised styles? Too often the choice for the British filmmaker has seemed to lie between critical approval combined with minimal box office or going all-out to emphasize the most garish, flamboyant and parochial aspects of popular cinema.

The best British films have always been those that transcended these artificial oppositions. Made without unnecessary extravagance but containing action, spectacle and visual magic, they are films that spring out of the native culture but articulate a broad vision that can ring chords wherever they are shown. They contain the sort of resonant imagery and psychological complexity one associates with the most determined European cinema, but within strong narratives that recall the best Hollywood films.

Producing films at that level requires a stronger nerve than British producers have generally shown. The important British companies, from Korda's London Films to Goldcrest, have attracted capital at a point where they seemed to understand the economic need to balance Hollywood extravagance with a strong dose of parsimony, but all have ended up committing suicide by spending huge sums of money on attempts to emulate Hollywood. No longer able to live with the difficulties inherent in producing films from a British base, they lost touch with reality and discarded common-sense. Still able to see the problem, they no longer knew where to find its solution, and seemed happy in consequence to embrace their own annihilation. Having started off making a big success with a little film, they ended up spending increasingly larger sums of money on bigger films until they had expended so much of their capital they could only go under. The first success disproved the thesis they ended up trying to vindicate, and they progressively discarded financial sanity in a crazy attempt to blot out the problems from their minds.

British filmmakers have always needed to face two ways, inwards towards the hopes and fears of the native audience to which they must address their pictures, and out to a broader, international public. Unable to develop an idea of filmmaking that was both British *and* international, they concentrated their energies on defining their position on either side of that spectrum, and lost any sense of what cinema really is for. 'I was fed up with English filmmakers who seemed to think that they were automatically entitled to have a film industry'[1] Michael Powell has remarked of the situation in the late 1930s. He went on to demonstrate, as Hitchcock had done earlier, just what a British international film industry would look like. Too few filmmakers have recognized that the argument for a British cinema could only begin when they showed a readiness to listen to people's dreams and nightmares, and play them back to audiences in exciting narratives that would enable those watching to know themselves a little better, and to feel a widening sense of possibility in the way they shaped their lives.

Beginning Behind

The pattern of industrial organization prevailing in Britain at the end of the nineteenth century made it inevitable that Britain's pioneer filmmakers would quickly find themselves crowded off the world's screens. This was not, however, immediately apparent to those photographers, instrument makers and lanternists who had been fired up to experiment with moving pictures after hearing reports of Edison's Kinetoscope, the original what-the-butler-saw machine, or witnessing the first projection of films made by the Lumière Brothers in 1896. It didn't require much capital to manufacture the equipment or produce the short films, and for some time it was possible for small craftsmen on the British model to keep up with the big boys in France or the US.

Early pioneers like Robert William Paul or James Williamson entered on their new enterprise with confidence, even though they were only individual craftsmen working out of small workshops and studios. Their past experience enabled them to produce and maintain their own equipment, and operate it with competence, but the fact that none had themselves initiated any of the significant developments in filmmaking or projects was an early indication of their unpreparedness for serious competition. Paul had the technical know-how to copy Edison's Kinetoscope when he realized the American inventor hadn't covered all the necessary patents, to make his own camera when Edison cut off the supply of films and produce a film projector, the Theatrograph, within two months of hearing about Lumière's invention. But, despite this ability to pick up on new innovations, and add refinements of their own, neither Paul nor any of the other pioneers found the backup necessary to generate significant leaps forward in the manufacture of equipment or the films themselves.

Scattered around the London suburbs, or in provincial towns like Sheffield, Brighton and Bradford, these pioneers had only limited access to capital resources, and their companies never grew to any real size. They became directors, screenwriters, producers, even actors, because that was the way to sell their equipment. Gradually film production became their main preoccupation, but only Cecil Hepworth became sufficiently involved to continue after the industry had hit its first crisis. As industrial enterprises, all were minnows by comparison with the Edison Corporation in the US, which had financial backing from Wall Street to finance a fine workshop, and a large staff. In France too, the Lumière Brothers operated on a much larger scale than their

British counterparts and, by 1902, Pathé-Frères had expanded to the point where it carried out all the functions relating to film production – from the manufacture of film stock to exhibition. None of Britain's filmmaking companies had this level of entrepreneurial energy. They reacted to events, never initiating them, and this trait became an increasing liability as time passed.

Nevertheless, Britain's early filmmakers set about the business of film production with some brio and not a little flair. Paul was soon making 50 short items a year; predominantly filmed vaudeville turns and trick films exploiting the new medium's capacity for visual magic. Equally productive, though somewhat more sophisticated, was James Williamson, a former portrait photographer and lanternist who was one of a group of filmmakers gathered in Brighton.

Cinema developed alongside the wireless and the telephone as communications media that would change the way people perceived the world around them. It is doubtful, however, whether these filmmaking pioneers had any sense at all of the new invention's potential significance. They may have felt a degree of excitement as they turned their cameras on a train arriving at a station, waves crashing on the beach, or a group of workers emerging from their daily grind in the factory, but these early pieces of reportage were seen as nothing more than 'animated photographs', a further step in the development of photography. A little later, as filmmakers began to expend the medium's storytelling capacities, they drew from the techniques developed for the magic lantern or diorama and audiences saw a woman interrupting her husband in the act of kissing the maid, or a miller grappling with chimney sweeps in front of a windmill.

It was natural to see these moving pictures as nothing more than a novelty, perhaps merely a passing gimmick; they were, after all, only shown as an additional turn on the music-hall programme. A little later, shows were put on at village fairs and halls by travelling showmen. Places dedicated to film presentation, the penny gaffes, did start to spring up at the beginning of the new century, but it was only with the emergence of long films around 1910 that cinema acquired any sort of institutional presence in British towns.

There is an extraordinary variety to the films produced in the early days of British cinema, showing the diversity of sources from which filmmakers drew their ideas. A film like *Mary Jane's Mishap* (1903), in which an uncouth maid who has been a little careless with the paraffin evaporates through the chimney, but returns in ghostly form to visit her grave, derives its fantasy elements from magic lantern shows, whereas *The Big Swallow* (1901), which shows camera and cameraman being swallowed up in a restless jaw, is more evidently a response to the medium's possibilities. One also feels the potential of moving images being explored in some simple documentary footage, as in the almost abstract shots of boys throwing snowballs, wind-surfing, skating and tobogganing in *Winter Sports* (1902).

Some films show their makers grappling with contemporary issues, without always the level of visual inventiveness applied elsewhere. Two films made by James Williamson, for example, deal with the hardships endured by the families of those who fought in the Boer War. In *The Soldier's Return* (1902), a returning warrior rescues his mother from the workhouse, while the demobbed soldier of *A Reservist before the War and after the War* (1902) steals a loaf of bread in order to supply the needs of his destitute wife and children. Both these films are somewhat stagey, but contemporary comment could be combined with visual fantasy, as is revealed by Cecil Hepworth's *The Perils of Modern Motoring* (1905), in which a policeman is left in a dismembered state after being mowed down by a car. After his pieces have been reassembled, both the driver and the passengers from the offending vehicle disappear in a puff of smoke.

It was the fact that the same individual could experiment with such a wide range of themes, subjects and styles that kept the spirit of invention alive, and encouraged some startling developments in film narrative, none of which had anything to do with theatrical forms of presentation. Williamson's *Fire* (1901) competently builds tension by running together the story of a man in a burning room and the fire brigade scurrying to his rescue. An even keener sense of anticipation is developed four years later in Hepworth's *Rescued by Rover* (1905), about a dog's role in rescuing a kidnapped child. Will the dog find the baby? Will the dog persuade the master that he knows something important? The way in which the film provokes these questions makes it possible, even today, to understand why this film was such a hit, selling 385 prints at £10 apiece. Many other films released at this time showed how widespread were the skills developed by Hepworth. The travelling showman William Haggar's *The Life of Charles Peace* (1905) may be less achieved but the sympathy it elicits for the ingenious villain who had been hanged in 1879 marks it out as a piece of genuine popular entertainment. Rather more in line with British cinema's future disdain for anyone outside the middle classes is Williamson's *Two Little Waifs* (1905), in which two adult gypsies are left to the flames while their daughter is carried off to her convalescence in a suburban garden. Not all the content is quite so melodramatic, and the same filmmaker's *Our Little Errand Boy* (1905) is a fabulous slapstick comedy about a plucky prankster who terrorizes his neighbourhood and, when pursued by the vicar, the shopkeeper, the matron and various others, locks them all behind the wire mesh of a chicken run.

It is around this time that the demand for films began to increase substantially and producers built larger studios to produce pictures that, while longer than before, were still some way short of what would become established feature length. The search for subjects that would appeal to audiences narrowed the range of films made, and resulted in a sometimes excessive reliance on

A final taste of freedom for the hero of *The Life of Charles Peace* (1905)

stories involving naughty boys, magic drinks, plucky dogs pursuing criminals and clothes left lying around for tramps to pick up. But a film like *When the Devil Drives* (1907), in which a train is taken over by the devil and taken at great speed under the sea and into the sky, shows that length did not necessarily constrict imagination, while *The Airship Destroyer* (1909), with its combination of romance and action in the story of an inventor who develops a missile that will destroy an airship, shows a filmmaker drawing material from contemporary anxieties about aerial combat.

Both the latter films were made by Walter Booth for Charles Urban, an American who had been sent to Britain in order to look after Edison's interests, then set up on his own as a distributor and exporter of French and American films. He sponsored documentary films of the Boer War and also travel and scientific films, and distributed the films of Williamson and others. Later he became involved with the Brighton-based G. A. Smith in developing the Kinemacolor process. With his entrepreneurial skills, and his international connections, he seemed for a time the man most likely to lead the British film industry away from its artisanal base, but he turned out to be no more responsive than anyone else to developments that were going to make things very difficult for the pioneers.

Initially there had been a substantial market for British films in the US, where demand remained for some time ahead of the production levels achieved by American filmmakers. But in 1908 Edison set up the Motion Picture Patents Company (MPPC), which included among its aims an increase in the share of the US market taken by domestic productions. To achieve this aim involved driving out the small importers. This was appalling news for the British companies, none of which had anything like the clout necessary to claim membership of the MPPC. Of the two European companies that did become members, Méliès had built its fortunes around the genius of one innovative filmmaker, whereas Pathé had deliberately set out on an internationalist path, making films not only in France but also in Britain, the US, Italy, Germany, Russia and Japan. Such small British companies as Cricks and Martin, Clarendon, British and Colonial and Urban came nowhere near that level of enterprise. Hepworth, it seems, even resented foreign filmmakers operating in England and trying 'to poach upon the natural preserves of other lands.'[1] Imbued with such smugness, British filmmakers inevitably fell behind.

While the French film industry expanded from its well-organized base, the Edison cartel encouraged the more effective organization that came from combining production and distribution in one company, and Edison's competitors like Shmuel Gelbfisz (Goldwyn), a former glove salesman from Lodz, or Lewis Zeleznik (Selznick), a jewellery dealer from Kiev, began to exploit the potential of the new medium in the US, many of the British pioneers decided to pack it in. G. A. Smith was among the first to give up, going to work with

Urban on developing his new colour process; Haggar retired in 1909 to run his own cinema; Williamson curtailed the production of dramatic comic films after his standing contract with the US was cancelled and directed his energies into educational filmmaking to escape 'the horrible nightmare of having my business directed by outsiders.' And Paul decided, after the failure of his expensive trick film, *The Butterfly* (1910), that production was 'too speculative to be run as a sideline to instrument making.' Even Hepworth shifted for a while into distribution after losing a regular order from the US for up to 40 copies of every film he made. Too late did he realize, as he later acknowledged, that he had been 'lured by the apparent security of our trade with America and other countries into feeling that change and progress need not be too seriously contemplated.'[2]

The withdrawal of these pioneers from the scene need not have been bad news for the industry; few American production outfits made the transition to new times and Méliès failed to keep up in France. The problem was that, in the UK, no enterprising producer stepped forward to fill the gap their departure created. Britain began to slip badly as a competitive producer of films, and the national market was increasingly ceded to imports from France and America. On a visit to England in 1914, Charles Pathé initiated what was to become a French sport, mocking the backwardness of British production. This he blamed on a lack of enterprise: 'There is no continuity of effort among your producers,' he said, 'They work too hastily and in too small a way.'[3]

A crisis of confidence among Britain's producers was the result of this sort of taunting, and from around this time one begins to detect in the press a sense that the nation's honour was threatened by its film industry's parlous condition. 'Hurrah! English Drama Again Takes Premier Position' ran the hopeful headline over a piece that described Hepworth's *Rachel's Sin* (1911) as 'a great triumph in film production' which was 'all ENGLISH'.[4] But, despite Hepworth's brazen nationalism, confidence in British filmmakers declined. As early as 1909, British and Colonial had brought over American directors and stars for its films. And when the London Film Company was formed in 1913 by Dr Ralph Tennyson Jupp, as an offshoot of his Provincial Cinematograph Theatres exhibition company, he relied heavily upon American producers and directors. With some reason did another Frenchman remark at this time that Britain had become no more than a colony of the American film industry.

The need to make films longer, in order to compete with American and French imports, also bred a more insidious form of dependence. For 15 years British filmmakers had experimented with the medium, developing film editing and camera effects to build suspense, and explore a world of magic and fantasy. Seen now, these early British films still have a feeling of freshness and spontaneity that derives from the natural performances of non-actors, and a loose approach to framing which allows interesting material to get in at the edge of the picture. But when William George Barker decided to bring to the screen a stage production of *Henry VIII* (1911), he cut British film production off from the innovations that had gone before.

Barker was a natural showman, promoting *Henry VIII* with the declaration that he would burn all the prints of the film within six weeks, and his own sense of the significance of what he had done is echoed in Rachael Low's description of this as 'the first really important feature film.'[5] But the only thing that was important about the film was its length and the ill omens it offered for the future. The development was welcomed by exhibitors, who felt that stage adaptations would enable them to attract a better class of customer, but they weren't to know what they were letting themselves in for. It was also paralleled abroad, where a French production of *Queen Elizabeth* was imported to the US by Adolph Zukor. But whereas film industries as vital as the French or American could absorb this new development, the British industry was put into a straitjacket by it.

Since the prints of *Henry VIII* were consigned to the flames at Ealing Studios, it's not possible to assess what merits Barker's production may have had, but some idea of the uncinematic monstrosity that was produced is suggested by a contemporary production of *Richard III*, which consists of 17 scenes played out from the stage to a static camera, interrupted by lengthy titles containing brief pieces of dialogue. The chase films swept away by this development may have been repetitive but they offered an excitement that no one can have secured from the sight of London stage actors running through potted silent versions of Shakespeare.

Slightly more promising as a source of cinematic entertainment were the melodramatic novels to which Barker and others turned for narrative material. But, as producers bowdlerized the romantic stories of Marie Corelli and Hall Caine, as well as literary classics by Dickens, Thackeray and George Eliot, the resulting films were all the evidence one needed that British filmmakers had lost confidence in their own ability to find and develop stories, and exploit the medium's potential. They stripped these books down to their narrative skeletons, then scattered a string of incidents on to the screen without caring whether they moved or excited the audience. With such a large literary storehouse to draw on, it all seemed so easy, even if the results were often dispiriting. In 1914, one commentator rashly predicted that the fad for adaptations wouldn't last much longer. After a brief flurry of original stories at the beginning of the First World War, it was back to business as usual and, by the early 1920s, some 95 per cent of film stories were adapted from the stage or novels.

The filmed play does not have to be stagey, nor the filmed book uncinematic, if the adaptation is imaginatively done. But there was little understanding at the time of how much work was required to develop high-quality screenplays.

Writers were poorly paid, rarely given a screen credit and never encouraged to take a fresh approach. Hepworth gives an account of the process of developing a script that reveals how undynamic was his approach to screenwriting, as well as how low a regard he had for writers:

> When I read a book or saw a play or studied a synopsis, there came into my mental vision a fairly detailed and consecutive pattern of what the film would be like. That pattern stuck in my head and gradually crystallized it out into a definite form, while the scenario was being prepared for me.[6]

There is no sense here of any engagement with the writer on what the script should be like, nor does Hepworth anticipate substantial work being done on the text after his initial moments of introspection. It's unsurprising that such an attitude failed to produce competent screenwriters, let alone exciting ones. Hepworth justified poaching from literature because of 'the advantage of a well-made plot, which was not at all easy to come by in original film scenarios'[7], but what this ignores is the responsibility of producers like him to foster the writing skills which would end British cinema's reliance on the novel or play, and novelistic or theatrical styles of storytelling.

Without writers there could be no new ideas about what cinema could do, and without new ideas there could be no sense of British cinema having a purpose. Instead of confronting their problems, producers fell back into a sorry-for-themselves analysis. A series of screenings were arranged in 1912 to 'demonstrate the high qualities of the British film'[8], and they proved rather the opposite. Producers responded to the critical backlash with a self-deceiving debate about whether British films did poorly because they were bad, or simply because they were suspected of being so. Instead of looking for new approaches that could galvanize the industry to deal with its problems, the call went up for a leader who would, in the words of one *Bioscope* editorial, be able 'to make order out of disorder, to organize agreement and concord with a strong hand, tactfully and helpfully, yet with a stern repression of pettiness and ignoble motives.'[9]. And filmmakers also began to argue for government legislation to protect the industry against marauding Americans. When the director Maurice Elvey heard of a proposal to tax all films imported into Britain, he declared, 'Why should the industry be protected. If it is not strong enough to grow on its own, let it die as soon as possible.'[10] Such a comment was not one, of course, to which any patriotically-minded Englishman could give heed.

Transition

There was much optimism about the prospects for British film production in the aftermath of the First World War. 'The industry', Hepworth later remarked, 'had enormously increased its prestige with the public, Parliament and the press. It had played no small part in tranquillizing things at home and inspiring 'national will to victory', and that was earnestly acknowledged by the Prime Minister.'[1] Unfortunately, most of this hopefulness was mere wishful thinking. Cinema admissions had indeed increased as people sought escape at the movies from the horrors of war, and the flow of French and Italian imports had been disrupted, but the screen-time made available had been almost totally absorbed by American pictures: by 1918 some 80 per cent of films shown in Britain were from the US. And, whereas filmmaking technique had been advancing in America, things had almost stood still in Britain. In reality, the basis for the prevailing sense of optimism was nothing more than a sense that, with hostilities now ended, everyone could get back to business as usual.

But 'business as usual' would not be enough to enable British producers to compete for audiences against American films. They hadn't grasped how popular American cinema had become with audiences worldwide. They saw Hollywood films, just as everyone else did, and many made valiant efforts to learn from American filmmaking styles. In 1920, for example, the notoriously rotund producer G. B. Samuelson made a trip to Universal Studios, where he produced six pictures to learn what he could about the American way of doing things. He could have stayed at home since, in the year of his journey, Famous Players–Lasky set up its own studio in Islington, to make films the American way. Yet British producers didn't appreciate the scale of what they were up against. Hepworth was to speak wistfully of 'a pressure in the air which we did not understand', saying that 'we worked on as best we could in spite of it.'[2]

Money was not initially the problem. The optimistic talk about the future of British films softened up sources of capital. Hepworth raised £100,000 to fund an expansion programme. Alliance, one of a number of new companies formed after the war, spent £90,000 on a grandiose production programme before seeing how a single one of its films performed in the cinemas. And two of the larger distribution companies moved into production: Ideal with funding of around £115,000, Stoll with some £400,000 in the bank. Such sums may have been trivial in comparison with the financial resources at the disposal of the larger American combines, but they provided a base that could have been built on. Commercial success would have lured forth more cash. Instead, within seven years, Hepworth had declared himself bankrupt and Stoll had withdrawn from the production business, having·lost some £200,000 from its various production ventures.

The production policy followed by Sir Oswald Stoll, a leading figure in the vaudeville world, was an imitation of Hollywood pursued with the aim of maximizing productivity and ensuring a steady supply of films for his distribution setup. Productivity he achieved – by 1925 a third of the films made in Britain came from Stoll's studios at Cricklewood – but he was never anywhere near achieving his intention to 'leave American buyers convinced of England's ability to deliver the goods.'

The problem was twofold. The market for British films was not sufficiently large to justify mass production of films at budgets high enough to ensure they reached real quality, and executives at Stoll didn't understand the difference between good stories and good cinema. A lot of money was spent on the acquisition in 1920 of the rights to a series of novels by H. G. Wells, Edgar Wallace, Marie Corelli and Conan Doyle, but little care was expended on ensuring that these books were transmuted into workable scripts. Things were much the same at Ideal, where Victorian novels and stage plays were preferred to books by contemporary worthies of literature. Films like *Lady Audley's Secret* (1920), the story of a bigamous marriage and a woman's cold-blooded murder of her devoted husband, were sensational without being plotted or shot with an eye to involving an audience. Alliance compounded its problems by allowing its production policies to be influenced by a consultative literary committee, on which theatrical big-wigs such as Arthur Wing Pinero played a leading role.

Factors such as the parasitic reliance on the stage and the book, the lack of attention given to screenwriting, the lack of flexibility in studio-based production and, at Stoll, a studio floor so constructed that it accommodated the noise and bustle of five films at the same time, had a deadening effect on anyone who came into the industry with new ideas or fresh visions. When the young Alfred Hitchcock was looking for a studio in which to learn the craft of filmmaking, it never occurred to him to knock at the doors of Samuelson's Worton Hall or Stoll at Cricklewood. Instead he went to work for Famous Players–Lasky, first as a subtitle writer and then as a screenwriter. Even here, however, the shortage of filmmaking competence was felt, causing the American company to terminate the project in 1924 with a complaint that 'the productions failed to reach a quality comparable to those made in the States.'[3] In four years, Famous Players–Lasky had given the go-ahead to only one screenplay from a British writer.

The poor quality of the films coming out of Stoll and Ideal did nothing to improve the reputation of British pictures, nor strengthen the hands of their producer–distributors in negotiating good terms for their cinema screening. And exhibitors were under increasing pressure from American practices designed to ensure it was US pictures which British audiences saw. Hollywood produced duds too, but could package them up with surefire-winners like the Chaplin shorts and insist that the cinema booker buy everything in the package. In this way exhibitors were forced to fill up their screens for months ahead with pictures they had never seen. Often the only opening they could offer British producers would arise because a blind-booked film hadn't turned up. As a result, British films were sometimes forced to wait up to 18 months to secure a release. For small British companies with limited capital resources, that delay could be terminal.

Just how tough it could be for the independent producer is evident from the history of Minerva Films. Set up in 1920 by actor Leslie Howard and director Adrian Brunel among others, with the hope that they could do something about 'raising the standards of British films', the company had only enough capital to produce six short comedies. Unable to get these onto the screen for 18 months, and lacking the clout necessary to raise the additional money for the six extra films they would need to secure foreign distribution, Minerva went under. Brunel was a serious casualty of the sluggishness of British production at this period. In 1922, he made *The Man Without Desire*, an imaginative account of a man who wakes from a sleep of several hundred years only to find he suffers from a lack of emotion. The film was a success but, for the next five years, Brunel could secure no further directing opportunities and passed his time writing stories, editing imported films and producing home movies. The sense of disappointment that hangs over the rest of his career reflects the loss of nerve that came from finding that, at the moment when his career seemed to be taking off, there were no opportunities to build on what he had achieved. 'Whenever I have had some sort of public success,' he reported in his autobiography, 'it has inevitably been followed by a period of personal financial distress and prolonged unemployment.'[4]

Occasionally, British producers were able to secure foreign revenue to supplement the returns available to their films from the home market, but no one managed to secure a regular outlet for their productions in the US. Hepworth and Stoll failed in their attempt to set up a permanent sales operation in America; Samuelson secured a short-lived distribution arrangement with First National Exhibitors' Circuit, and various other films secured some sort of release. But the problem was that British exhibitors didn't produce a sufficiently reliable supply of quality product to ensure that any of these efforts were long-lasting. In 1922, the year in which audiences were offered such striking films as Rex Ingram's *The Four Horsemen of the Apocalypse* and Fritz Lang's *Die Niebelungen* cycle, not to mention Douglas Fairbanks' spirited

Filming Ivor Novello in *The Man Without Desire* (1922)

version of an English story, *The Adventures of Robin Hood*, of the 422 British films offered to American exhibitors only six found buyers.

There were quality films made in Britain during this period, but their producers pursued a non-commercial approach. Hepworth's obsessive desire to make 'English pictures, with all the English countryside for background and with English atmosphere and English idiom throughout'[5] didn't keep him up-to-date with audience tastes. *Comin Thro' the Rye* (1922), for example, exploits the beauties of the English countryside and constructs an allegorical subtext out of the changing seasons, but the narrative approach dilutes the dramatic potential inherent in its tale of a simple girl robbed of her true love by a heartless flirt, the sort of woman who is 'very useful for amusing men on rainy days.' The passivity of the wronged girl is a trait she shares with the hero of Guy Newell's *Fox Farm* (1922), a sensitive farmer abandoned by his go-getting wife after he has been blinded in an explosion. Even before his accident, he's much given to lighting his pipe, slumping in a chair and arguing that it's no use pushing against fate. Afterwards, he becomes loquacious about the Stoics, 'men who took what came, because they knew that grumbling made no difference.'

Worthy as such sentiments may be, they are not the stuff of powerful drama. The low intensity of these rural idylls shows up the problems created by the failure of the commercially-minded companies to generate anything other than fusty, studio-bound melodramas, as unsuccessful in their way as the airy, de-sensationalized productions of their more creative competitors. Newell and Hepworth might define their own styles against those of Stoll and Ideal but, since neither was particularly successful, there was no pressure operating on the one to be more 'commercial' or the other to be more 'artistic'. Both followed the route that came most naturally to them, with relatively unsatisfactory results all round.

The career of George Pearson provides an interesting example of the commercial and creative impulses fighting against each other in one person. Pearson came to films from school-teaching when he was already 37. Welsh–Pearson, the company he set up in 1915, remained small, making only three or four films a year, thus resisting the pressures for mass production that prevailed at the larger studios. But, much more than a filmmaker like Hepworth, he had learnt to find stories that would have genuine popular appeal. In 1914, Gaumont's London office commissioned him to make *Ultus, the Man from the Dead*, an attempt to match the success of the French company's *Fantômas* series. The film and its three sequels are well-constructed crime stories, told with speed and punch.

Pearson challenged the rest of British cinema's reliance on middle-class theatre by commissioning original stories that could appeal to a more popular audience. His sensitivity to audience tastes also led to his developing Britain's

Alma Taylor against the English landscape in *Comin' Thro' the Rye* (1922)

Criminal action in George Pearson's *Ultus* (1915)

first homegrown film star in Betty Balfour, whom he put into a series of films featuring the character of Squibs, an impish Piccadilly flower girl. The films are simple, unpretentious and amusing. In *Squibs Wins the Calcutta Sweep* (1922), for example, the energetic heroine suddenly comes into money, with which she spreads happiness to her neighbours and enjoys the high life, thereby offering audiences an opportunity for vicarious wish-fulfilment. The film is not particularly well constructed, and the subplot featuring Squibs' sister's desperate life in Paris with a murderer on the run is poorly connected to the scenes of rejoicing back home, but the central character's vitality carries the story.

However, Pearson's lack of interest in the methods of play construction led him towards even more unfocused ways of organizing his films, aiming for a sort of primitive naturalism – 'nothing more than the capture of things seen, life in the living, and by selection and arrangement, the flow of the human tale.'[6] He described his 1924 film *Reveille*, an episodic account of how a group of humble people had been affected by the war, as 'a scrapbook of pictures of life caught in the living, no hero, no villain, no plot, no tying up of loose threads.'[7] His 1926 film, *The Little People*, was publicized as 'just a bit of life caught by the camera'.[8] Unfortunately audiences did not warm to such tales and their commercial failure led to Pearson losing control of his own company. As a result, the creative phase of his career came to an end.

Pearson's enforced demotion within his own company, and the distaste shown by his partners for experiments that veered too sharply away from the comedies that had established Welsh–Pearson's reputation, is generally taken as evidence of the conservatism inherent in the film industry. Pearson is seen as the first British director to be sacrificed on the altar of his art. Nevertheless it does show considerable misjudgement to make films that had little to do with popular taste at a time when it was so difficult for British filmmakers to find an audience. Pearson hoped that the sense of authenticity in his films would 'carry feeling and understanding to an audience,'[9] but it was odd to imagine he could achieve genuine popularity by avoiding suspense and dramatic conflict.

Pearson's strategy led him to ignore, rather than deal with, the increasing crisis within British film production. Those small producers who were so intimidated by the problems of securing significant distribution that they simply carried on producing small, cheap pictures which, according to Hepworth, 'helped to build up and succour the very evil which was bringing about their downfall', inevitably went under first. But even more ambitious filmmakers like Samuelson and Hepworth were pushed out by the difficulties involved in making film production profitable. Production declined sharply. In 1923, some 25 per cent of the films shown to the trade were British; the following year it was only five per cent. In 1926, only 26 films went before the cameras.

To some extent this decline in quantity was coupled with an improvement

33

in quality. Nevertheless, the general contraction of the industry did further damage to its already shrivelled morale. Conscious that British audiences were almost wholly uninterested in British films, some members of the industry increased their efforts to secure through persuasion and publicity what the films so patently could not. In 1918, an attempt had been made to form a British Screen Club to influence the press in favour of British films. Similar thinking lay behind the setting up of the British National Film League in 1921 to 'encourage the production and exhibition of British-made films'. Its activities led to the British Film Weeks of 1924, which involved screening a programme of British pictures, accompanied by the sort of ballyhoo which left the public, according to critic Paul Rotha, 'hypnotized into readiness to applaud the worst picture in the world because it was British.'[10] Unfortunately, the films, which included Hepworth's *Comin' Thro' the Rye*, did nothing to support the claims made for them. It must have begun to seem that there was nothing the British film producer could do to challenge the place of American films on the nation's screens. Certainly, the Americans assumed that the victory was won; 'Not even on the horizon,' remarked Marcus Loew in 1926, 'can I see the nucleus of a British film-producing industry.'[11]

But although these were indeed dog days for British film production, film producers were emerging who understood the need for modern styles of production, bigger budgets and more ambitious showmanship. If neither Herbert Wilcox, Michael Balcon nor Victor Saville started off with much in the way of imaginative flair, they did at least know what was required to build successful enterprises. All three came from the Midlands and had been at the sharp end of the business as salesmen for distribution companies. When they launched themselves into production in 1922, Balcon and Saville with *Woman to Woman*, the story of a shell-shocked officer who comes out of amnesia to discover the truth about his sordid past, and Wilcox with two films of which the second, a florid melodrama called *The Flames of Passion*, was a hit, they used the same director, Graham Cutts, and judged it worthwhile incurring the expense of bringing over American stars, Betty Compson for *Woman*, Mae Marsh for *Flames*, in order to increase their films' marquee value at home and abroad. The strategy worked in both cases, and the producers were able to turn their initial successes into the resilience required to survive the setbacks that followed.

Wilcox remained always the showman, often directing his movies even though, like Saville in the same role, he was always more competent than gifted. He was committed to middle-of-the-road filmmaking, which he defined as 'escape entertainment of pleasant people in pleasant surroundings doing pleasant things', had an eye for a subject that could be exploited, and was fascinated by stardom. He loved to watch the crowds that gathered at Waterloo Station to greet the actresses he brought over from the US for his productions.

Dorothy Gish, for example, featured in his *Nell Gwynn* (1926) and *Madame Pompadour* (1927).

Balcon was unique among these *émigrés* from the Midlands in that he remained only a producer. Having started his working life in business (with the Dunlop Rubber Company), he saw himself as an impressario rather than a producer–director, and he consistently sought to develop an environment which stimulated the creativity of others. Through the successive phases of his career – at Gainsborough, Gaumont-British and then at his own Ealing Studios – he was to show that his talent lay in finding the most talented people available, giving them the best context to work in, inspiring and stimulating their efforts and intervening where necessary to ensure that the best possible film came out of the production process. Balcon was the sort of producer the British film industry had needed for a long time. He had the eye for detail and concern for quality lacking in Stoll or Samuelson, as well as the sort of business acumen that neither Hepworth nor Pearson had ever displayed.

Not, of course, that all the policies of the mature Balcon emerged at this period. He was himself later to acknowledge the inadequacy of a production policy that drew so heavily on stage plays, particularly at a period before the arrival of sound when it was impossible, for example, to do more than allude to the savagery of Noël Coward's attack on his social set in *The Vortex* (1927). Even so, some impressive films did emerge, notably *The Rat* (1925), whose pulp subject matter and lowlife setting invites comparison with the popular work of Pearson, while the script, although untidy, is much more engaging. Also, the performance of Ivor Novello as the impoverished hero whose charming vulnerability wins the hearts of all the girls, as well as that of a bored woman surrounded by too much luxury, and Cutts's mobile camerawork, put it in another class. The film deserved its popularity and its sequel.

Novello, who had initially developed *The Rat* for Brunel, was to join with Cutts' assistant, Alfred Hitchcock, in demonstrating that adapted stageplays didn't need to constrict cinematic invention as long as script and direction were entrusted to someone who could convey ideas in visual terms. *The Lodger* (1926) opens dramatically with the shot of a screaming girl, then shows the news being spread abroad, causing fear and panic throughout the city. This might be the prelude to any adapted stage play, a stimulating montage before the proscenium arch is fitted over the screen. But, although most of the rest of the film, until its chase finale, is played out within one house, where the lodger's strange behaviour arouses suspicions of his guilt, Hitchcock's interest in using the details of daily life to build anticipation and stir emotion ensures that the action never seems confined. With good cause did *Kine Weekly* subsequently hail the film for giving 'promise of a genuine reaction against the deeply-rooted Wardour Street superstition that America will only buy pictures similar to her own.'[12]

35

The Lodger represented a substantial step forward for British filmmaking. Its release had, however, been held up for some time on instructions from C. M. Woolf, a shrewd film salesman who had played a key role in financing the first projects of both Balcon and Wilcox. The re-editing he demanded has generally been taken as evidence of just that Wardour Street backwardness to which *Kine Weekly* alluded. But while it's true that Woolf's disapproval of the film's distinctive angles and extreme lighting contrasts does betray a degree of conservatism and, in his later campaign against *The Man who Knew Too Much* (1934), he was clearly the enemy of anything even moderately original, Woolf was not a simple philistine. Brunel, no less committed than Hitchcock to an 'artistic' direction for British films, was later unstinting in his praise of a man who 'by his faith and support set the pace at a time when we most needed it' and credited him with contributing 'very considerably to the renaissance of the British film production industry.'[13] Given that the re-editing of the film reduced the number of title cards from 300 to 80, it is reasonable to assume that Woolf's intervention considerably improved the film, and that Woolf's commercial experience provided a valuable lesson both for Hitchcock and Balcon.

What was being fought out over *The Lodger* was a debate about how far it was possible to combine a concern for art with the values of popular cinema. Hitchcock was triumphantly able to achieve this sort of synthesis, but it is not surprising that Woolf was suspicious of the highbrow values that were being propagated around this time, and decided to challenge their deployment on this film. The formation of the Film Society in 1925, which aimed to make British filmmakers aware of the creative possibilities of the medium by screening the most artistically adventurous films being made in Russia, Germany and elsewhere, had caused some confusion in the commercial film industry, which rightly saw the Film Society's platform as a blast against the prevailing aesthetic orthodoxies. Brunel, in fact, was advised by Gainsborough executives that continued attendance at the society's screenings would damage the reputation of the films, such as *The Vortex* and *Blighty*, that he made for them. But the company was inconsistent enough to employ Ivor Montagu, a Film Society stalwart, to re-edit *The Lodger*.

It is easy enough now to mock the film industry's seeming paranoia about the Film Society screenings. After all, what sort of threat was a group of film people who got together with interested artists, writers and sculptors on Sunday evenings to screen foreign films? Shouldn't producers have welcomed the society's aspiration to fertilize British film ideas and draw new talent into the cinema? Or were they really unnerved by its stated intention to improve 'standards of taste and executive ability.'?[14] But what their reaction shows is just how little awareness there was among Britain's film executives of cinema's artistic potential, and how little discussion had gone on about what sort of cinema British producers should develop. 'We were in the business of giving the public what it seemed to want in entertainment,' Balcon later recalled. 'We did not talk about art or social significance.'[15]

One might have expected the intense difficulties confronting British film producers to stimulate discussion; instead it seems to have narrowed their perspective. Nevertheless, Balcon did take practical measures of his own to develop more technically sophisticated films, by setting up productions in German studios, and working with European technicians whose superiority to their British counterparts was recognized. Although Balcon was not the first to make films in Germany, he was the first to do so on a regular basis. And while there were crudely economic motives in, for example, sending Hitchcock to reconstruct English and Oriental settings in Italy and Germany for his first film, *The Pleasure Garden* (1925), it did at least show that he was as aware as the Film Society's membership of the backwardness of British films.

Balcon could reasonably feel defensive about the sort of criticism of British cinema that began to appear from the Film Society milieu, particularly in the pages of *Close Up*, a journal founded in 1927. These writers criticized the industry for being a second-rate imitation of Hollywood, but that was because they despised American cinema and the 'box-office bogey'[16], not because they appreciated the economic gap between the two industries. They depicted British cinema as indifferent to art, lacking drive and sense of direction and, in their distaste for the commercial orientation of the system, failed to suggest any ways to reform it. Pulling apart the British film industry was the only solution offered. They proposed getting rid of the philistines found along Wardour Street, London's Film Row, wiping out the middle-class personnel who had been creeping into the director's chair, or introducing a bunch of amateurs into the business. 'Oh, it's a mess,' remarked one desperate commentator. 'And yet one sincerely wishes them well, but there just doesn't seem anything to say.'[17]

But while the gap between the filmmakers and the critical culture could seem an unbridgeable chasm, there were people with feet in both camps who were discussing how to wrest British cinema away from its dual dependence on the stage and American models. In a letter to the *London Evening News* of the late 1920s, Hitchcock expresses his own sense of how Hollywood models could be redeployed in a British context:

> The Americans have left us with very few stories to tell. But there is no reason why we should not tell stories of *English* boys who leave the village and make good in the city – why rural drama should not be found and filmed among the mountains of Wales and moors of Yorkshire. Our history – national and imperial – provides a wonderful storehouse of film drama.[18]

37

And Hitchcock's films do demonstrate that a British filmmaker could learn from Hollywood, but yet create distinctive national films, and without breaking with the commercial filmmaking culture as *Close Up*'s writers proposed.

A similar position was put by Anthony Asquith in his first feature film, *Shooting Stars* (1928). The son of the former British Prime Minister, Asquith combined an intellectual grasp of film with commercial aspirations (although he lacked Hitch's grasp of the popular idiom). He had studied the latest Russian, German and French film theories, spent six months mixing with movie people in Hollywood, then gone on to train at British Instructional Pictures, a maker of successful non-fiction films which moved into drama production in the late 1920s. Asquith's début feature is fascinating both because its setting in a bustling film studio gives some impression of what it was like to shoot a picture in Britain at the end of the silent era, and because of what it argues as the future for British films. There are two films being shot side-by-side in the studio. Both are Hollywood-style productions, one a soppy Western, the other a slapstick item featuring a Chaplin lookalike. The actress playing in the Western abandons her cowboy lover for the comic after he promises to take her to Hollywood and put her name up in lights, but the scandal that follows wrecks her career. The cowboy, by contrast, stays faithful to his British films, however limited their ambition, becomes a director and goes on to make serious pictures. The message is twofold. British cinema must grow up, but it can only do so by building on everything it has already created, even when that includes silly Hollywood ripoffs.

Filmmakers and critics were not the only ones worrying about the state of British filmmaking, nor was the film industry the only British enterprise losing out to American competition. The popularity of Hollywood films made them the most obvious indicator of the general shift in world trade. In holding British films responsible for their own failure, industrialists were encouraged by the willingness of US producers to assert that the aim of the American film industry was 'to Americanize the world.'[19]

General concern about the parlous state of British film production was expressed throughout the 1920s. A letter to *The Times* of 1923, for example, drew attention to 'the dangers arising from the Americanization of the British Empire from the excessive number of American motion pictures shown', but things came to a head in 1924. Production had sunk so low that in November, Black November, not a single film went into production in any of the country's studios. Public attention was galvanized by a publicity gambit from the American distributors of *The Phantom of the Opera*, who persuaded a brigade of British soldiers to escort the print from Southampton to London. These indicators of the native film industry's weakness encouraged The Federation of British Industries to intensify its campaign to bring attention to the way in which the disappearance of British films from the world's screens impacted on 'the prestige of the country as a whole, and thereby the prestige of British

Cowboys in Cricklewood – the studio setting of *Shooting Stars* (1928)

industry also'. Even the Prime Minister, Stanley Baldwin, got in on the act, speculating upon 'the enormous power which the film is developing for propaganda purposes, and the danger to which we in this country and our Empire subject ourselves if we allow that method of propaganda to be entirely in the hands of foreign countries.'[20]

It shows how little the FBI really understood about film production that their proposals to improve the situation focused on increasing the quantity of production, rather than stimulating a few high-quality pictures that might promote British prestige abroad. A National Film Studio, combining the small companies into one strong conglomerate, had been proposed, but this idea made no more headway than a proposal to negotiate a reciprocity deal with the Americans, whereby they would take a certain number of British films into national distribution in return for free access to British screens. The notion that won through involved stopping the American companies' strong-arm booking tactics and reserving a space in the domestic market for British films by requiring that exhibitors and distributors handle a proportion of domestic product. The measure would compel American distributors to back British film production, ensuring a rise in the number of British films. What it wouldn't do was ensure good pictures, and Herbert Wilcox saw at once that such legislation would create an 'awkward squad' of British films which would immediately become the laughing stock of the world.'[21] He argued, along with Balcon, Pearson and Woolf, that it would do nothing to achieve the FBI's objectives. But a proposed clause in the new act to disallow for quota any film of low standard of production and entertainment value was dropped because of the difficulties involved in determining which films should be excluded.

The drafters of the legislation overlooked the imbalance between the British and American markets. The US had 20,000 cinemas, the UK only 4,000; 80 million people a week went to the cinema in the US, against only 20 million in the UK. The average budget for a British film was £7–10,000, against £100–120,000 in the US. The 1927 Cinematograph Act imposed a distributors quota of 7.5 per cent, and an exhibitors quota of five per cent, both rising to 20 per cent, but it did nothing in itself to shift the economic balance in favour of British producers. However, thanks partly to the arrival of the sound film, this small measure was to change the nature of the British film industry in ways that could hardly have been foreseen by the legislators, and enable it to 'project England' more effectively than it had ever done before.

Reaching England

The Cinematograph Act of 1927 put producers in a strong position for negotiations with financiers. There was now a captive market for British films, and that market would expand steadily through the ten years the act was set to remain on the statute book. The first beneficiaries of this new climate were two would-be moguls who seized the opportunity to considerably expand their existing film holdings. 'The City is certainly more inclined to look kindly on the film trade than before, and thus a considerable weight that has handicapped us in the past is removed'[1], remarked John Maxwell, as he launched British International Pictures (BIP) as a public company with interests in production, exhibition and distribution. Maxwell, a former solicitor from Glasgow, had moved into exhibition in 1912, then distribution in 1923. In 1926 he built studios at Elstree and made his first tentative move into production with *The Woman Tempted*. Encouraged by the new legislation, he sought to become a big player on the local production scene. His main competitors were two merchant bankers, Isidore and Maurice Ostrer, who had acquired a stake in Gaumont-British in the 1920s. The new legislation encouraged them into a buying spree that led to their picking up such distribution companies as Ideal and C. M. Woolf's W&F Film Services, and sufficient cinema circuits to build a chain of 316 theatres. As well as continuing production at Gaumont-British, the company took a stake in Balcon's Gainsborough company. These two film combines were strong enough to focus filmmakers' creative and entrepreneurial energies, but not so dominant that they crushed out other centres of initiative.

The fresh availability of finance also drew into the industry people with a less developed understanding of cinema or business matters than Maxwell or the Ostrers. New companies were set up by public subscription, and there was a substantial increase in the number of films produced. Studios were built and additional stages added on to old complexes. But this was not, at first, a boom with roots, and many of these new operations were to be swept away when the arrival of sound led to an increase in the cost of production.

As its critics feared, the legislation quickly established an area of production where cheapness was the only important criterion, with film being treated as so many yards of celluloid filled with moving figures. There were not many talented British filmmakers, and American distributors were not simply being awkward when they decided to do no more than fulfil the letter of the law by distributing films from far-off parts of the British Commonwealth that nobody wanted to see. And Maxwell reinforced their argument by importing European directors and stars to make BIP's more ambitious films. *Piccadilly* (1929), for example, had foreigners in all the key positions: the German E. A. Dupont as director, Alfred Jünge as art director, Werner Brandes as lighting cameraman, as well as Olga Tschechova and Jean Bradin as the film's stars.

Soon, however, distributors were able to secure cheaply-made films from small studios set up to supply their needs, and some American companies began to make their own 'quota quickies'. A production environment that sought to minimize expense was not especially stimulating to creativity, and some idea of the cynicism involved is evident from the instruction given to Adrian Brunel by the bosses at MGM that he couldn't make any improvements in the film he had made for them lest his cuts shorten the film below the act's definition of a full-length picture.[2] 'All vaulting ideas of film as an art had to be abandoned,' remarked George Pearson. 'Only as a capable and speedy craftsman could one survive in that feverish and restless environment.'[3] Pearson made no fewer than eight quota films in one year at Julius Hagen's Twickenham Studios, where one small stage was occupied around the clock, and pictures that had been scripted in a fortnight were filmed in another two weeks. From this industrious factory, and from others across London, came a never-ending flow of costume melodramas, musicals, detective stories and films in every other sort of genre.

The quota legislation is generally depicted as a disastrous blow to the British film industry, dragging down its reputation and perpetuating the sort of mediocrity that previously characterized the output of Stoll and Ideal Studios. But whereas in the early 1920s, cheapie production had constituted almost the entirety of British filmmaking, in the 1930s there existed a more ambitious production sector running in parallel. In this context, the low-budget production area, by providing continuous employment, usefully offered directors and technicians opportunities to develop craft skills and promote their potential. The quantity of talented filmmakers coming through the quota mill was not substantial. Nevertheless, it did provide a stepping stone for some significant figures. The Hungarian *émigré* Alexander Korda gained a foothold in British production by making *Service for Ladies* (1932, *Reserved for Ladies* in US) and five other pictures for Paramount. David Macdonald made a series of quota quickies before going on to a larger budget with the striking comedy-thriller *This Man is News* (1938), and Michael Powell built a reputation as a director of energetic quota films before making his mainstream début with *Edge of the World* (1937), about the depopulation of a remote island in the Shetlands. Sadly, neither Pearson nor Brunel, the two most distinguished industry veterans working the quota seam, was able to use this production area as the springboard to a comeback.

The quota film also offered directors the chance to work outside box office constraints and experiment with the medium's possibilities, as Hitchcock did with *Number 17* (1932), his offbeat haunted-house Gothic. And, although many quota films were, inevitably, bland transpositions of stage plays, there was an area of quickie production which, by taking stories of murder, robbery and blackmail from the newspapers, prepared British cinema to deal with tougher issues than its obsession with middle-class theatre allowed. Quota filmmaking also made the argument for narrative simplicity that sometimes escaped the more prolix mainstream filmmakers. As a result, Brunel could argue that killing off the quickie at the end of the decade was a mistake since it was possible to make 'really fine, unspectacular pictures', and 'we were evolving a technique that showed what could be done when facing fearful odds.'[4] The quota, in short, forced *some* British filmmakers to be realistic about the economic constraints operating in British filmmaking, and to look to what could be achieved within them rather than simply hoping that film budgets could rise on some magic carpet to figures close to those of Hollywood pictures.

As significant as quota in changing the nature of British film production was the arrival of the sound film. In some ways, by seeming to justify the adaptation of stageplays and musical comedies to the screen, sound perpetuated the worst aspects of British film production. One can easily understand the ferocity with which the more creative British filmmakers positioned themselves against the new development. It was for them that Paul Rotha spoke when he declared: 'The dialogue film, at its best, can only be a poor substitute for the stage.'[5] And filmmakers like Brunel, Asquith and Powell worried about the loss of camera mobility and editing flexibility inevitable with the early sound technology. But if sound set back filmmaking style by several years, it offered a great boom for the British film industry. Drawing on the verbal and musical skills of comedians and other performers who were established in theatre and the music hall, filmmakers were able to make up for their failure to develop indigenous styles of visual comedy, and to produce relatively cheap pictures that enjoyed genuine popularity. Their success in this area so changed the way British films were perceived that, in 1932, a year when a large number of exhibitors substantially over-filled their quota, the American showbiz journal *Variety* reported on 'the complete stranglehold the home-made pictures had established at the local box office.'

Herbert Wilcox was among the first to realize the opportunities sound created for British filmmakers. He had been quick to fit out his Imperial Studios with the necessary equipment, and produced *Splinters* (1929) as his first sound film. The script, about a soldier taken out of the trenches not, as he fears, to be shot, but to organize an army concert party, is just a rudimentary framework within which to present a number of variety turns. If it is difficult now to concur with the *Bioscope* reviewer's judgement that the film 'surpasses in technical achievement anything of its kind ever made in Britain, and at times soars to heights of directorial brilliance',[6] it's still possible to understand how

43

an audience that had been accustomed only to silent films might warm to the various acts on display. More easily comprehensible is the enormous success Wilcox enjoyed in the following year with *Rookery Nook* (1930), the first of the Ben Travers farces he brought to the screen. However token the attempts to open the play out from its Tudor house setting with shots of sea waves, a train coming into a station and a village street, the result is still entertaining.

The most popular films of the 1930s were those built around Britain's first superstars. Among the many comic performers Balcon developed for Gaumont-British, such performers as the histrionic Cicely Courtneidge and the dapper, completely unexportable, Jack Hulbert, none matched the success of musical performer Jessie Matthews. She danced with zest, sang sweetly and had a fine sense of comic timing. And her posh accent was sufficiently artificial to be laughed at, where a more natural intonation would have alienated audiences. She first made an impression in an adaptation of J. B. Priestley's rambling tale about a group of travelling performers, *The Good Companions* (1933), and followed that with *Friday the Thirteenth* (1933), which recounts the activities of a group of characters immediately before the crash of the bus in which they are riding. Her major musical films included *Evergreen* (1934), an untidy but profitable adaptation of a West End stage success; *First a Girl* (1935), in which Matthews amusingly impersonates a female impersonator in a British version of the German *Viktor und Viktoria*, and the fascinating *It's Love Again* (1936), in which Matthews is a struggling dancer who takes on the character of a fictional celebrity dreamed up by two desperate newspaper men. The films are always set against glamorous backgrounds, with Matthews offering herself for audience identification as the outsider trying to enter a world that seeks to exclude her.

By contrast, the films made to exploit the vitality, comic talent and phenomenal singing voice of Grace Fields are at their best when set not against a showbusiness background, but in the midst of depressed working-class communities where Fields stands as a beacon of cheerfulness and hope. If *Looking on the Bright Side* (1932) is sometimes spoilt by the fact that the director, Basil Dean, seems to be under the impression he is making a sophisticated Hollywood musical, the scenes in the tenement block where Fields and her songwriter lover first meet are genuinely stirring. And there is passion as well as poetry in *Sing as We Go* (1934), one of the few films of the 1930s to make any reference to unemployment. Framed by the story of the closure of Greybeck Mills, and its reopening, the centre of the film is a tour of popular culture articulating the message, 'If we can't spin, we can still sing.' In her spirited struggle to survive in Blackpool, Fields becomes a waitress, a song plugger, a potential beauty contestant and a human spider in a sideshow. The naturalness and energy in Fields' performances made these films popular with both middle-class and working-class audiences.

Jessie Matthews signs pictures for her fans

Gracie Fields was the mainstay of the production programme at Basil Dean's Associated Talking Pictures (ATP), where, towards the end of the decade, Dean developed another star in George Formby. He's the smiling innocent who so trusts the sharks he meets in his various roles – newspaper reporter, army recruit, spy, racing bike rider or whatever – that he continually lands himself in trouble, forcing him back on reserves of charm, and his skill with a ukelele, to secure his escape. Formby's films, with their straightforward plots and repressed naughtiness, were first-class family entertainment, making him the top box-office attraction of the late 1930s.

The regular production of films featuring these performers gave their production companies some sort of economic foundation to build on, as well as allowing producers like Balcon and Dean a glimpse of what a popular British cinema might achieve. Dean was too much of a cultural snob to get the message, but Balcon sought to emulate the success of these pictures in his more serious, dramatic movies. However, while it was comparatively easy to cobble together a story around a popular star, the British industry was not yet well organized when it came to finding a steady output of ideas for dramatic features and developing them into workable scripts. The lack of competent screenwriters, and of directors with strong creative drives clearly limited executives' freedom of movement. 'Financiers and impresarios you can buy two a penny,' the documentarist John Grierson lamented in 1931. 'Directors who have something to say and the power to say it, you can only close your fingers and wish for.'[7]

As head of production for Gainsborough Pictures and, from 1932, also for Gaumont-British, Michael Balcon had to make over 20 pictures a year. In order to wean the company away from a reliance on theatre plays, he set up a major script department which drew on the talents of writers like Frank Launder, Sidney Gilliatt, Val Guest and Michael Pertwee, as well as occasionally giving jobs to young writers like Christopher Isherwood. The result of this openness to new ideas began to pay off when films like the Gilliatt-scripted *Rome Express* (1933), a streamlined comedy thriller, became hits at the box office.

The working principle of Balcon's life was that a 'film producer is only as good as the sum total of the colleagues with whom he works', and he understood better than anyone else at the time how to turn the studio into a source of creative energy. In order to ensure that every department at the studio was of the best, he set up training schemes for new entrants to the industry. He also imported cameramen, make-up staff and editors from Europe and America, so that those working at the studio could learn the more advanced techniques. Most important of all, he inspired the people who worked for him with a vision of what they were doing. Just as the Hollywood moguls built an, albeit mythic, vision of the American dream, so Balcon, from a Jewish immigrant family, felt that films should 'express England'.[8] This conviction brought forth the rebuke from Michael Powell that Balcon was 'suburban'[9], but it was the sense of purpose Balcon gave to his employees that distinguished Gaumont-British from other local studios. This interest in national subjects could have led to cosiness as it tended to during Balcon's time at Ealing Studios, but at this period he was under pressure from the Ostrer Brothers to maintain a diversity in his output and aim for the international market. Powell unfairly argued that Balcon had 'lost his soul' in thus producing a programme of films, but the range of his output was a strength. His only major mistake lay in the way he responded to the demand for international films.

Basil Dean called ATP the Studio with the Team Spirit, and its qualities as a place to work are suggested by the fact that such distinguished directors as Carol Reed, Thorold Dickinson and Basil Dearden emerged from Dean's tutelage. Dean's weakness was his belief in the stage as the ideal source of film material, as a result of which the only films from ATP that secured broad popular appeal were those featuring Gracie Fields and George Formby. Dean saw the theatre as the inherently superior form, setting up his company initially 'to combine the current influence of the film studios with the wealth of past achievement of the theatre'.[10] One of his early projects was a film version of John Galsworthy's *Escape* (1930), which he proposed to the writer as a way to enable theatre to 'regain influence' over the screen. The film was a flop but Dean continued to produce, as Dickinson put it, what were essentially 'canned plays'.[11]

Something of the difference between working for Dean or Balcon and for John Maxwell can be gleaned from the fact that denizens of the latter referred to BIP's script department as the Borstal. The company's head of production, Walter Mycroft, had been a founding member of the Film Society, but he doesn't seem to have had very much interest in nurturing talent. There were competent individuals in the script department, just as there were good cameramen working on the studio floor, but the environment didn't encourage any of these individuals to stretch their creative powers. 'The story department of BIP fulfilled my worst fears,' remarked Michael Powell. 'It was a Saragossa Sea of hopeful scriptwriters, an Isle of Lost Scripts.'[12] While Balcon was encouraging his writers to come up with original stories, and steadily reducing the company's reliance on the theatre, BIP remained largely stagebound. The company not only had no interest in encouraging innovation, but its fear of creative daring amounted sometimes to paranoia. One Borstal inmate, Rodney Ackland, was expelled from the company when it was discovered that he had written a highbrow play while employed as a BIP screenwriter. And the experiments with sound that Hitchcock carried out in films such as *Blackmail* (1929) and *Murder* (1931), as well as the narrative innovations of *Rich and Strange* (1932, *East of Shanghai* in US), seem to have irritated Maxwell even more than similar developments did C. M. Woolf. Ackland records Hitchcock's account of how BIP treated its directors:

47

Test for sound – Anny Ondra with Hitchock on the set of *Blackmail* **(1929)**

> At the slightest sign of originality in approach or technique a director might well be regarded as a menace and any departure from the hoary formula adhered to by the executives could be considered highly presumptuous.[13]

The lack of ambition in the output of slapstick comedies, innocuous romances and bland dramas from BIP demonstrated Maxwell's willingness to accept the economic constraints of British film production, while doing little to encourage new approaches to low-budget filmmaking. He had a good chain of cinemas, as well as a strong network of contacts in Central Europe. Knowing how much he could expect to earn on a regular basis from each market, he tailored his budgets accordingly. With quality technicians creamed off from other studios, he could make cheap films so that they looked good and brought in a respectable profit. Since he had no ambition to sell his films in the US, there was no reason why he should be more adventurous.

A Board of Trade Memo in 1940 was to remark on Maxwell's notoriety for 'pursuing a policy with which the rest of the industry is at variance' but bitter personal experience lay behind his low-level ambition. In 1928 he had found, when attempting to sell BIP films to the US, that the doors were 'barred in the faces of UK producers'[14], and the excitement that *Blackmail* caused at home was not matched in the US. In other companies, however, as the production industry expanded and the films improved, it was natural that filmmakers would begin to think seriously about aiming for a share of the US market. After all, it was one of the aims of the quota legislation to foster an industry that could promote Britain just as American films promoted America and, with only ten British films a year grossing £100,000 at the local box office, the financiers backing British film companies began to push for expansion.

Encouraging them were the new links between British and American film companies that grew out of the quota legislation. While Warner Brothers and Twentieth Century-Fox had set up their own production companies to produce British pictures, other US distributors relied on local suppliers. Paramount, for example, as well as providing Korda with the money he needed for his first English films, made a deal with Wilcox's British and Dominions company to supply them with 12 pictures annually on budgets of £30,000 apiece. And Dean set up ATP with backing from RKO, although he was to be rapidly disappointed in his expectation that the company would provide him both with technical expertise and favourable distribution in the US. Not only was the company interested exclusively in cheap pictures for the local market, but also Dean had to go through the ignominious process of securing cast approval on his pictures from Solly Newman, the head of the company's UK subsidiary, whom he regarded as both 'illiterate' and 'over-shrewd where money was concerned.'[15]

The relationship between American distributors and British producers was an unequal one, but when British studios started to make films that went down well in America, executives became optimistic that they could turn the new relationships formed with US companies in their favour, and brushed aside Maxwell's repeated warnings that 'as their films were produced in a manner most acceptable to their own people, there was no reason why they should go outside for pictures.'[16] The first internationally successful British sound film was *Rome Express* from Gaumont-British, but its box-office performance was soon eclipsed by that of *The Private Life of Henry VIII* (1933), Alexander Korda's calculated attempt on the international market. With a story sufficiently English to appease nationalist sentiment and Britain's only international star, Charles Laughton, in the central role, the picture deployed every lesson Korda had learned from his sojourns in Europe and Hollywood about pleasing an audience. The film was fast, funny, naughty and irreverent. It was a masterpiece of international cinema which brought Korda all the financial backing he could need and a dream deal with United Artists that led eventually to a partnership in the American company.

The problem for British producers seeking to emulate Korda's achievement was to define what an international British film might be. Wilcox, always one to strike while the iron was hot, signed a deal of his own with United Artists, then remade his silent film, *Nell Gwynn*, presumably thinking its mix of history and sexiness made it sufficiently like Korda's hit to clean up. But it was a flop, and Wilcox moved on from UA to make successive deals with Universal and RKO. Eventually he concluded that history without salaciousness was the answer, making *Victoria the Great* (1937) and its followup, *Sixty Glorious Years* (1938, US title *Queen of Destiny*) as stately pageants, more solemn than exciting. Graham Greene sarcastically remarked of the latter that 'Both the director and the star seem to labour under the impression that they are producing something important'[17], and the film's success was enough to assure Wilcox that Hungarian naughtiness should give way to solemn patriotism.

Despite his own patriotic convictions, Balcon initially avoided national subjects in pursuit of his new-found belief that 'films had to be less and less parochial and more and more international in appeal.' Made on exceptional budgets of around £100,000 after Gaumont-British had arranged distribution through Fox, neither *Jew Süss* (1934, *Power* in US) nor *The Tunnel* (1936, *Transatlantic Tunnel* in US) had much to do with Britain. *Jew Süss* featured Conrad Veidt as an ambitious aristocrat at a German court, whose intrigues lead to his being put on trial under an old law forbidding sexual relations between Jews and Gentiles, and the film was made because of its relevance to the contemporary situation in Germany. *The Tunnel* was the British version of a film that had already been made in France and Germany, about a crazed engineer who sacrifices his family in order to complete the construction of a link between Britain and America. Both are spectacular, well-scripted pictures, but neither has the sort of commercial edge that would justify the high financial

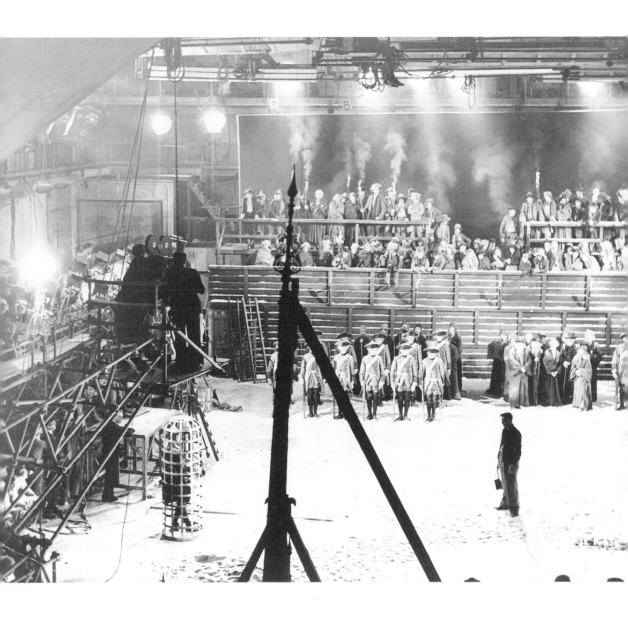

The big movie – the execution scene of *Jew Süss* **(1934), filmed at the Gaumont-British studio**

expectations their investors had of them. These were films that had been grafted onto the Gaumont-British production programme, rather than emerging out of the script department as projects with potential that called for higher expenditure. Films made in such a way were unlikely to be breakout hits.

The clash between Balcon's nationalism and the Ostrers' requirement that he pursue international popularity led to the signs of strain that are evident in much of the Gaumont-British output, and it is easy to understand why Balcon became so disillusioned with the idea of international production. Cicely Courtneidge was put into a soldier's costume and sent off to war in pursuit of her simple-minded husband in the clumsy *Me and Marlborough* (1935). Raoul Walsh was brought over from the US to direct *O.H.M.S.* (1937, *You're in the Army Now* in US), the improbable tale of an American hoodlum who takes on the identity of a murdered gambling companion and finds himself in the British Army, where he slowly comes to understand the habits of self-effacing Englishmen. It was perhaps the heightened awareness, evident in this film, of what distinguished the Americans from the British that produced such a weird send-up of the archetypal Englishman in the company's popular adaptation of Rider Haggard's *King Solomon's Mines* (1937). 'So unlike the home life of our dear Queen,' the character played by Roland Young comments in the presence of some wild African dancers. His *sang-froid* comes so naturally that, when death seems imminent, he remarks: 'It seems too bad that just when we get to where there's a fortune in diamonds, the mountain should decide to sit down on it.' But the quest for patriotism with adventure could also lead to an adaptation of C. S. Forester's true-Brit *Forever England* (1935), in which a lone sailor keeps a German ship occupied until it can be sunk by a British destroyer, and dies a hero's death in the process.

The quest for American success sometimes made Balcon's production programme an uneasy mix of the oppressively patriotic, the blandly spectacular and the uncomfortable hybrid. But it also contained films by Hitchcock dealing with British stories that avoided the sort of grandiosity which afflicted so many of the pictures pitched at the US market, and had as much wit as *The Private Life of Henry VIII*. Recognizing that audiences could never identify with nobs, Hitchcock's films showed ordinary people going through extraordinary experiences: 'The upper classes,' he remarked, 'are too "bottled up" to be of any use as colourful screen material, too stiffened with breeding to relax into the natural easiness and normality required by the screen.'[18] But the characters played by Leslie Banks in *The Man Who Knew Too Much* (1934), or Robert Donat in *The 39 Steps* (1935), are archetypically English in their capacity to muddle through, triumphing over the dark forces ranged against them by their flexibility of mind. With his powers of observation, his smooth, fast-moving narratives and his ability to make characters live on the screen, Hitchcock set himself apart from the rest of British cinema.

Comic splendour. Cicely Courtneidge on parade in *Me and Marlborough* (1935)

Madeleine Carroll and Robert Donat escape in handcuffs under Hitchcock's gaze – a scene from *The 39 Steps* (1935)

Despite Hitchcock's example, Korda argued that 'stories that dig too deep into national roots start with a handicap.' He was essentially a European filmmaker, and he was drawn to pictures that featured lavish costumes and spectacular sets. His market was the world, and he wasn't particularly concerned to toady either to the British or the Americans. He may have made his name with a story from British history, but that was simply calculated opportunism as he showed by following with similar, though less amusing and successful, treatments of the lives of *Catherine the Great* (1934) and *Rembrandt* (1936). He made films like *Sanders of the River (1935)* and *The Four Feathers* (1939), featuring courageous British aristocrats going off to fight for the British empire, not out of a sentimental admiration for those times, but because the Empire provided good stories, as Hollywood also found at the time. And while the plot of *The Ghost Goes West* (1935), about an American millionaire who buys a ghost-inhabited castle from an impoverished Scottish laird, might suggest an uncomfortable balancing act between the demands of the two national audiences, the appointment of a Frenchman, René Clair, to direct, suggests that Korda was simply impressed by the story.

While Korda's freedom from nationalist hangups may be refreshing, too many of the films that came out of his Denham Studios lacked either the narrative drive of *The Four Feathers* or the wit of *The Ghost Goes West*. No amount of pouting by Marlene Dietrich or posturing by Robert Donat could reveal why anyone thought the audience would want to watch the dull account of the Russian Revolution offered in *Knight Without Armour* (1937). And, despite Korda's avowed belief in 'lightness', little effort seems to have been made to mute the pompous misanthropy evident in the company's two H. G. Wells adaptations. *The Man Who Could Work Miracles* (1936) amusingly shows a simple bank clerk trying to grasp the potential of the miracle-working powers he has been given, but frames this story within a portentous divine commentary on 'that little planet under the sun', occupied by 'such silly little creatures, swarming and crawling.' And although *Things to Come* (1936) offers a spectacular account of the horrors of mechanized warfare, no one was thinking of the native audience when putting into the mouth of Raymond Massey a description of Britain as 'that last dismal vestige of ancient predatory soldiery, the last would-be conquerors.'

Much more commercial calculation was required to justify the cost of these pictures: *The Man Who Worked Miracles* came in at £133,000; *Things to Come* at £241,000. Since the American slump that created a space for *Henry VIII* and some of Korda's succeeding films quickly passed, subsequent pictures had to be not just good, but exceptional, if they were to break through the resistance of American audiences to foreign films. But neither Korda nor his regular scriptwriter, Lajos Biro, had the will to hone scripts for international consumption. Graham Greene fairly remarked of the amorphous string of

Korda's extravagance – *Things to Come* (1936) filmed on the backlot at Denham

sequences that made up *Rembrandt* that 'no amount of money spent on expensive sets, on careful photography, will atone for the lack of a storyline, the continuity and drive of a well-constructed plot.'[19] And Robert Donat cannot have been the only one who complained to Korda about a 'silly and unproductive attitude towards scripts', which he credited as being at 'the root of the failure of so many British films.'[20] Korda's shirty reply suggested he wasn't willing to listen to such a criticism from an expensive star. Certainly that was Donat's experience, writing from the set of *Perfect Strangers* (1945): 'No script to go on – just a mass of blarney from A. K. Our first complete script arrived five days ago – we have been filming for sixteen weeks! Isn't it wicked.'[21]

Korda enjoyed the attentions that his relatively exotic origins attracted from the British press. Now that he owned his own studio by the banks of the River Colne he could play the mogul to the technicians, artists and directors he had gathered there. But never a great organizer, he was bad at deputizing authority to others. 'His weakness,' the critic C. A. Lejeune perceptively remarked, 'is that he plays a lone hand. His final authority is unshared and undeputed.' The result was unproductive chaos. Rights were acquired in literary properties that would never be filmed. Pictures were started, had money thrown at them, and then put to one side. There was no process for acclimatizing the many foreigners who came to the studios to a different language and culture. Writers and technicians were put on contract, then given nothing to do. And nothing much was done to develop the careers of talented contract artists like Laurence Olivier, Vivien Leigh and Valerie Hobson at Denham.

The press adored Korda, because he represented 'quality and the big time', but the extravagance was a matter of concern to his backers, the Prudential Assurance Company. In 1938 they moved in to take control of Denham Studios. It was not simply that London Films had registered a loss of £330,000 for the fiscal year 1936. The Prudential, like all other financial institutions involved in films, had been put in a panic by revelations about the activities of Max Schach, one of several central Europeans renting space from Korda. During the boom sparked by the success of *Henry VIII*, banks, insurance companies and everyone else with money to lend had been pouring money into films. Almost 100 new companies had been formed, and Schach had been able to secure over a million pounds in bank guarantees to finance not only such expensive disasters as *Dreaming Lips, Love from a Stranger* and *The Marriage of Gorbal*, but even films that were never made. Schach's reckless overspending, lousy scripts, and ineffective financial management made Korda appear a model of good filmmaking. That didn't, however, help him when dealing with the Pru.

Everywhere the signs were that the British film industry was overheating. Production rose from 153 films in 1932 to 212 in 1936, and the returns were insufficient to justify such expansion. The bid to crack the American market hadn't worked, as Isidore Ostrer explained, due to 'the fact that we are not

57

accorded playing time in the most important situations, these being almost exclusively controlled by American producing interests.' British filmmakers were in trouble, and even Maxwell was only able to sustain profitability by cutting back production.

As early as 1935 Herbert Wilcox had been forced to resign from his British and Dominions company following the failure of his bid for US success. Subsequently, both Dean and Balcon had trouble with their respective boards. ATP could always come up with a few money-spinners in its annual output, but the lavish location and studio work on *Whom the Gods Love*, Dean's film on the life of Mozart, irritated board chairman Sir Stephen Courtauld, who began to argue that Dean was doing too much stage work, and had alienated George Formby. After the company had declared a loss of £96,678 for the year ending June 1937, Dean was, in his own words, 'asked to walk the plank'.[22] He was to retire altogether from films, declaring himself 'tired of knocking my head against a brick wall.'[23] Although Gaumont-British also declared a loss in 1937, of £98,000, Balcon's departure from the company was precipitated by the prospect of Maxwell, a man whose production philosophy he abhorred, taking a stake in the company, and a general sense that he wasn't going to be able to continue the same broad-based production policy as before. Maxwell never did join G-B, but Balcon's departure was followed by the closure of the company's larger Shepherd's Bush Studio. Production was henceforth to be concentrated on a steady output of 'marketable product', which meant basically low-budget comedies from the likes of Will Hay and the Crazy Gang.

Balcon moved, with several of the scriptwriters and directors he had brought up through Gaumont-British, to the American company, MGM. He anticipated new openings for Anglo-American coproduction, in which British talent could be deployed with American actors on films financed by the Americans and given proper distribution in the US. MGM had been responsible for some of the worst quota quickie outrages, and its new willingness to finance British-based production was the result of legislative changes which brought American companies deeper into British film production.

When the 1927 Cinematograph Act came up for review, there was agreement that the quota had stimulated domestic production and should be renewed, but that the quickie had to go. Only Maxwell fought a rearguard action to defeat a measure imposing a minimum (though not very onerous, £7,500) cost for quota-registered films, and allowing more expensive films to be registered for double or triple quota. The latter measure made it worthwhile for the Americans to try and do what the British had failed at, making British films which would go down well in America. Warner Brothers responded by announcing it would bring Hollywood stars to Teddington Studios. Fox set up New World Pictures to make British films, and Columbia Pictures engaged Irving Asher, who had been making quickies for Warners, to initiate a production programme that led to such interesting pictures as *The Spy in Black* (1938, *U-Boat 29* in US) and *Q Planes* (1939, *Clouds Over Europe* in US), both of which tapped into contemporary anxieties about the prospect of war.

It was MGM that seemed to take the whole business most seriously. Nevertheless, Balcon seriously overestimated the confidence of the company's boss, Louis B. Mayer, in British talent and his new head of production. While Mayer was willing to finance films from Gainsborough if they brought him Hitchcock's *The Lady Vanishes* (1938), and would pay £150,000 for six films from Robert Donat, that didn't amount to a love affair with the British film industry. Balcon could expostulate all he liked about the depth of British talent but, for Mayer, the film industry remained in Hollywood. Thus the script that Sidney Gilliatt, among others, had worked on, for *A Yank at Oxford* (1937) was taken back to Hollywood and then passed around to the resident heavyweights, including Ben Hecht, who wouldn't touch it, Herman Mankie-wicz and Scott Fitzgerald. In other areas too, Balcon was finding that Mayer's promise of autonomy was worthless. 'I had to be in charge,' he later said, 'when it came to the actual making of the films. It was, for me, the only way to work.'[24] Unsurprisingly, he left after completing only the one film, and his position was taken over by his erstwhile colleague, Victor Saville. Ironically, *A Yank at Oxford* is the least British of the three films produced by MGM in Britain. The other two were *The Citadel* (1938), from A. J. Cronin's novel about a once-idealistic doctor who becomes a cynical practitioner to the upper classes until the death of his friend on the operating table leads to a revival of his old principles, and *Goodbye Mr Chips* (1939), a hymn to the glories of the English public school. Both films starred Donat; neither had a British director.

Some of the same thinking that led Balcon to MGM persuaded Hitchcock, in 1939, to sign a deal with David O. Selznick and emigrate to Hollywood. He wanted the best stars, effective US distribution and adequate finance, and no longer felt the British industry could deliver his requirements. He did not immediately contemplate any drastic change in his filmmaking aesthetic, since his first Hollywood picture, *Rebecca* (1940), was based on a British book and used British actors, and it was some time before he made a completely American picture. Balcon took Hitchcock's departure hard, as well as that of another protégé, Robert Stevenson, feeling it reduced the chances of realizing his conviction that 'London could and should be the capital of the film world.'[25]

The failure of British cinema's first big drive on the international market-place provoked some serious reflection about why British films had only limited offshore appeal. More sensitive than their counterparts at the beginning of the decade had been to the technical qualities of Hollywood films, the critics of the time constantly drew attention to the gap between the aspirations and the achievements of British films. They were not always fair in their criticism: few today would agree with the *New Statesman* reviewer who wrote of *The Lady*

Vanishes that 'the English should leave amorous wisecracking to the nation which invented and alone understands that art.' But Dilys Powell could reasonably complain of *Jamaica Inn* (1939) that there was 'hardly any suspense, hardly any of the building up to a climax which makes the dullest American film tolerable'[26], and enthuse about Carol Reed's *A Girl Must Live* (1939), saying it showed how the British could make 'a comedy which has the speed and glitter and impudence of the best American comedies.'[27] Much the same point was made by the *Kine Weekly* reviewer, who commented that the film's dialogue coupled 'wit and wholesome vulgarity with a sureness of touch that, until now, has been the irresistible prerogative of the Americans.'[28] This sensitivity to American qualities was coupled with a new willingness to accept that commerce and art had to go hand in hand. 'And it is wrong,' remarked Graham Greene on *Goodbye Mr Chips*, 'to despise popularity in the cinema – popularity there is a *value*, as it isn't in a book: films have got to appeal to a large undiscriminating public: a film with a severely limited appeal must be, to that extent, a bad film.'[29]

Critics also drew attention to the failure of British films to exploit the potential of British life. Greene remarked on how seldom the nation's directors used the camera 'to establish a scene, a way of life, with which he and his audience are familiar.'[30] And John Grierson persistently praised Hitchcock for putting ordinary people on to the screen, while attacking Asquith for making films that reflected 'a leisure-class England which has lost contact with fundamentals, with the toiling earth and the men who go with it.'[31] As the cinema of froth, of romantic never-never-lands where poor girls fell in love with handsome officers, was now seen to have failed, filmmakers were increasingly willing to listen to Grierson's expostulation: 'The damned thing has no roots, and what is the use of saying otherwise.'

Throughout the decade, Grierson had been sponsoring young filmmakers to go out and record the lives of ordinary working people. The result in films like *Shipyard* (1934/5), an impressionistic study of the life of a shipbuilding town, or *Night Mail* (1936), a poetic record of the journey of the Postal Special from London to Glasgow, were films that revealed how much was being missed by the filmmakers who created fabulous fictions behind the walls of the studio – what Grierson described as 'the cinema's capacity for getting around, for observing and selecting from life itself.' At a time when the feature industry was undergoing a re-examination and the documentary movement was split between filmmakers who felt that they should reach out to a cinema audience, and those like Grierson himself who preferred to exhibit films outside the theatre (e.g. town halls, schools, etc.), the possibility was open for some sort of rapprochement between the documentary and the fiction film.

Where previous discussions about the Britishness of British films had been coloured by official concerns about national status, and cinema's role in boosting American economic might, filmmakers increasingly focused on the possibility that good stories might be British stories. 'I am sure,' said Balcon, 'we can get into the American market, but it will be with films of genuine British character. We shall become international by being national.'[32] This position was not only the culmination of ideas that had been knocking around in Balcon's mind for the past six years or so, it was also a declaration of a new confidence in the possibility of British cinema, and a final casting off of the inferiority complex that had impaired British filmmakers since 1918.

The fact that British films of the early 1930s don't reflect pressing economic and social realities is sometimes blamed on the censorship system. Jeffrey Richards, for example, claims the result of the strictures imposed by the British Board of Film Censors (BBFC) was 'that the British screen in the 1930s was dominated by innocuous musicals, comedies and detective stories.'[33] The argument is an easy one to assemble. The BBFC aimed to ensure that British films were as bloodless as possible, contained no criticism of any foreign power and no attack on any established British institution such as the clergy or the judiciary, avoided all political, religious and social controversy, and did nothing that would risk causing offence or inflaming public opinion. Also, the process of pre-censorship by what Thorold Dickinson called 'ex-colonels and maiden aunts in long flowered frocks' made filmmakers complicit with the censors in keeping everything a touch daring, challenging or controversial from the screen. Lord Tyrrell, the former diplomat, who became BBFC President in 1935, notoriously declared that 'we may take pride in observing that there is not a single film showing in London today which deals with any of the burning questions of the day.'[34]

But the argument is too neat, and dependent on the assumption of a desire on the part of filmmakers to express themselves about contemporary realities that was being repressed by the censorship system. There is little evidence of the existence of that urge in the early part of the decade. Balcon, for one, was not aware of any frustration on the part of his filmmakers, unless he was dishonest when remarking in his autobiography, 'It is puzzling to me in retrospect that none of my films . . . in any way reflected the despair of the times in which we were living.'[35] Given that there is little sign in early 1930s films of political comment disguised as fantasy or allegory, it is reasonable to assign limitations of these pictures more to filmmakers' sensibilities than censors' rules.

It is only around 1935, shortly after Lord Tyrrell's appointment, that filmmakers became actively conscious of censorship as a real restriction on their freedom of expression. Victor Saville joined together with the story editor of Gaumont-British and worked out that filmmakers who took all the BBFC's rules seriously wouldn't be able to make *Cinderella*. In 1936, outrage was expressed when two submissions to the BBFC to film Walter Greenwood's bestseller, *Love on the Dole*, were turned down. The following year Graham Greene, having struggled to write a script from Galsworthy's *Twenty-One Days* – about a murderer who killed himself and an innocent man who was hanged for the suicide's crime – within BBFC rules that forbade the representation of either suicide or a failure of British justice, joined with J. B. Priestley, Bernard Shaw and H. G. Wells in speaking out against the censorship system.[36] It was perhaps the argument that this imposition of middle-class morality was holding back the British cinema which led to the matter becoming an issue of public concern. Following a series of attacks on the BBFC in the House of Commons during 1938, Lord Tyrrell was persuaded to relax his stance.

Thanks to the changing critical climate, the new ideas circulating among filmmakers and the relaxation of the censorship rules, the British films made at the end of the 1930s were much tougher and more emotionally charged, than anything that had gone before. 'How the financial crisis has improved English films!'[37] remarked Graham Greene in 1939, but the process had started earlier. *Brief Ecstasy* (1937), for example, is a powerful drama centring on a woman who has married her professor and abandoned work for a life 'sitting all day knitting jumpers for my husband', who is then thrown into a whirlpool of desire when her one-time lover arrives at the marital home. The following year Arthur Woods directed *They Drive by Night* (1938), which makes evocative use of such ordinary English surroundings as a dance palace and the roadside cafés along the Great North Road for the story of an ex-convict hunted for a murder he didn't commit, who comes back to London to hunt down the real killer, a weirdo with books like *Sex in Relation to Society* and *The Thrill of Evil* in his briefcase. In *On the Night of the Fire* (1939, *The Fugitive* in US), Ralph Richardson plays a small-town barber whose desire to be shot of a miserable life, 'earning a few quid a week and no hope of making anything more' leads him first to an act of casual theft, then murder. After accidentally bringing about the death of his wife and child, he sets up his own suicide. It was of films like these that the exhibitor Sidney Bernstein may have been speaking when he said:

> The public has always wanted good British films, not the million-pound 'epics' which so often bore them, but the good, honest, unpretentious stories in which we have shown such promise — the records of everyday life.

'Real people — Real problems — a human document' declared the poster for *There Ain't No Justice* (1939), about a boxer who walks out on the crooked world of the professional fighter. The same director, Pen Tennyson, also made *The Proud Valley* (1939) which, with Carol Reed's *The Stars Look Down* (1939), exploited the BBFC's new leniency towards stories with an industrial setting. Both show life in a mining town with some degree of realism and Reed's picture, about a community in which the miners are browbeaten into

Low-life thriller – actor Emlyn Williams with director Arthur Woods during filming of *They Drive by Night* (1938)

working a coal seam which the proprietor knows to be dangerous, links itself to the documentarist sensibility with an opening voiceover referring to those 'simple working people who take heroism for granted as part of their daily lives', and a concluding epilogue that calls for the world to be 'purged of its old greeds.' Despite its distracting romantic plot, this was campaigning cinema which put a case for the nationalization of the mines as strong as the argument presented in *The Citadel* for a National Health Service.

Filmmakers were attempting to link in to contemporary realities. WAR CLOUDS OVER EUROPE read the banner headlines at the opening of Reed's earlier film, *Bank Holiday* (1938), a picture whose setting suggests escapism but whose narrative argues for the need to face up to the dark side of life in order to find meaningful happiness. Margaret Lockwood plays a nurse who, on the eve of a bank holiday, has to console a man whose wife has just died in childbirth. Preoccupied with the thoughts of his suffering, the trivial concerns of her lover become increasingly aggravating as they hang around with the crowds at Brighton. He seems over-concerned about what people think of them, to lust after her but not deeply love her. Fearful that the widower will take his life, she rushes back to London, to a man grieving for a woman who once said to him: 'don't be silly, there's no hurry, we've all our lives.'

The mood of *Bank Holiday* reflects that of a nation knowing that war must come, but other films dealt more directly with the storm clouds building up on the other side of the Channel. Just how seriously intended was the concocted story of *The Lady Vanishes* is clear from an early script which opens with a cut from a shot of Nazis strutting to geese on similar manoeuvres. The message is even more explicit in *The Four Just Men* (1939), a tale of derring-do in which some chaps set out to warn the nation of a demonic plan to destroy the British Empire, leaving world domination in one man's hands. Like so many of the films that were to be made during the Second World War, *The Four Just Men* doesn't only draw attention to the nature of the enemy; it also presents an evocative picture of just what it is that is under threat – 'all the roads and rivers, fields and woods and hills that make up this funny old island.'

The maturing of British cinema between 1939 and 1945 is often seen as a particular response to the conditions of wartime, when filmmakers were called upon to communicate to audiences an idea of 'what we are fighting for.' But filmmakers were only able to rise so impressively to the challenge because of what had happened in the preceding decade. While some filmmakers were making expensive films positioned in a European never-never-land, believing that placeless films were preferable to British films, the documentarists and, to some extent, the makers of quota pictures, were dealing with a more everyday level of life. When the technical skills of the big-budget filmmakers were combined with the ideas of those working at a lower level, the result was the possibility of a thriving national cinema.

Rushing to the seaside – Hugh Williams at the railway station for the start of
Bank Holiday **(1938)**

Dark Conflicts

The 1940s were a highpoint of British filmmaking. The Second World War gave filmmakers a role, as reporters and commentators on the contemporary situation and providers of entertainments that enabled audiences to deal with their anxieties. Official encouragement, genuine popularity and a sense of purpose helped further heal the self-doubt and hesitation that had previously constrained British filmmakers. The rise in cinema admissions and consolidation of the industry's structure meant that, when the restrictions on subject matter were lifted at the end of the war, filmmakers could fully stretch their imaginations on stories that seemed relevant to the post-war mood. The result was that, for a few years, directors like Carol Reed, David Lean, Michael Powell, Robert Hamer and Alexander Mackendrick created masterpieces. But the new financing structure collapsed under them and, as the cultural energy build up during the 1939–45 period became depleted, these filmmakers were only occasionally to work again at the same level of intensity. And British filmmaking was never quite the same again.

The production industry was much less active during the war than it had been before, producing an average of only 69 films annually, and as few as 46 in 1942. If there was any substance in the argument that high quantity was necessary to bring about a certain level of quality, this retrenchment would have been disastrous. Instead, the concentration of energies, combined with the prosperity that came with rising cinema admissions, from 19 million weekly in 1939 to over 30 million in 1945, enabled some filmmakers to create pictures of high quality.

Although the panic order for cinemas to close and production to cease was rapidly rescinded, many film studios were to be requisitioned by the military throughout the war. ABPC (the company into which BIP had been absorbed), for example, lost its Elstree base. By the spring of 1940 only six of the 19 pre-war studios were still operating. But this was in many ways a blessing. Too many studios had been built in Britain during the production boom and, at a time when filmmakers were anyway keener than they had been hitherto to get out among ordinary people, they found they were no longer constrained by anxious accountants determined to maximize the use of studio space. Among those who found wartime location shooting refreshing was the actor Michael Redgrave who credited much of the quality in *The Way to the Stars* (1945), Asquith's atmospheric picture about life on an airforce base, to 'the atmosphere of those three weeks at Catterick, which could never have been created in the studio.'[1]

Filmmakers were constricted as to subject matter by the requirement that their films contribute in some way to the war effort. That was the deal to keep British filmmakers in business which Alexander Korda had proposed to government, and supported with his propaganda film, *The Lion Has Wings* (1939), combining documentary footage with patriotic clips from earlier feature films and a contemporary narrative full of pontifications on Britain's purpose in going to war. Balcon echoed Korda with his pledge that Ealing Studios would 'grasp with both hands the opportunity of putting every phase of the war on to the screen.'[2] Scripts had to be submitted to Ministry of Information (MOI) officials for vetting. If the film presented an image of typically English virtues – independence of spirit, toughness, sympathy with the underdog – or put the case for the ideals of freedom and parliamentary democracy, then the filmmakers could have the stock they needed, and the necessary artists would be released from the ranks. The MOI could also be helpful in liaising between film companies and government departments, and even put finance into the occasional film such as *49th Parallel* (1941, *The Invaders* in US), Powell–Pressburger's skilful piece of star-studded propaganda. If the MOI didn't approve, things were more difficult.

That filmmakers didn't feel hamstrung by the need to defer to the MOI reflects their own desire to 'do their bit'. But the ministry was anyway not run by the maiden aunts of the BBFC but by members of the intelligentsia who took a reasonably broad view of wartime cinema, and recognized that effective propaganda was subtle propaganda. As well as vetting projects, the MOI ran an Ideas Committee to notify filmmakers of issues that needed developing into film narratives. It was then up to the industry's writers to find amusing and diverting ways to explore these important questions, sustain morale and present an image of British strength to the outside world. Being asked to write stories that would distinguish an idiosyncratic, individualistic and, in some ways, rather odd group of people from the militaristic, regimented and brutal régime they were fighting against, was a challenge to which many found they could rise.

In some ways filmmakers enjoyed more freedom than before. Under the censorship rules in force throughout the 1930s, they would not have been able to cast aspersions on a foreign power, tackle the relations between capital and labour, or take an irreverent view of the army. But a nation now so proud of its right to freedom of speech could not exempt British institutions from criticism. *Love on the Dole* (1941), with its depiction of the grimness of life for the unemployed in the Salford slums, was finally given the go-ahead. And many films attacked the sort of conservative attitudes which held back the British war effort. The message of *The First of the Few* (1942, *Spitfire* in US), a biopic of the life of R. J. Mitchell, is that the Spitfire was made possible by one man taking on short-sighted business executives and parsimonious government authorities. Similarly, the hero of *The Foreman Went To France* (1941, *Somewhere in France* in US) has to overcome managerial indifference and bureaucratic obstruction to cross the Channel and recover machines that might otherwise fall into the hands of the Germans. 'Nothing in the King's regulations against using commonsense,' remarks the Cockney in the group that's been persuaded to dump their official load and carry the machines through war-battered France. This critical strain culminates in *The Life and Death of Colonel Blimp* (1943), which argues that the gentlemanly values appropriate to the Boer War and the First World War are no longer suitable for fighting the Nazis. 'War starts at midnight' screams the bald-headed general when his steam bath is interrupted by a plucky Home Guard soldier who has launched a premature start to a military exercise. The films was advertised as the BANNED film because of Churchill's doubts about its message, but no serious attempt was made to stop it being made or shown.

The enemy was the more usual butt of filmmakers' criticism, particularly in comedies which showed warm-hearted, slightly muddled Englishmen winning through against the demon aggressors. In *Sailors Three* (1940, *Three Cockeyed Sailors* in US), Tommy Trinder and his companions get drunk and end up on a German ship which, more by mishap than demon cunning, they occupy and deliver to their commander. The amateurishness of Will Hay doesn't stop him winning over some Nazis, giving the others a good lesson in the English way of doing things, and bringing home their secret weapon in *The Goose Steps Out* (1942). But the apogee of imaginative anti-Nazism comes in *Let George Do It* (1940, *To Hell with Hitler* in US), when George Formby, who otherwise divides his time between playing his ukelele and trying to crack the code a bandleader is using to broadcast messages to the Germans, dreams a sequence in which he flies over Berlin in a Zeppelin, lands at a Nuremberg rally and challenges the Führer himself, 'You, Adolf, put a sock in it.'

Similar themes were treated more romantically in Carol Reed's *Night Train to Munich* (1940, *Gestapo: Night Train* in US) and Leslie Howard's *Pimpernel Smith* (1941, *Mister V; The Fighting Pimpernel* in US). The latter features a seemingly placid English schoolmaster who is, in fact, smuggling refugees out of Europe. Like the comedy films, these tales of the British winning through by skill and intelligence carry their propaganda messages lightly. A point may be slightly rammed home as when, in *The Foreman Went To France*, the brutality of the Germans in shooting refugees and bombing cities to kill innocent civilians is several times reiterated, but there is never any point in these pictures where one feels the dramatic structure is being distorted for purely message-directed ends.

One cannot say the same for those films which make specific connections between earlier events in British history and now. *Lady Hamilton* (1941, *That Hamilton Woman* in US), which Korda made in America with Vivien Leigh and Laurence Olivier, works most of the time as a love story, but the messages that constantly obtrude about men whose 'insane ambition' makes them want to destroy what others had built are not organic to the main narrative. 'You cannot make peace with dictators, you have to destroy them,' Nelson asserts at one point for the benefit of inattentive members of the audience. Nor are viewers left to make for themselves the link between the 'nation of arch fanatics led by an arch fanatic' that confronted *The Young Mr Pitt* (1942) and Britain's contemporary enemies. Presenting a very sanitized view of Pitt's career, the film ends up a hagiography of Churchill. These films showed that using the past as a mirror through which to view the present was an approach of limited value during wartime.

Similar signs of strain were present in films that offered images of heroism. *Ships with Wings* (1941), for example, tells the improbable story of a flyer who loses his commission after an attempt to impress the admiral's daughter leads to the death of her brother. He takes up a job as a pilot shuttling planes between a Greek island and the mainland, but is eventually able to vindicate himself when his old ship reaches the Aegean. Recruited for a tricky mission, he pinions a German plane under his own, crashes into a dam, floods a German base and goes out in a blaze of glory, having saved the British fleet from likely destruction. A peculiarly bad film which is made all the more dreadful by scattered shots of Greek swains sitting beside ancient pillars and playing their pipes, *Ships with Wings* represented a turning point for Balcon, who had supervised the film's production at his Ealing Studios. He concluded that the approach was 'too heavily fictionalized' to go down with an audience that was having to deal with the everyday realities of war. 'From then on,' he recalled, 'we learned to snatch our stories from the headlines and they had the ring of truth.'[3]

This coming-together of documentary and fiction filmmaking was the most significant aesthetic development of the period. 'It took a war to compel the British to look at themselves and find themselves interesting,'[4] Dilys Powell was later to remark. Although the MOI Film Division, under Sir Joseph Ball, had been hostile to the documentary movement, his successors Kenneth Clark and Jack Beddington arranged for their GPO Film Unit to be absorbed within the Ministry. The documentarists were natural allies of the government, well practised in tailoring their own ideas to the demands of their sponsors, and exploring ideas about British character that it had become important to validate in order to distinguish the natives from their foes.

Whereas Grierson had concluded in the late 1930s that 'in the commercial cinema there is no future worth saving,' Harry Watt hoped to 'crash the commercial cinemas'[5] with story documentaries. Having shown the potential

69

of this genre in *North Sea* (1938), his film about fishermen caught in a storm, he demonstrated with *Target for Tonight* (1941), which follows an air-crew on a raid across the Channel, that films about the truth of war could secure a large audience. The logistical problems involved in constructing a narrative out of fast-moving events restricted the potential of this genre, but other impressive story-documentaries were produced. Churchill's favourite was *Desert Victory* (1943), a loosely-structured account of the Desert Campaigns, but the most remarkable documentary of this period was Humphrey Jennings' *Fires were Started* (1943). Set on the home front, it follows a crew of firefighters working through the night to control the blaze at an East End warehouse. Situating the men in their community, the film astonishes with its unstrained truthfulness and poetic intensity.

Balcon saw the potential for bringing into mainstream cinema the observational powers of the documentarists, and their capacity for evoking a quieter form of heroism than that displayed in *Ships with Wings*. Both Albert Cavalcanti, the onetime head of the GPO Film Unit whose Brazilian origins had made him unacceptable as a civil servant, and Watt joined the tight group of filmmakers Balcon had gathered round him at Ealing. Described by the studio's publicist-turned-producer Monja Danischewsky as 'the Nanny who brought us up,'[6] Cavalcanti helped Ealing's filmmakers to develop the semi-documentary style of films such as *San Demetrio London* (1943), which recounts the true story of a group of sailors bringing a wrecked oil tanker back to port.

But when these documentary imports came to direct films of their own, they revealed distinct personal leanings. Watt's *Nine Men* (1943) depicts a group of soldiers making their last stand in a desert hut, which has a dramatic intensity that pushes it to the edge of documentary fiction. And Cavalcanti's *Went the Day Well?* (1943, *Forty-eight Hours* in US), draws upon a broader range of influences. While setting up the calm surface of village life in a realistic manner, the film does so only as a contrast to the savagery that ensues: a priest is shot while making a stand against 'the enemies and oppressors of mankind', the Post Office lady kills a German with an axe and is promptly bayonetted herself, and the vicar's daughter disposes of the Quisling squire, to whom she had been amorously linked. In the way it lays bare dark emotional rumblings normally concealed beneath the constraints of village life, *Went the Day Well?* suggests Cavalcanti had learned as much from the Surrealists he worked with in Paris as from Britain's documentarists.

To Michael Powell documentary was nothing more than a refuge for 'disappointed feature filmmakers or out-of-work poets',[7] but the wartime films he made within an immensely fruitful collaboration (the Archers) with the Hungarian Emeric Pressburger, with the two of them sharing credits for production, direction and screenwriting, take on documentary concerns in ways which indicate that the absorption of the documentary filmmakers into commercial filmmaking was only an incidental part of a process with roots deep in wartime culture. *A Canterbury Tale* (1944) centres, like *Went the Day Well?*, around a sinister village squire. But while Cavalcanti uses his traitor to question the existing social order, Powell–Pressburger's Thomas Colpepper remains the guardian of the best English traditions. He has taken to disrupting romantic trysts in the village by pouring glue into the hair of those girls who step out with soldiers; his motive being to encourage the largest possible number of servicemen to attend his lectures, where he speaks of the mysteries of the countryside. There is a significant divide between Cavalcanti's surrealism and Powell's romantic mysticism but, within their bizarre plot, the Powell–Pressburger team also show us how land girls were being absorbed into the rural workforce, and the sort of connections that were being formed between British and American soldiers. The film both fulfils the Powell–Pressburger partnership's aim to produce 'original stories, written for the screen, keeping pace with events and trying to put into action what people were thinking and saying at the time,'[8] which is what the more obviously documentarist filmmakers were also trying to do, and articulates its own vision of the mystical forces in nature, culminating in the healing miracle that arrives for each of the three Canterbury pilgrims on their way to the cathedral.

The documentary impulse was inherent in the contract filmmakers made with the MOI at the beginning of the war, but it could absorb the poetic romanticism of Powell–Pressburger, the sophisticated visual and verbal montages produced by Humphrey Jennings, another documentarist with surrealist roots, in such 1941 pictures as *Words for Battle* and *Listen to Britain*, as well as films in the realist tradition. And it's significant that a strand of films showing how a group of individuals from different social backgrounds could be brought together by war and learn to forget their divisions, generally regarded as the supreme achievement of wartime 'realism', was anticipated in Powell–Pressburger's *One of our Aircraft is Missing* (1941), in which a bomber crew bales out over Holland and works its way home with help from the Dutch resistance. A similar focus on the war's effect in shattering class barriers is present in *In Which We Serve* (1942), where the trigger to unity is a torpedoed destroyer rather than a crashed plane, *The Gentle Sex* (1943), which follows a group of women as they are trained to become competent fighters, and *Millions Like Us* (1943), which brings together a mixed group of girls in an aircraft engineering factory.

'Realist' films like these drew ecstatic praise from the local critics, whose enthusiasm for the national cinema was a new phenomenon. Writing shortly after the end of the war, Roger Manvell spoke of a 'cinematic poetry peculiar to British films' while Dilys Powell suggested that the films made during the war had 'set the English film on the path in which masterpieces may be created.' Such enthusiasm may have had as much to do with the excited nationalism of wartime, as any subtantial appreciation of these films' merits, and it should not be supposed that British filmmakers had universally gone from being dull and unimaginative to become masters of the cinematic art. Just as stagebound as anything produced before 1939 is *When We Are Married* (1943), in which three middle-aged couples are thrown into a frenzy upon discovering that the parson who married them all those years ago wasn't qualified to do so. The script of *They Met in the Dark* (1946), in which James Mason is a discharged sea captain hunting down those who delivered fake orders to his ship, is a textureless and muddled affair. Nor did the documentary impulse make much impact on the films of Herbert Wilcox, whose 'patriotic' pictures always had a preachy tone. In her primping performance as Amy Johnson in *They Flew Alone* (1942), Anna Neagle is allowed to express none of the deeper motivations for her character's decision to defy convention and take up flying, and the film never tries to make anything of its contrast between Johnson's individualism and its concluding images of girls marching, clearly anything but individuals.

What these filmmakers miss is the level of emotional intensity that both the realist filmmakers, whom the critics approved of, and those of a more melodramatic or fantastic disposition, whom they didn't, seem able to conjure, for almost the first time, in the films they produced during the war. The deprivations and adjustment entailed by war taught British filmmakers how to orchestrate strong emotions. Whereas Hitchcock's last British film, the pre-war *Jamaica Inn* (1939), could be said to be dealing with a similar area of subject matter to, say, *Hatter's Castle* (1941), the emotional level struck by the latter is a world away from the former. Hitchcock sets an innocent woman against Charles Laughton's squire, a criminal buffoon, and a gang of smugglers, but there is never any real conflict, and the ending is almost comic. *Hatter's Castle*, by contrast, is remorseless, depicting the destruction of a family by the pressures created by its patriarch's social aspirations.

But it was at Gainsborough Studios, where production head Maurice Ostrer believed in making films that offered the audience 'good themes and good laughs'[9] that filmmakers produced the most distinctive melodramas of this period, entertainments created at the opposite extreme to the realist dramas. Tightly budgeted, aiming to thrill and drawing upon the talents of performers such as Margaret Lockwood, Phyllis Calvert, James Mason and Stewart Granger, these full-blooded pictures were among the most popular films released in the latter stages of the war. In *The Man in Grey* (1943), Lockwood plays a ruthless woman who enters the house of an old schoolfriend as a governess and takes up with the man of the house. After killing her former friend, she is ready for her final triumph but instead is killed by his riding whip. It's a grim vision of the past, heavy with conflict, loss and unhappiness. There's a somewhat lighter tone to *The Wicked Lady* (1945), another big hit, in which Lockwood is the aristocratic wife whose passion for living and sense that if 'I can't live while I'm alive, I'll go mad' leads her into a double life as a highwaywoman.

What Dilys Powell missed when she described *The Wicked Lady* as a concatenation of 'the hoary, the tedious, the disagreeable,'[10] as did other critics who saw Gainsborough's films as a reassertion of an old escapist tendency in British cinema, was how much of an advance such films offered on everything of a similar sort that had gone before, and how they touched the sentiments of audiences who could no longer respond to stories of gallant endeavour quite as they could when it seemed that defeat was an imminent possibility. While the films made at the beginning of the war appealed for people to forget selfish desires and apply themselves to the common good, to put aside class divisions in order to confront an enemy that threatened everyone equally, the Gainsborough films addressed themselves to the frustrations and the pain that came after continuous self-sacrifice.

What happens in many of the significant films that emerge after the war is that the claims of the community and the individual are set against each other, bringing together Ealing realism and Gainsborough melodrama in a tremendously fruitful, if brief and explosive, relationship. Ealing Studios made films as untypical of itself as *Dead of Night* (1945), a collection of mostly unsettling tales of the fantastic and of hidden desires that erupt from below, *Pink String and Sealing Wax* (1945), in which the son of a strict father becomes the unwitting accomplice in a woman's murder of her husband, and even a costume melodrama, *Saraband for Dead Lovers* (1948, *Saraband* in US).

Powell and Pressburger brought an energy to films exploring this conflict between wartime values and those of the post-war world that reflects their increasing disaffection with the new England. In *I Know Where I'm Going* (1945), Wendy Hiller plays a go-ahead girl who, when forced to choose between the sort of rural mysticism the filmmakers previously invoked in *A Canterbury Tale* and a 'good' marriage, is only reluctantly brought round to accept the former. *Black Narcissus* (1946) chronicles the breakdown of a community of nuns set up in the Himalayas, riven by inner conflicts and pulled apart by the intrusion of romantic figures from outside. The conflict is played out for the last time in *The Red Shoes* (1948), where the ballerina played by Moira Shearer initially lives unproblematically for her dancing, until she falls in love with a composer. Forced to acknowledge the impossibility of achieving perfection in both love and work, she is driven to self-destruction. The old wartime community that could absorb individual needs, the filmmakers are saying, is no more. However, it's impossible for anyone who lived through those times to settle down to cosy domesticity, the world without adventure that Marius Goring offers Shearer. *The Red Shoes* is a declaration by Powell–Pressburger that they don't find post-war, welfare-state England a particularly brave or challenging place in which to live.

73

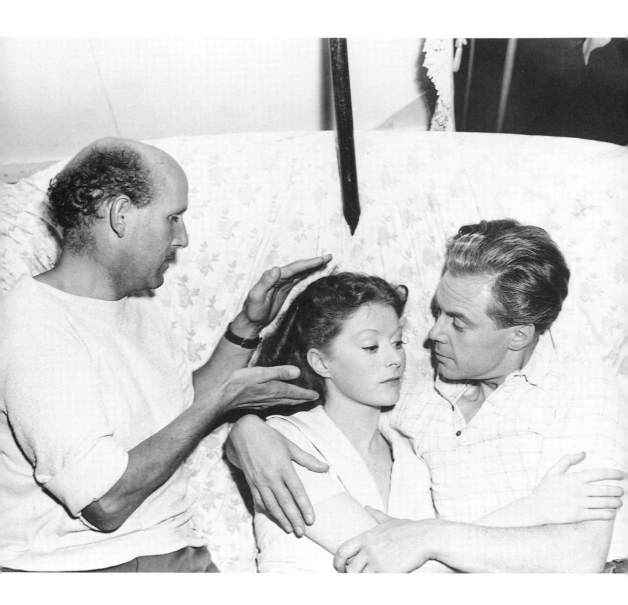

Michael Powell sizes up Marius Goring and Moira Shearer for
The Red Shoes **(1948)**

The films of David Lean show a similar drift towards a darker vision of the choices facing individuals in post-war society. The domestic world which draws the suburban housewife away from the temptations of an illicit romance in *Brief Encounter* (1945) is quite as cosy as that depicted in an earlier collaboration between Lean and Noël Coward, *This Happy Breed* (1944). The fact that the film was hailed by critics as a triumphant piece of realism, even though the woman's choice between a passionate affair and married contentment is as melodramatic as that offered by any Gainsborough melodrama, reflects the kudos Lean had acquired as director of *In Which We Serve*, the critic's touchstone for quality. Lean's realist reputation was enlarged by his first Dickens adaptation, *Great Expectations* (1946) but, by the time he came to film the extraordinary expressionist opening to *Oliver Twist* (1948), questions were being asked. Critics were even more profoundly unnerved when Lean took a new approach to the *Brief Encounter* story with *The Passionate Friends* (1948), where the husband is a much more potent, interesting and violent character than the would-be lover, again played by Trevor Howard. Finally, with *Madeleine* (1950), Lean ventured into costume melodrama, telling the story of a nineteenth-century woman who may, or may not, have murdered her French lover. The critics were appalled.

But, however rapidly the filmmakers who built their reputations during the war may have disillusioned the critics, with their narrow concept of what the nation's filmmakers should be doing, British filmmakers had reason to be confident in 1945. They had built a strong relationship with audiences both at home and abroad. In the US, thanks to an agreement that major distributors would give eight films annually a full circuit release, pictures such as *The 49th Parallel*, *Target for Tonight* and *In Which We Serve* had done remarkable business. And there was now a British company as large as any American maker, under a leader, J. Arthur Rank, who wanted to breathe life into the dream that British films could conquer the American market.

Rank was a businessman who pursued a grander vision than Isidore Ostrer or John Maxwell had ever done. The third son of a successful Yorkshire miller, he had the contacts necessary to raise all the backing he needed. Having started in films by putting a few thousand pounds into a short religious picture in 1933, he went on to form British National, a production company, in association with Lady Yule, the wealthy widow of a Calcutta jute merchant. He built a large studio at Pinewood and went into distribution with General Film Distributors (GFD). Then, as the industry reeled from the production slump of the late 1930s, Rank extended his stake in the business. He took over Denham from Korda in 1938 and by 1941 had acquired a controlling interest in Oscar Deutsch's Odeon cinema chain and the Gaumont-British set-up – both its cinemas and its filmmaking companies. Between 1941 and 1947, Rank's companies were to be responsible for financing half the films made in Britain.

Rank controlled most available studio space, two cinema circuits (over 600 theatres) and the largest British distribution company.

With cinema admissions expanding rapidly, Rank was not only in a buoyant financial condition, but also in a strong position to negotiate a deal, which would secure his films a fair return from the US market, with major American companies increasingly concerned to protect their UK earnings. As well as negotiating from strength, Rank had a realistic perception of just how tough he would have to be. There was no question of simply negotiating a deal with one American company, as producers had done in the 1930s, and then just hoping for the best. When his attempt to buy Korda's stake in United Artists didn't work out, Rank poached two of the company's employees and put them in charge of an international distribution operation, Eagle Lion Films. Then, realizing the cost and risk of setting up an American operation only for his own films, he backtracked and arranged for UA to handle his company's big-budget pictures. He then opened discussions with Universal, a company in which he had taken a 25 per cent stake back in 1935, whereby Rank's smaller films would be packaged with the pictures of an independent US production company, and sold in a block to exhibitors. But this sophisticated attempt to deal with exhibitor resistance to British films was ruled illegal by the US Justice Department in 1946 and had to be replaced by a less ambitious system, in which Rank's films were sold on their merits. While continuing negotiation with the Americans, Rank also bought cinema circuits in Canada, New Zealand, Australia, Egypt and South Africa.

Many set the odds on Rank achieving his ambitions very low indeed, seemingly believing that, as Eric Ambler was later to remark, 'a policy of selling British cars to America with their steering wheels on the right would have had the same chance of success.'[11] And Michael Balcon, now convinced that making big-budget films to please the Americans was a sure way for the British film industry to commit suicide, began a campaign through the Cinematograph Films Council to draw attention to the amount of control Rank, with his dangerous policies, now had over the film industry. The resulting Palache Report, named after its chairman and published by the CFC in 1944, articulated Balcon's concern that the British cinema was becoming a 'channel for disseminating the ideas and aspirations, no matter how worthy in themselves, of one or two dominating personalities in this country,'[12] and backed his view that the British industry should concentrate on a regular output of low-budget, authentically British films.

But Rank was a disarming opponent. He offered Balcon's Ealing Studios favourable distribution through his company's domestic and foreign network, with 'independence as far as production was concerned'[13] together with a licence to go on producing low-budget British films. Balcon was sensible enough to forget his scruples and accept. Similarly, although Rank turned down Sydney

Box's first independent feature, *29 Acacia Avenue* (1945), on the grounds that the innocuous story about an aborted premarital romp was 'immoral', and offered him £40,000 to put the film on the shelf, he was later to give Box the job of running Gainsborough's production programme.

In any case, by strengthening his position abroad, Rank had made himself unassailable at home. The ministers and officials at the Department of Trade to whom the Palache Report was submitted were less concerned about the inner workings of the film industry than with how to respond to Treasury demands that they work to secure foreign currency. Rank's argument that he needed the studios, the cinemas and the distribution network if he was to ensure that his films performed in foreign markets was, therefore, one that relevant officials were predisposed to accept. And, given the rather jaundiced view that civil servants had by then formed of the movie business, it is not surprising that they preferred to commend Rank for observing 'the normal standards of commercial efficiency and honesty, which have not so far been conspicuous within the film industry' than listen to the arguments presented by Palache that budget control on Rank's film productions was inadequate. In short, the DOT accepted that the existence of a conglomerate like Rank offered the best 'prospects of making first-class films, of acquiring an export market.' Balcon was forced off the CFC, where places were found both for Alexander Korda, who shared the new mogul's enthusiasm for 'bigger and bigger films,' and for Rank himself.

For a time Rank produced films that really could compete against American pictures. Powell and Pressburger brought their Archers outfit under the umbrella of Rank's Independent Producers company where they made all their films from *The Life and Death of Colonel Blimp* to *The Red Shoes*. After the phenomenal success of *In Which We Serve*, the Italian producer Filippo del Giudice, whose belief in high-budget artistic filmmaking was in line with Rank's, attached his Two Cities company to Independent Producers, and made through it such films as the Lean–Coward *This Happy Breed*; Laurence Olivier's rampantly patriotic version of Shakespeare's *Henry V* (1945); Thorold Dickinson's unbalanced *Men of Two Worlds* (1946, *Witch Doctor* in US) and Carol Reed's *Odd Man Out* (1945, *Gang War* in US), the story of a dying gunman's desperate search for charity on the streets of Belfast. To make *Brief Encounter*, Lean's Cineguild team joined Independent Producers as a separate company, as did Wessex, a company formed by former Crown Film Unit filmmakers Ian Dalrymple and Jack Lee.

The success of Independent Producers owed nothing to Rank's skills as an impresario; he had none. He benefited from the way the highly productive film industry of the 1930s had given filmmakers such as Powell, on quota films, and David Lean, as a film editor, an opportunity to develop their creative skills and judgement. And it was the filmmakers' good fortune that their first creative maturity coincided with Rank's willingness to give full scope to their talents. Independent Producers may not have been a particularly well-managed production outfit but the filmmakers had developed sufficient self-discipline to ensure that, while the films might become increasingly expensive, they were always tightly constructed and realized the potential in their subject matter. And a competitive working environment drew out from directors and writers the best they could achieve. The creative excitement generated leads sometimes, in the work of Lean and Powell–Pressburger, to moments of creative delirium.

A more controlled production context had been established by Balcon at Ealing, where his belief that filmmaking was essentially a team activity had been strengthened by the importation of documentary filmmakers who were accustomed to working in tight-knit groups. Even after projects had been assigned to particular producers, directors and writers, they remained studio properties, discussed at round-table discussions involving all the key people who worked there. 'The various projects were not regarded as competitive,' Danischewsky recalled, 'so we read each other's scripts and kicked in with our suggestions and contributions to all the films.' To strengthen the sense of group identity, set designers, editors, publicists and others graduated through the studio's hierarchy and became directors, writers or producers. With this coherent team, in many ways bonded to the studio, Balcon set out to make films that mirrored what was happening to British society and fulfilled his aim of building up 'a native industry with its roots firmly planted in the soil of this country.'[14]

For a time Ealing was as closely in touch with the hopes and frustrations of post-war audiences as were the directors and writers working for Rank's Independent Producers. Both explored the breakup of wartime solidarity, the liberation of former restraints on individual selfishness and the irruption of dark, subversive and irrational forces to tear down the cosy myths so assiduously cultivated during wartime. Behind the façade of normal family existence in an East End street, in *It Always Rains on Sunday* (1947), lurk strong, violent desires. The RAF officer who was so noble in conflict becomes the devious villain in *Cage of Gold* (1950). The willingness of England to welcome foreigners into its communities, celebrated during wartime in the pleasantries of *Tawny Pipit* (1944), is thrown into question by the searing melodrama of *Frieda* (1947), where the 'kindly, good-natured people' of Denfield become vicious xenophobes when the stranger amongst them is a blonde German girl. And the willingness of the British aristocracy to yield place without a show of force is thrown into serious doubt by the calculated viciousness of *Kind Hearts and Coronets* (1949), as the disowned son of a noble line works murderously through the family tree in order to claim his birthright.

British filmmakers would not for much longer feel free to look behind the placid surface of English life. The history of Gainsborough Pictures shows just

Extra-marital passion – Googie Withers and John McCallum steam it up for director Robert Hamer in *It Always Rains on Sunday* (1947)

Robert Hamer prepares Joan Greenwood for the trial scene in
Kind Hearts and Coronets **(1949)**

how strong were the forces dragging them away from conflict and passion, towards gentility. Here Rank's insistence that he was in films to make money, that he wouldn't interfere because he knew nothing about production, was challenged by his lack of vision and, eventually, his weak stomach for full-blooded costume melodrama. Gradually he undermined the potential of one of his most profitable production centres. Key personnel, including Frank Launder and Sidney Gilliatt, left in anger to join Independent Producers after Rank had failed to support deputy production chief Ted Black in his determination to maintain a broad range of productions against Maurice Ostrer's desire to focus on costume melodrama. Without the depth of talent to draw on, and with a Rank veto placed on a sequel to the phenomenally successful *The Wicked Lady*, Maurice Ostrer, who took over Black's responsibilities, was unable again to match the verve of the early period pictures. He was in turn replaced by Sydney Box who, while reinstating Black's policy of maintaining a broad range of films and enlarging the script department, run by his wife Muriel, to develop original stories and train new writers, gave a twist to the company's film production that looks more like deference to Rank's demand for moral uplift than a full-hearted pursuit of the popular audience.

The early Gainsborough melodramas, while they never allowed the villainess to prevail, offered insight into the sensations of an evil life dedicated to, sometimes perverse, pleasure. That openness to liberated desire is cut off in the films which the Boxes produce. The heroine of *The Good Time Girl* (1948) never seems to be enjoying herself. She has a miserable time, leaving home for a job in a club, escaping from reform school to hang out with drunken hoodlums and joining up with some soldiers for a bout of petty thieving that culminates in murder, and the film never allows one into the girl's experience. It's always angled towards the case for more funds to be allocated to reform schools set up for 'the salvaging of these youngsters whose natural growth has been marred by bad upbringing, bad companions, bad luck.' Muriel Box claimed for the film that the issues it covered were 'treated seriously and with sincerity.'[15] Something of the same librarian's desire for accuracy seems to have afflicted Gainsborough's later nods in the direction of costume melodrama. Of the promisingly-titled *Bad Lord Byron* (1949), for example, Box remarked that 'nothing was artificially concocted,'[16] but the film is also deathly dull to watch as various figures from Byron's life come into a court room to debate whether he was a great poet or a great cad.

The Gainsborough films that best characterize the desire of filmmakers to close their eyes to the darker currents in society, to make believe that the world really is as cosy as some wartime films made it out to be, are *Holiday Camp* (1947) and the three sequels set amongst the jolly Huggett family. *Vote for Huggett* (1948), for example, shows the family patriarch played by Jack Warner making a stand against a corrupt local councillor, then with the help of the local youth club and three eccentric old ladies, exposing the property transactions that stand in the way of a lido and public garden being built to serve the local community. The sanitized, simplified, view of the world offered in films like this anticipates later television styles, and mark the beginning of the closedown of any willingness on the part of British filmmakers to confront the difficulties of contemporary life.

The drift to comedy started by *Hue and Cry* (1947), in which a group of kids foil some crooks, took Balcon's studio in a similar direction, but there is a spirit of anarchy in the early Ealing comedies and a recognition that, since there can be no final victories, the little people must sustain their rebellion. Typical are the films written by T. E. B. Clarke, such as *Passport to Pimlico* (1949), about a community whose discovery that it is an independent Burgundian principality enables the inhabitants to forget for a while the realities of post-war austerity, and *The Lavender Hill Mob* (1951), about a bank clerk who robs a bank. Even so, a process of gradual denial creeps into Ealing's output, most clearly represented in *Train of Events* (1949), a film that brings together many of the characters who people post-war movies, only to kill them off or put a stop on their moral infractions. A blitz baby hungry for love tries to get her hunted German lover away to safety in Canada; an actor, taunted by his wife for being still soft and weak, replies he's been 'toughened' by military service and proves it by strangling her, and a conductor plans to elope with his pianist mistress. These troubled souls are mostly killed in the train crash. Only the conductor and his lady survive, but the incident ends their romance. The train is driven by Jack Warner, Mr Huggett himself, who the following year takes the part of a reliable policeman out to put a stop to juvenile delinquency in *The Blue Lamp* (1950). That film is generally taken as marking a shift in Ealing's focus from the sources of energy to the forces of repression.

The impression that post-war production was almost totally dominated by Rank and his subsidiary companies is largely accurate. During the war, ABPC had been confined to a small studio at Welwyn, producing low-budget crime melodramas. Production continued in this vein afterwards, with films like the Georges Simenon adaptation *Temptation Harbour* (1946) and John Boulting's prosaic account of Graham Greene's *Brighton Rock* (1947, *Young Scarface* in US). And when Alexander Korda returned from America, where he had been supporting Britain's propaganda effort, with the intention of competing with Rank, he had to use bravado and charm where Rank had cash. Also, he didn't easily gauge the mood of a country emerging from war. *Perfect Strangers* (1945), which he directed for MGM, seemed glib in its presentation of the changes war had brought to a married couple, changing him from timid clerk to authoritarian naval officer, and her from drab housewife to confident member of the WRNS, but the film was popular nevertheless.

After a period as head of MGM UK, Korda reconstituted London Films,

Pinkie on the phone – in the studio for *Brighton Rock* (1947)

On the streets – onlookers gather for an exterior scene from *Brighton Rock* (1947)

bought and modernized studios at Shepperton, took over a controlling interest in the British Lion distribution company and purchased the Rialto Cinema in Leicester Square as his showcase. But the larger films he made showed how out-of-touch he was with audience tastes. *An Ideal Husband* (1947), a film version of Oscar Wilde's play, is a lavish but stagey production set in 1895, when 'Britain ruled the world and held the purse', showing the dilemma facing a government minister whose murky past catches up with him. There followed such extravagant follies as *Bonnie Prince Charlie* (1948) and an *Anna Karenina* (1947) in which Vivien Leigh vainly tried to bring some of the same magic to the role as Greta Garbo had 12 years earlier. Some compensation for these flops was provided by Carol Reed's *The Fallen Idol* (1947), an adaptation of Graham Green's short story about a young boy's loss of innocence, and Anthony Asquith's *The Winslow Boy* (1948), an adapted stage-play about the struggles of a naval cadet's father to prove his son's innocence of theft.

Korda lacked the resources to lure away a significant number of Rank's key directors. But if Rank controlled the source of the more creative ideas, his company didn't have the management necessary to ensure the continuance of his production policy. Rank was so convinced that making expensive films was the way to break through into the American market that he made no attempt to rein back costs. While the magnificence of the result could justify the fact that *The Red Shoes* cost twice as much as *The Life and Death of Colonel Blimp*, there were many cases where the extravagance worked against the final result, and Michael Powell has recalled that he became 'impatient at the complacency of my associates about the mounting costs of our films.'[17] Just how weak were Rank's budgetary controls can be seen from their dealings with Gabriel Pascal, the Hungarian producer whose brief career was built on his having persuaded George Bernard Shaw to trust him with the film rights to his plays. But while *Pygmalion* (1938) had been directed by the reliable Asquith, Pascal himself took over the reins on *Major Barbara* (1941). His pernickety attitude and lack of experience led to the film going almost 100 per cent over-budget. Rank, having carried the can on that occasion, then allowed spending on *Caesar and Cleopatra* (1945) to reach the mind-numbing figure of £1,280,000, twice as much as *The Red Shoes*. The film is so dull and wordy that it bears out in every frame Powell's assertion that Pascal 'knew as much about directing as a cow does about playing the piano.'[18]

Rank was a company without the creative leadership to support its chairman's ambitions for the world market. While Gainsborough was becoming enfeebled, nothing was being done outside Ealing and Independent Producers to bring on talent or set up new centres of production strength. Rank's ambitions in the US were dependent on the company's films all being of a certain quality, but there was an insufficient understanding of what made a production unit like Ealing work, and the model was not copied elsewhere. As a result, many of the films emerging from Rank were of poor quality. Although the sums remitted back from the US were much lower than expected, and continuing high taxation rates caused a drain on domestic box office receipts, no attempt was made to rein in film budgets. The company also started making silly mistakes. Gainsborough's executives were pushed very much against their will into an expensive production of *Christopher Columbus* (1949), simply because a lot of money had been spent on a script. Muriel Box's complaint, of course, was that the script was 'inaccurate,'[19] critic Richard Winnington's that the film 'contrives with something like genius neither to inform, excite, entertain, titillate or engage the eye.'[20] And Rank interpreted his own difficulty in understanding *The Red Shoes* as evidence that he had a disaster on his hands. He rushed it into UK cinemas to ensure that the shareholders didn't notice. Sensibly he allowed UA to enjoy the benefits of a mega-hit in the US.

The Gater Committee on Film Production Costs, which reported in October 1949, was in no doubt that the film industry had brought its latest crisis down upon its own head, through creating 'a general atmosphere of extravagance and unreality, leading to a disregard of expense which would not be tolerated in other forms of business.'[21] Rank, however, argued with equal conviction that it was all the government's fault. His case was not without foundation. In July 1947, while Rank was in America negotiating with the five major companies, the British government responded to its own problem, a serious dollar shortage, by trying to slow down one of the major outflows and imposing a 75 per cent levy on remittable income from foreign films. It was a stupid decision, indicating only the severity of the government's dollar crisis, and it is incredible that it should have been implemented without any discussion with the country's major exhibitor. Rank, however, seems to have been taken unawares by a move that provided a disastrous demonstration of how ineffective he was in protecting the interests of the American companies. 'All my work was thrown away. My two months in America went for nowt,'[22] he was to complain.

Rank had funded his forays into production on the back of profits accruing from the exhibition of US pictures but, instead of standing firm with the American companies when they announced a boycott of British screens, he decided to boost his own company's production. If Rank seriously thought that his directors could work to order and effectively fill the gap in the release schedules, notwithstanding the audience's proven affection for US pictures, then he really did know very little about film production. After the tax had been abolished and the boycott lifted, Rank compounded his incompetence by deciding to keep the best playdates for his mix of low-budget featurettes and big-budget pictures. The Americans must have felt as if he was taking revenge on them for what had happened, but they had the final laugh since most of Rank's films weren't very good. Rank could blame the government all he liked, but it was his own policies which had antagonized the Americans, alienated audiences and significantly increased the company's overdraft.

Rank's wilful demolition of his own dream suggests he had simply had enough of trying to create a niche for British films in the American market. Certainly he was never again to be as actively interested in the company as he was in the late 1940s. In 1959 Rank claimed that 'Britain would now have a healthy industry and a very successful market'[23] if it had not been for the insensitivity of the Department of Trade. It may be that it was their actions that tipped the balance for Rank, and decided him against pushing on with his ambitions. After all, if the British government knifed him in the back when he was pursuing their patriotic interest, what was the point of going on? If so, it is difficult to know how he would have stood up to the long haul that still awaited him. British filmmakers could come up with films that would overcome the resistance of American exhibitors to non-Hollywood products, as the $5 million grossed by *The Red Shoes* suggests, but they wouldn't do so in sufficient quantities until Rank had developed more sophisticated ideas about how to cajole the right sort of product from his writers, directors and producers. The upward spiral on which film budgets were set suggests that Rank might have had to go on losing money for a long time before hitting on a way to achieve a steady supply of sellable films. Also, it is difficult to know how well Rank's negotiating position would have held up after cinema admissions had started their precipitate decline in the mid-1950s.

But now, with hopes of a breakthrough into the American market dashed, there were signs of retrenchment everywhere in British filmmaking. Rank closed down its smaller studios at Shepherd's Bush and Islington (the old Gaumont-British studios) as well as Denham and Highbury. The budgetary cutbacks gradually drove the directors gathered in Independent Producers to London Films, but Korda was having problems raising cash to fund production, and his British Lion company was on the verge of bankruptcy. The 45 per cent quota imposed in October 1948, in a futile attempt to support the films encouraged into production during the American boycott, had to be lowered to 40 per cent when 1,600 cinemas claimed exemption on the grounds that there simply weren't enough films to show, and it was reduced again to 30 per cent in 1950 (the level at which it remained until its abolition 23 years later). In early 1949, 17 studios were idle, over a third of the film technicians' union's members were unemployed and British filmmaking, as a writer in the *New Statesman* put it, was 'facing disaster'.[24]

Indian Summer

British filmmaking ticked over during the 1950s, for the most part without any great ambition, or yen for artistic adventure. Filmmakers settled down to live with the Americans, having decided against launching any further substantial challenges on their home turf. The UK government, following the example of the French and Italians, instituted measures to strengthen the ability of local producers to secure a reasonable return from the domestic box office, and filmmakers developed undemanding forms of cinema, mainly comedies and war films, that would reliably appeal to native audiences. Meanwhile, cinema admissions declined steadily, from 1,365 million in 1951 to 501 million in 1961, reinforcing the impression of limpness that hung around the whole of the British film industry.

The powerhouses of film production in the previous decade nearly all wilted in this atmosphere. Only Alexander Mackendrick at Ealing and David Lean seemed able, to some extent, to sustain their earlier initiatives, the one by focusing an acerbic eye on the state of England, the other by applying his extraordinary craftsmanship to such international films as *The Bridge on the River Kwai* (1957) and *Lawrence of Arabia* (1962). Powell and Pressburger made their last disillusioned statement on the post-war mood in *The Small Back Room* (1949), the story of an explosives expert's struggles against drink and pain that was their first film after the defection to Korda. They turned to florid over-statement with *Gone to Earth* (1950) and, by the time the duo came to make *Ill Met by Moonlight* (1956), it is difficult to dissent from Powell's own judgement that 'we'd run out a bit of ideas'.[1] The tough treatment of childhood Carol Reed had offered in *The Fallen Idol* gave way to feyness in *A Kid for Two Farthings* (1955) while Robert Hamer, expelled from Ealing, shifted from the controlled savagery in *Kind Hearts and Coronets* via the eccentric *Father Brown* (1954, *The Detective* in US) to such routine comedy assignments as *To Paris with Love* (1954) and *School for Scoundrels* (1959). And at Ealing itself, Balcon's post-war ambition for a cinema that would project 'the true Briton to the rest of the world' as a 'leader in social reform, champion of civil liberties'[2] had shrivelled by the end of the 1950s to a commitment to make films about 'day-dreamers, mild anarchists, little men who long to kick the boss in the teeth.'[3]

There were complex reasons behind the shift in each individual's creative potential. Powell and Pressburger couldn't find the stories that expressed what they wanted to say to a contemporary audience, Reed suffered a loss of nerve after making two exceptional films with Graham Greene (*Fallen Idol* and *The Third Man*). Lean drew strength from being such a cerebral filmmaker, while Mackendrick had the advantage of being a (Scottish) outsider in the very English setting of Ealing studios. Hamer, by contrast, was not only unable to flourish inside Ealing, where his projects were now considered too risqué, but unable to thrive outside.

But the general inability of the film industry to support and encourage creative adventure was the responsibility of the two major companies, which were now in the hands of former accountants who had not cast off their old ways of thinking, John Davis at Rank and Robert Clark at ABPC. Michael Powell noticed the development of a 'civil service' mentality within Rank at the time of making *The Red Shoes*, but his argument that 'there is something after all to be said for lavishness, improvisation and a certain amount of waste'[4] was not likely to make much headway with John Davis, managing director of Rank from 1948, who disliked creative people, considering them extravagant and unreliable. He remarked in 1953 that 'film producers have grown fat, lazy and unimaginative.'[5]

Davis was the worst sort of person to have at the head of a monopolistic company. Whereas Arthur Rank could argue in the 1940s that the diversity of production activity within the company eliminated the dangers of monopoly, Davis did away with alternative centres of initiative. He didn't appreciate that a production company would only flourish if there were several channels, run by people with diverse sensibilities, through which to filter projects. Production was now centralized at Pinewood Studios, with Davis's former personal assistant Earl St John, a onetime exhibitor, put in charge of making 'inexpensive films without artistic pretensions, films that had no other object than to provide good family entertainment and show a profit.'[6] Strong-willed producers previously housed under the Rank umbrella, like Filippo del Giudice, George Archibald, Joseph Somlo and Sydney Box all left, along with the prestige directorial talent, and their companies were consolidated into J. Arthur Rank Productions. The majority of screenwriters were dismissed and half the production staff sacked. This was asset-stripping on a grand scale, only the assets were stripped by the company's managing director and then thrown away.

With neither Rank nor ABPC willing to undertake adventurous production, the initiative passed to independent companies like John and James Woolf's Romulus Productions, the Boultings' Charter Productions and numerous others. None of these operations, however, was strong enough to take on the role of nurturing talent or providing a supportive home for creative filmmakers. Finance was on a film-by-film basis for the most part, with assistance coming from the new National Film Finance Corporation. Successive government reports since the late 1930s had recommended setting up a national film bank, but it was only in the wake of the 1948 production crisis that the government seriously contemplated making funds available to the industry. Some stop-gap funding was provided immediately for British Lion and this was followed, in April 1949, by the setting up of the National Film Finance Corporation which the Board of Trade provided with a revolving fund of £5 million (expanded to £6 million in 1950). This money was initially paid out to distributors as a stimulus to set up a network of satellite producers but, after the corporation had trouble recovering the £3 million invested in Korda's British Lion, money was directed into individual projects which they thought had commercial potential, as the percentage of the budget (usually 30 per cent) that couldn't be raised from a distributor. Between 1950 and 1961, the NFFC helped into production almost half the 730 British first feature films produced.

The second government measure increased producers' bargaining power with financiers by reserving for British films a portion of the money taken at the domestic box office. Although the returns accruing to a particular film from the Eady Levy, as it was called, were limited both by the size of the box office in any particular year, and that film's success in the market-place (the levy was paid out in proportion to a film's success), the promise it offered did make it easier for independents to raise cash.

Like previous government action to boost the native film industry, Eady strengthened the ties between British and American production. The legislation's loose definition of a 'British' film, as one made by a British company in a British studio using a certain percentage of British crew, could be applied to a picture made by a British subsidiary of a US major, using an American director, writer and key cast. Together with the agreement that led to the lifting of the Ad Valorem duties, which required US companies to invest a certain proportion of their earnings in Britain, Eady led to a considerable increase in British-based American production. MGM, Fox, Warner and RKO made a substantial number of films out of London, many of them spectaculars rather than authentically British productions, and a number of producers like Albert ('Cubby') Broccoli and Sam Spiegel moved from America to the UK.

The fragmented production environment provided fewer opportunities for untried directors. Recognizing this, the NFFC set up an independent unit, Group 3, to finance low-budget films. This was a good idea, but the organization lacked effective leadership. Its chairman was John Grierson who had never been particularly interested in responding to the requirements of the commercial marketplace, and production control was in the hands of John Baxter, a one-time director whose films had been of the prosaic but worthy variety. With budgets of around £50,000, the preference was for gentle tales with a non-urban setting such as *The Brave Don't Cry* (1952), about a Scottish mining disaster; *Conflict of Wings* (1953, *Fuss Over Feathers* in US), in which East

Anglian villagers fight for the cause of bird sanctuaries against the needs of the RAF; *Judgement Deferred* (1951) and *Brandy for the Parson* (1951), both of which are smuggling stories. But what aroused resentment from people in the film industry had nothing to do with the merits of these films, which critic Raymond Durgnat reasonably characterized as 'sub-Ealing comedies so timid as to be positively ingratiating,'[7] nor the production programme's lack of profitability. It was felt by John Davis and others that the government was backing unfair competition with the commercial companies. For Davis, therefore, this feeble attempt at sponsoring new talent was unacceptable 'socialism'. Group 3 was closed down in 1955.

Absorbing many of the energies that had been concentrated in Independent Producers, Korda's London Films was able for a time to resist the drift towards cosiness. Somewhat chastened by his recent flops, burdened by the NFFC loan and prevented by his reputation for extravagance from raising substantial finance elsewhere, Korda kept away during this period from glamour, lavish sets and spectacle. Although production controls were never tight at London Films, he reduced costs and increased production. And for the more ambitious film projects he developed a coproduction arrangement with David O. Selznick, the producer who had lured Hitchcock to Hollywood.

It was with Selznick that London Films made one of the most remarkable films of the late 1940s, *The Third Man* (1949). Although Korda was now more of a financier than an active producer, it was his suggestion that led Graham Greene to visit Austria to see if he could find the background in the four-power occupation of Vienna which would inspire him to extend his one-line story: 'I had paid my last farewell to Harry less than a week ago, when his coffin was lowered in the frozen February ground, so that it was with incredulity that I saw him pass by, without a sign of recognition, among the host of strangers in the Strand.'[8] The film Greene developed with Carol Reed is a strong thriller that maximizes the potential of its locations. It also contains in the character of Colonel Calloway, the world-weary Englishman responsible for alerting the innocent American writer of pulp novels to his former friend's evil doings, a perfect symbol of Britain's position after the Second World War, standing in the middle between battered Europe and gung-ho America.

'Great Britain has lost an empire and not yet found a role' taunted Dean Acheson, the American Secretary of State, around this time. The dilemma of which he spoke was felt by filmmakers as they sought to make films that dealt with the pressing contemporary issues, at a time when the initiative in world affairs had passed decisively to the Americans. For a while they could believe, like the politicians, that an independent nuclear deterrent, the skills of their scientists and a special relationship with America would give the UK a portion of its old status. The scientist who threatens to blow up London in the film John Boulting directed for Korda, *Seven Days to Noon* (1950), does so in order that the whole world will be made aware of how a scientific dream had been corrupted. In Lean's film *The Sound Barrier* (1952), the central character, an engineer, is portrayed as a more deeply ambivalent figure, driven by his ambition to build a plane that goes faster than the speed of sound, seemingly prepared to accept the loss of his son and a pilot in pursuit of his dream, but actually torn by a deep sense of what he has lost.

One year later, Rank made *The Net* (1953), also concerned with aviation, but here there is no attempt to confront the possibility that there is danger within the scientific project itself. The hero is credited with wholly worthy motives, to 'make this all one place' so that 'we may learn to trust one another and live in peace', and the only opposition to his dream comes from bureaucrats as obstructive as those who tried to restrain the foreman who wanted to go to France, and an interloper who plots to take the plane across the Iron Curtain. Where the nuclear scientist in *Seven Days to Noon* is shot, and the engineer in *The Sound Barrier* ends the film a shattered man, the scientist in *The Net* is rescued from danger and goes off home to resolve his marital problems.

Tame films of this sort show directors and writings giving up the struggle to deal with contemporary anxieties. Lean and the Boultings drifted towards less intense forms of filmmaking, and the concerns evident in their early 1950s pictures were pushed out to less prestigious areas of film production. These became, in fact, the almost exclusive preserve of Hammer Films, a company that had been making skilfully-marketed pictures with an eye on the US B-movie market since the late 1940s. In 1955 the company picked up the film rights to a popular sci-fi TV series. The resulting film, *The Quatermass Xperiment* (1955), tells of a spaceship returning to earth with only one being on board – a monster gestating inside the skin of a crew member. The film was immensely popular and had so clearly struck a chord that Hammer carried out a rethink of its production policy. This led, through *X The Unknown* (1957), which parodies the complacency of the authorities towards the radiation threat and *Quatermass 2* (1957), in which the visiting monsters come much closer to taking over the world, to the cycle of horror films that started with *The Curse of Frankenstein* (1956), moving away from immediate contemporary concerns towards mythological narratives that touched some of the same fears and terrors.

But if film executives were to be believed, the majority of the audience was less interested in salving their fears about wars and conflicts ahead than in looking back to the time when Britain had a role to play in the world. Like the crooks pursued by the hero in *Calling Bulldog Drummond* (1951), for whom 'life in peacetime seemed unbearably flat', or the ex-officers who take over their old ship for smuggling runs across the Channel in *The Ship that Died of Shame* (1955), or *The League of Gentlemen* (1960), for whom robbing a bank promises their 'finest hour', many filmmakers seemed to feel that there

BBC cameras record the final appearance of a monster in
The Quatermass Xperiment **(1955)**

was nothing to do, now the war was over and the hopes of peace had faded, than go back to the site of old glories. 'The H-bomb looms ahead,' remarked the critic William Whitebait, 'and we daren't look at it, we creep back to the lacerating comfort of "last time"'. From the demonstrations of British pluck and enterprise in *The Wooden Horse* (1950), the first of a series of escape pictures, and the celebration of one woman's heroism in the Anna Neagle-starring *Odette* (1950), through action films such as *The Dam Busters* (1955), *The Battle of the River Plate* (1956, *Pursuit of the Graf Spee* in US) and *Sink the Bismark* (1960), there is a sense of well-known events being played out for an audience that already knew about them. The celebrations of selflessness and sacrifice are much as they were in the wartime films, but this time there seems little point in asserting them, nothing to be argued for. These pictures function as rituals of reassurance, demonstrating that when there was a job to be done, the British got down to it. They have nothing new to say about the war. And when a new note does enter in, it sounds with despair. The British commander who has to bring his team through the desert in *Ice Cold in Alex* (1958) seems hysterical and incompetent by comparison with the Dutch South African who accompanies them but is working for the Germans; and the message of Ealing's *Dunkirk* (1958) is summarized in one character's closing statement, 'Somebody's made a muck of it but I don't think it's the army.' One understands from these films why critic Gavin Lambert remarked of his departure from England in 1956 that the country 'really seemed in the doldrums, like it had lost the war almost.'[9]

Why did Ealing chose to make *Dunkirk*, about the evacuation of the British Expeditionary Force from the French beaches? Perhaps they saw it as a last call for help to come to a failing Britain. In other war films, however, the purpose is revealed by insistent preachiness, as in *Reach for the Sky* (1956), where the story of Douglas Bader, the determined pilot who, despite losing both his legs in an accident, went on to command the air force during the Battle of Britain, is told as a story that 'was not only an example to those in war but is now a source of inspiration to many in peace.' In other areas of filmmaking too, stories seemed to be chosen for the potential they offered for homily. Films about juvenile delinquency, for example, from *Cosh Boy* (1952) to *Violent Playground* (1958), never explore the inner worlds of their characters, only demonstrate what a terrible threat to organized society such behaviour represents. And the interminable squabbles of the couple in *Escapade* (1955) are staged to make the point that expounding the pacifist cause, the main activity of the male member of the pair, isn't enough, and that the only hope for the world rests with their children, untouched by the complex, screwed-up emotions of the older generation. Their eldest son aims to prove this by stealing an aeroplane to gain publicity for his pompous declaration that 'We boys do not wish to kill the children of any other school.'

Escapade's director Philip Leacock specialized in the unsullied emotions of

Back to wargames – Jack Lee coaxes the actors in *The Wooden Horse* **(1950)**

childhood. In *The Kidnappers* (1953, *The Little Kidnappers* in US), two orphan boys demonstrate their deep needs to a stern grandfather by kidnapping a baby. But more complex emotions creep in at the fringes of the tale, where the grandfather's ostracism of the man his daughter loves leads to several fraught emotional scenes. And much the same process of intensification at the edges goes on in *The Spanish Gardener* (1956), where another little boy is prevented by his possessive and emotionally repressed father from developing his relationship with a gardener. The culmination of the drama, an explosion of emotions during a thunderstorm, has parallels in other Rank-financed movies of the time, when the lid comes off and all the emotions that have been barely repressed throughout the film come pouring out as if from some Pandora's box. Such a lightning-spattered ending is found, for example, in *Passionate Summer* (1958), where for most of the film the schoolteacher on a Caribbean Island has been keeping at bay the emotions directed towards him by a troubled pupil, the headmaster's wife and an air hostess.

In these films the sorty of sticky emotional conflicts which the production system seemed determined to cleanse from its films fight their way back into the movies. Elsewhere, filmmakers attempted to substitute frenetic drama for intense conflict. Set in places where many things happen, these films followed multiple story lines in a way that clearly anticipates a later staple of TV drama programming. Hospitals were to become a setting later in the decade for 'Doctor' films, 'Carry Ons' and such tepid dramas as *Behind the Mask* (1958), but the genre can be traced back to *White Corridors* (1951) where, amidst the routine romantic squabbles, and an occasional lecture on the working of the NHS, two strong stories evolve: a researcher develops a drug that will kill infections resistant to penicillin and his lover secures herself a registrar's post against nepotistic competition, by skilfully operating on a patient her rival has misdiagnosed. *Front Page Story* (1953) is set in a newspaper office, where a harassed editor played by Jack Hawkins deals with homeless children, a scientist wanting to spill atomic secrets, a journalist's crisis of conscience and a wife who plans to walk out on him. Hawkins' qualities in this sort of role were deployed again in a film that brought together the American director John Ford and former Ealing writer T. E. B. Clarke, *Gideon's Day* (1959, *Gideon of Scotland Yard* in US), where he plays a slightly muddled police officer who, in true English fashion, only reveals his mettle under pressure.

Ealing's films of the 1950s also deal with communities, not torn apart by inner rivalries but bonded in solidarity against an external aggressor. Increasingly what they came to oppose was the process of change – social, cultural and economic. By the time the studio came to make *The Titfield Thunderbolt* (1953), about a village's attempt to preserve their branch line against nasty entrepreneurs who have set up a bus service, gentle anarchy has given way to nostalgia for Olde England.

Balcon's strengthened determination to impose his own world-view on the studio's pictures accounts for the declining ambition of Ealing's production at this time. Arthur Rank was no longer applying pressure on him to make bigger, more ambitious pictures, and Balcon was very much his own man. The films give an increasingly wide berth to messy problems like sexuality and violence and, whereas Ealing's films during and immediately after the war had interrogated what was happening to England, many of those made in the 1950s just don't seem interested. Balcon's desire to avoid 'socially objectionable' subjects and 'to make pictures worthy of that name' (whatever that was supposed to mean) provided a cover for turning the studio's face away from the world.

The solidarity and sense of community that had once been Ealing's strength now began to work against it. Filmmakers were rarely imported from outside (Thorold Dickinson, who was allowed in to make *Secret People* in 1952, could be regarded as an 'old boy' since he had worked at the studio during Basil Dean's time) and, with five directors responsible for two-thirds of the films made at the studio between 1942 and 1955, there was little competition inside the studio, and no exposure to fresh ideas from outside. With a secure nest under Rank, and a distribution deal through Universal in the US, there was little contact with the marketplace, which could have driven the studio to search out new styles and new areas of subject matter. There had developed, according to art director-turned producer Michael Relph, 'a public school ethos' which 'stopped us growing up'.[10]

Attempts from within to knock the dust off Ealing cosiness were crushed by Balcon. Robert Hamer planned to follow *Kind Hearts and Coronets* with a sexually-charged film set in the West Indies, with Vivien Leigh in the key role, but this was cancelled two weeks before shooting began and he quit the studio in a huff. Charles Crichton's desire to make a film of Kingsley Amis's *Lucky Jim* was vetoed, even though the book is hardly risqué or coarse. In fact, the only film director who flourished within the Ealing set-up, by focusing upon the studio's evasions and working sufficiently within the grain for his deviations from it not to be too embarrassingly apparent, was Alexander Mackendrick. There are sometimes signs of strain, as in the clumsy development of a conflict between husband and wife in *Mandy* (1952, *The Crash of Silence* in US) over whether or not their deaf-and-dumb daughter should be sent to a special school. Nevertheless, the film deploys sounds and images with intense effect as it explores the inner experience of a little girl closed off from the world, for whom her family is a cage tightened around her and preventing her from communicating with the world. Where *Whisky Galore* (1948, *Tight Little Island* in US) depicts a Scottish community determined to outwit officialdom and salvage the whisky from a shipwrecked boat, *The Man in the White Suit* (1951) treads into that tricky area for British filmmakers, industrial relations,

Alexander Mackendrick talks with the sound engineers about *Mandy* **(1952)**

to suggest that when workers and management come together, it may have more to do with their own selfish interests than those of the broader community. After the timid *The Maggie* (1953, *High and Dry* in US), Mackendrick's Ealing oeuvre culminates in *The Ladykillers* (1955) where a gang of bank robbers, masquerading as an unlikely string quartet, engages in a battle of wills with an unutterably sweet and totally irritating landlady, symbol of Ealing's (and England's) determination not to think about the modern world, smothering the horrors and the nightmares in gentility.

The constraints Ealing placed upon Mackendrick were constructive, because they forced him to find original narratives that used Ealing's increasingly stale formulae against itself. William Rose, the American writer of *The Ladykillers*, went on to write scripts outside Ealing that again deal with England's infatuation with old things, and resistance to change, but distil these through cosy middle-class couples. Although relatively fresh and interesting, neither has anything like the same energy as his screenplay for Mackendrick. *Genevieve* (1953), one of Rank's biggest successes of the decade, was directed by another old Ealing hand, Henry Cornelius, who left the studio after making *Passport to Pimlico*. The vintage car of the title is driven by a married duo who bicker, moan and make love all the way to Brighton, then challenge a less permanent couple to a race back to London. Genevieve wins by driving herself across Westminster Bridge. The fleapit at the centre of another Rose script, *The Smallest Show on Earth* (1957, *Big Time Operators* in US), directed by Ealing's Basil Dearden, is eventually burnt to the ground by its old commissionare: 'It were the only way weren't it', he says to the cooing couple who inherited the place in a town stinking of glue from the local factory, together with staff so lost in the past that they still enjoy looking at Hepworth's *Comin' Thro' The Rye*. Although they make a go of the cinema for a while, by showing desert pictures and pushing up the heat so that they can sell cool refreshments, their only aim is to get back to middle-class life, but with enough money to avoid any more 'petty, stupid problems.' The indictment of British nostalgia is more amiable than sharp, and the ideas are much less interesting than anything in Mackendrick's films.

But despite Mackendrick's creative vigour, Ealing didn't flourish at the end of the decade. In 1955 Balcon sold the studios to the BBC to resolve a longstanding debt problem, moving his production unit on to MGM and then ABPC, but failing to find at either place the sort of working context that would re-energize his production programme. Everywhere else, however, the late 1950s saw filmmakers of every hue turning to comedy as they struggled to hold on to audiences and prevent their defection to television. 'It is safer to make comedies,' explained Ken Annakin in 1958, 'because they are the only pictures which, in Britain, bring back any profit at all to the people who put up the money.'[11]

Joan Greenwood and Alec Guinness in a quiet scene from
The Man in the White Suit **(1951)**

The same scene before the cameras, and the spectators

Desperate film projectionist – Bill Travers gazes on Peter Sellers' confusion in *The Smallest Show on Earth* **(1957)**

Thus Launder and Gilliatt launched their 'Saint Trinians' series with *The Belles of Saint Trinians* (1954) and continued to produce films about mischievous schoolgirls until 1966. They also made such one-off comedies as *The Green Man* (1957), in which a vacuum cleaner salesman sets out to prevent a sour-faced captain of industry from being blown up. The Boultings went from thrillers and melodramas to initiate a series of often strained films making fun of British institutions. These take in the law (*Brothers in Law*, 1956), the redbrick universities (*Lucky Jim*, 1957), the foreign office (*Carlton-Browne of the FO*, 1958) and the trade unions (*I'm All Right Jack*, 1959). The latter gains its incisive bite from a performance by Peter Sellers as the Machiavellian union chief Fred Kite, but too many of the other Boulting films take facile swipes at absent-minded professors or barristers, and ignorant, lazy bureaucrats.

In the same year as *Genevieve*, Rank found a bankable comedy series in the 'Doctor' series initiated by *Doctor in the House* (1953), and Norman Wisdom introduced his winning blend of slapstick and sentiment with *Trouble in Store*. Later came the 'Carry On' films, launched by *Carry On Sergeant* (1958), films as defiantly un-Ealing as one could conceive, with their emphasis on the inability of institutions (army, hospital, school, etc.) to contain the animal natures and the sheer potential for vulgarity of the humans within. In thus celebrating anarchy, the 'Carry Ons' put themselves as far outside critical respectability as the contemporary films being made by Hammer.

Some of the more interesting comedy films were made outside these generic contexts. *Top Secret* (1952), for example, touches on Cold War issues with its story of a sanitary engineer abducted to the Soviet Union in the belief that he is a bomb expert holding the secrets of a devastating new weapon. All innocence, he calls out 'Good old England. Up the Empire!' to a group of communist students from the UK gathered at the bar of his hotel, promises to do something about the 'blooming awful' state of Soviet plumbing and ends up making a deal with Stalin with the insouciance of George Formby addressing himself to Hitler. Later in the same decade, when British filmmakers had lost their interest in international affairs, the same actor, George Cole, plays the inadequate gang-leader in *Too Many Crooks* (1959), a film whose insights into the cold realities of contemporary marriage derives from the story of a kidnapped wife who plots revenge when her husband shows himself less than interested in paying over her ransom. The film contains an extraordinary kidnapping scene involving a broken-down hearse and the not-very-firmly-sealed coffin that contains the victim.

Whereas the cinema of the late 1940s had forced audiences to confront the realities of post-war Britain, the mainstream films produced at the end of the following decade diverted their anxieties into laughter. That was just how the circuit bosses liked things, believing that the best way to hold on to their audience was through 'family entertainment', and arguing through the Cinematograph

Exhibitors Association (CEA) that filmmakers should avoid treating themes and incidents that 'were offensive to the reasonable taste and standards of those whose patronage was necessary to the health and future of the industry.'[12] Although an X certificate had been introduced by the BBFC in 1951, only six such films were shown on the Rank circuit between 1951 and 1957. Things hotted up thereafter, but the company's Annual Report of 1960 complained that X-films were being misused 'to the detriment of cinema entertainment.'[13]

This assumption that films had to be bland to be entertaining, and refusal to acknowledge that movies could usefully enable audiences to deal with fears and nightmares, went along with an unwillingness to acknowledge that audience tastes and sensitivities were being shifted by television. At every level, the major companies took a stand against the new medium. Films were made which attacked the small screen. Ealing's *Meet Mr Lucifer* (1953) defined the new medium's effect on audiences as largely negative and, by distinguishing the communal address of cinema from television's attention to the individual, established a line of attack that was to be much used later. Rank's *Simon and Laura* (1955) pursued a different tack, mocking TV for the phoniness of its images of life through the story of a married couple in a TV soap, who are represented as cooing doves on the screen when in reality they always bicker and squabble. Cinema, the film asserts, presents the more full-blooded experience. It was a strange position for a Rank film to adopt and, after the launch of the Sunday night series, 'Armchair Theatre', in 1956, television presented dramas with more grit in each minute than many feature films had in their whole duration. Also, through documentaries and slots on magazine programmes, the medium opened up questions about class, colour and sex that many filmmakers seemed convinced could not interest an audience.

Inevitably, television's influence seeped into movies. TV's initiative with *Quatermass* brought two successful movies to Hammer and a change in its production policy, while sitcoms like *Inn for Trouble* and *Whacko!* became cheap features. Films like Basil Dearden's *Sapphire* (1959), dealing with racial prejudice and mixed marriages, and *Victim* (1961), which cast Dirk Bogarde as a homosexual barrister who decides to take a stand against social hypocrisy, would not have been possible if television had not already put such issues on the agenda. Nor was the movement all one way. Norman Wisdom was snapped by up Rank after he had proved what he could do on TV, and the cosy cop series *Dixon of Dock Green* (1955–76) was clearly a lineal descendant of Ealing's *The Blue Lamp*.

These interconnections argued for a close symbiotic relationship between the two media. The film companies, however, were pledged to fight the new medium to the last ditch. Rank's policy of having nothing to do with television prevented Balcon from becoming involved in any of the bids to secure a commercial television franchise in 1955, and ensured that the film industry had no stake in the new medium. And in 1958, when over eight million households had television licences, the various trade associations formed the Film Industry Defence Organization (FIDO) in an attempt to ensure that none of the nation's producers sold their films to television. This really was an attempt to bolt the stable door after the horses had bolted. Korda died in 1956, but he had sold a series of his films to ABC and, following the presale of London Films' version of *Richard III* (1955) to a US network, had announced plans to develop films for pay-TV. Korda had seen that producers would have to look to television as an alternative source of revenue. FIDO simply ignored that fact, even as admissions slumped in 1957 to just above the 900-million mark.

Rank and ABPC were still the powers in the land but, when it came to British filmmaking, they really weren't very interested anymore: their cinema revenues were considerably more important to them than film production. Therefore, they decided to put their energy into a battle they could only lose, and not just because of television but also because they did so little on their own account to improve the cinemas, and to provide an environment which would lure potential audiences away from their increasingly comfortable homes. Their economies ensured that the fleapits would remain forever fleapits, until the time came for them to close. It was an uninspiring policy.

Dirty Words and Pop

Given the timidity of British cinema in the late 1950s, it is easy to understand the anger with which Lindsay Anderson blasted British filmmaking for being 'snobbish, anti-intelligent, emotionally inhibited, wilfully blind to the conditions and problems of the present, dedicated to an out-of-date, exhausted national ideal.'[1] For the filmmakers of Anderson's generation, there was a double frustration: both that there was no vital British cinema they could celebrate as critics, and that the film industry had shrunk to the point where it offered no easy point of entry into the industry. Finding it impossible to break into movies after the production slump of the 1940s, before television offered an alternative route to aspiring filmmakers, people like Anderson, Tony Richardson and Karel Reisz worked instead within sponsored documentaries, while writing about the sort of passionate, personal filmmaking that seemed to be possible in France, Italy, even India, but not in Britain.

Free Cinema, which had Anderson as its spokesman, was always more certain of what it was against than what it stood for. He was brilliant at invective, and making general statements about the need to communicate a politically responsible set of values, but neither he nor any of his friends were screenwriters, nor were they motivated to work with writers on ideas that were their own. Despite their rousing calls for a cinema that was 'vital, illuminating,' and their polemic against a national cinema divorced from contemporary realities, they turned to a series of novels set in the English provinces for material out of which to make their first movies.

Nor did this brief fashion for working-class subjects derive directly from their critical campaigns, except insofar as Richardson had directed *Look Back in Anger* on the stage in 1956, and that production marked the cultural watershed from which a fashion for 'realism' seemed to flow. It was Jack Clayton, a director trained in the traditional film industry, who persuaded Romulus Films to finance a version of John Braine's *Room at the Top*, a representative sample of the disillusioned provincial novel. The resulting film, released in 1958, centres on a bright, ambitious young man, living in a charmless northern town, who marries out of his working-class background in a cynical pitch to advance himself. The film was a big success, partly because of its openness about sex (made possible by the appointment of John Trevelyan to head up the BBFC), but also because the hero's class resentment brought to the surface emotions that British cinema normally repressed.

Jack Clayton and Laurence Harvey discuss whether there's
Room at the Top **(1958)**

Clayton's film cleared the way for a cycle of films with proletarian heroes who, for all their bluster, see their dreams shrivel in melancholy and their little rebellions crash to the ground. Defeat is built into the genre. Typical is Arthur Seton in *Saturday Night and Sunday Morning* (1960), described by the film's director Karel Reisz, as 'a sad person, terribly limited in his sensibilities, narrow in his ambitions and a bloody fool into the bargain'[2] who ends up throwing a stone towards the housing estate that is his final destination, declaring with more bravado than honesty, 'It won't be the last one I'll throw.' Vic Brown in John Schlesinger's *A Kind of Loving* (1962) settles for telly-watching inanity within marriage, while Billy Liar in the same director's 1963 film turns away from the girl who offers him the chance to fulfil his ambitions in London. The same actor, Tom Courtenay, plays the Borstal boy in Tony Richardson's *The Loneliness of the Long Distance Runner* (1962) who loses the race he's trained for as a way to spite the governor.

The directors of these films, tourists in working-class cultures for which they felt little sympathy, saw only what they wanted to see. Worried about the impact of television on social habits, and disillusioned with British life, they constructed films depicting the destruction of traditional cultural forms, the dead-end nature of the proletarian life and the tawdriness of sexual relationships leading inevitably to closure in marriage. The films had a sense of urgency that the rest of mainstream British cinema at the time largely lacked, but their directors didn't have enough personal contact with the lives of their characters to offer visions that rang true.

Standing apart from these films is Lindsay Anderson's feature début, *This Sporting Life* (1963), where the director's jaundiced view of the world seeps into every frame of the film. The prevailing mood is disgust; at the pathetic inarticulacy of the great ape on a rugby field, Frank Machin, and the blocked emotions of his landlady and lover, who has given up hoping for anything since her husband's death. The film that results from the clash of wills between these two characters is a story of desperation that demonstrates the Gothic aspects of Anderson's sensibility. All the more pity, therefore, that, in his sweeping dismissals of British cinema where there seemed nothing to praise beyond Humphrey Jennings' poetic documentaries, he refused any engagement with the darker elements in the native cinematic culture. He was sufficiently confused by the English way of repressing emotion to characterize *Kind Hearts and Coronets* as characteristic of Ealing movies in being 'emotionally quite frozen,' and so fastidiously determined to stay aloof from bland commercialism that he took no interest in the horror genre (even though his later use of the Frankenstein story in his 1982 film *Britannia Hospital* suggests how much of a contribution he might have made in this area).

'Why no films,' asked Anderson in 1958, 'on Teddy Boys, nuclear tests, loyalty of scientists, bureaucracy, etc.'[3] Why, one might ask in reply, did

Karel Reisz on the water to film a scene from *Saturday Night and Sunday Morning* **(1960)**

**Lindsay Anderson talks with Karel Reisz, his producer on *This Sporting Life*
(1963)**

Anderson never develop stories that engaged with just these issues, even when Joseph Losey, an American who came to Britain in the early 1950s as a refugee from the communist witch-hunts, could deal with them in an assignment for Hammer. *The Damned* (1961, *These are the Damned* in US) compares the violence of contemporary youth to the behaviour of a scientist who has locked up a group of children for experiments. Losey's films during the 1950s and into the 1960s did just what Anderson seemed to be asking British films to do, posing questions about contemporary society in strong, engaging narratives. Films such as *The Sleeping Tiger* (1954), where a psychologist's efforts to reform the mugger he's picked up off the street are subverted by his own drives and the desires of his wife, *The Criminal* (1960, *The Concrete Jungle* in US), in which Stanley Baker plays a loner trapped between the violent prison system and the criminal underworld, or *The Servant* (1963), in which butler is pitched against master, focus on tensions in British society much more interesting than anything opened up by Anderson's contemporaries.

The tepidity of most British cinema during the 1950s made Anderson resistant to the values of commercial filmmaking, and this cut him off from the possibility of developing his critical argument through filmmaking. A concordat between Anderson and the horror genre was ruled out not only by Anderson's fastidiousness, but by the inability of Hammer Studios to provide an environment in which filmmakers with a strongly defined sense of individuality could flourish. An iconoclast such as Anderson could never have settled into directing films about mummies, werewolves and vampires, and Hammer was too much a market-led company to encourage fresh approaches to the monstrous. James Carreras, its salesman, would pitch projects to distributors on the basis of title and poster. If they liked the idea, the film would go to script stage. If they didn't, it would be dropped. In this way, Hammer became a victim of its own phenomenal success, always going for the big thrills and unable to get away with offering anything less than what was expected from a 'Hammer' film.

Only for brief moments did the studio venture away from the formulae and try out different ideas, even when, as with *The Damned*, the studio cut the film in defiance of its director's wishes. Among a series of films designed to cash in on the success of Hitchcock's *Psycho* (1960), for example, was Seth Holt's *The Nanny* (1965), made with the visual flair of his earlier Hammer picture, *Taste of Fear* (1961), and telling the powerful tale of two sisters, both dependent in their own way on the woman who brought them up, who pay no attention to the declarations of their son and nephew that it was nanny who killed his sister and now wants to kill him.

The success of Hammer encouraged other companies into working the same seam. Anglo-Amalgamated, for example, enabled Michael Powell to make an astonishing, if short-lived, comeback with *Peeping Tom* (1959), which was

Joseph Losey prepares a moving scene for _The Sleeping Tiger_ (1954)

scripted by Hammer hand Leo Marks and follows the murderous career of a seemingly gentle young focus-puller who has been psychologically damaged by his father's pain experiments and gets his kicks from filming women in their death agonies, inflicted by the bayonet at the end of his tripod. In the middle of the decade, Michael Reeves stamped his mark on the horror genre with *Witchfinder General* (1968, *The Conqueror Worm* in US), his last film made at the age of 23 for Tigon, set amidst the witch hunts of the English Civil War.

By the late 1960s, Hammer had ceased to become an effective production centre but its influence was still at work. Films like Ken Russell's *The Devils* (1971), with its hysteria and erotic frenzies, or Nic Roeg's *Don't Look Now* (1973) would not have been possible without the developments in Gothic instigated at Hammer's Bray Studios (although Roeg had also worked, as a cameraman, on Roger Corman's *The Masque of the Red Death* (1964)). Both Roeg and Russell could engage with popular cinematic forms in a way that the directors around Anderson could not. Reisz has recalled that when he broke ranks and made a melodrama, *Night Must Fall* (1964), he was accused of selling out and going commercial.[4] This aesthetic refusal went along with an unwillingness to develop a strategy for ensuring a continued capacity to make their sort of films. Woodfall, the company set up by Tony Richardson and John Osborne to exploit the profits from *Look Back in Anger*, with the aim of proving 'that good films, ones that showed British life as it really is, could be made cheaply', nevertheless had no particular strategy for trying to bring down the budgets of films from the £100,000 or so they were costing to the £30,000 level that, for example, French filmmakers worked to. Thanks to American investment, Woodfall was to flourish, but at considerable cost to its original brave intentions.

The lack of any programme for changing the industry is all the more striking given the obstacles that the likes of John Davis persistently put in their way. Davis didn't think much of the 'kitchen sink' films, and asserted that a realistic minimum budget for a first feature was in the order of £250,000 as a way to justify his blocking their exhibition on his company's circuit. Rank, it is said, had to be 'blackmailed'[5] into showing Woodfall's *The Entertainer* (1960), even though Laurence Olivier had the lead role. And it was proving almost impossible to secure any exhibition for *Saturday Night and Sunday Morning* until a booking became available at a London showcase cinema, and the audience turnout proved this was a film with legs. And Peter Brook's powerful adaptation of William Golding's *Lord of the Flies* was a long time on the shelf before securing a release in 1963.

As Rank and ABPC's interest in production declined, their influence over exhibition in Britain increased. Everyone was closing their theatres, but the independents and smaller circuits closed proportionally more, thus shifting the proportion of the box office take in favour of the conglomerates which owned

Peter Brook takes a child's eye view of *Lord of the Flies* (1963)

the larger and more salubrious houses. In 1958, Rank had amalgamated the Odeon and Gaumont circuits, in defiance of an earlier undertaking not to do so. The result was that producers wishing to secure a reasonable return from the British market had to persuade either the Rank or the ABPC booker to take their film. With only two circuits to book, and programmes changing less frequently than hitherto, fewer films were required. And while both conglomerates needed independent producers to supply them with quota films (they showed 49 British first features between them in 1963), the supply was sufficiently buoyant that they could pick and choose. Even the films of Allied Filmmakers, a company formed by Bryan Forbes, Richard Attenborough, Basil Dearden and Michael Relph with backing from Rank, sometimes found it difficult to secure a circuit booking.

In 1963, many producers were having as much difficulty securing screenings for their films as their predecessors had in the early 1920s. British Lion, the independents' major distribution channel, had 18 films awaiting release, a situation David Kingsley, the company's managing director, blamed on the hostility of the circuits to its policy of dividing films between the two of them. However, the sort of routine farces and imitations of earlier successes being handled by British Lion were hardly a match for spectacular films like *El Cid* (1961), *Dr No* (1962), *The Longest Day* (1962) and *Lawrence of Arabia* (1962) that were now coming down the line from American companies, with a 'British' tag on them.

It was a peculiarly difficult time for the independents. The contracting industry of the 1950s had not nurtured new talent or new ideas, as happened in the 1930s and 1940s, so that, apart from the Free Cinema directors, it was mostly a case of the same old people trying to make films. The need to compete with television, and with the sort of films the Americans were making, meant that producers had to make spectaculars, which they couldn't afford to do, or the sort of brave and adventurous pictures that the circuits were reluctant to accommodate. And there was little hope that government intervention would bring about a more flexible cinema industry. The Monopolies Commission was, in fact, asked to report into 'the supply of films for exhibition in cinemas' in 1963. Its 1966 report, while confirming the claim that the 'uniquely rigid' two-release system 'discouraged the production of certain types of films', concluded that there were 'formidable and probably expensive practical problems in the way of adopting any of the proposals'[6] put forward for ameliorating the situation. Something must be done, but nothing could be done, seems a fair summary of the commission's conclusion.

The lack of strong leadership in the independent sector reflected the absence of any new producer talent. It was the veteran Michael Balcon who blocked Sydney Box's takeover of British Lion in late 1963, and had the unenviable task of trying to put an end to faction within the board. And it was Balcon who, as part-time chairman, steered the policies of Bryanston, the main source of independent finance. Seeing that the independents would be slowly strangled so long as they relied exclusively upon the British circuits, he sought to establish connections to Hollywood. In 1961 he formed a link-up between Bryanston and an American company, Seven Arts, designed to build a US foothold and enable Bryanston to finance more ambitious projects. Whereas the company had formerly been limited to films which cost between £150,000 and 200,000, it could now stretch up to £700,000.

The problem for Balcon and the Ealing cronies who mostly peopled the Bryanston board was how, after years of looking inwards to British themes, to define the international film. In the event, they entrusted Alexander Mackendrick with a colourful story, *Sammy Going South* (1963, *A Boy Ten Feet Tall* in US), about the journey of a small boy, orphaned by an air-raid on his Port Said home, who crosses Africa on his own to find relatives in the south. It's an intriguing, nicely-made film, but hardly calculated to excite the contemporary audience (even though John Davis would approve of its family entertainment value) or connect with the contemporary cultural ferment.

The pop explosion that eclipsed *Sammy Going South* at the box office was the end of the road for Bryanston, and Balcon's career in commercial filmmaking. Bryanston was sold to the TV company Associated Rediffusion in 1965 and the whole rickety infrastructure of an independent British film industry was simply swept under by waves of American finance, with AFM ceasing production in 1964 after Bryan Forbes' ponderous *Seance on a Wet Afternoon*. The directors, however, were to flourish. Thanks to American backing, they no longer had to worry about the small size of the British market, the limitations of the native cinematic culture or their responsibility to show Britain on the screen. American companies took away all their troubles, offering substantial budgets, 100 per cent financing and access to world markets. It was a fool's paradise, but they weren't to know that, and it was hardly surprising that few worried much about the maintenance of British-financed production. By 1967, some 90 per cent of the films made in Britain were backed by American companies.

Established British companies had exploited the first whiff of pop vitality, with ABPC putting the saccharine personality of Cliff Richard through his paces in *The Young Ones* (1961), a let's-have-a-show musical where all possibility of an interesting inter-generation clash is defused by the fact that its hero works for, and adores, his father, the property developer who wants to destroy the youth club; and *Summer Holiday* (1962), in which Cliff and the Shadows drive a London bus to Rome, pursued by the mother of the teen star they are thought to have kidnapped. But it was an American company, United Artists, which put together the talents of Richard Lester, a London-based American who had acquired fast-cutting wizardry on live TV shows, and a phenomenon far bigger than Cliff, the Beatles, for *A Hard Day's Night* (1964). Since setting up UA's London office in 1961, George Ornstein had already launched the 'James Bond' series with *Dr No* (1962), *From Russia With Love* (1963) and *Goldfinger* (1964), establishing the world of glamour, action and intrigue in which the neo-thug Bond moved, each time taking on an evil villain bent on destroying and dominating the world, but always finding time to tryst with beautiful girls in exotic locations. Ornstein also snatched Tony Richardson's *Tom Jones* (1963) from under the nose of Bryanston, sealing the British company's fate and bringing UA a considerable return on an investment of only $1.3 million.

In March 1965 UA announced record profits. After that, there was no holding back the flow of American capital into the British industry. All the majors and two of the mini-majors set up production subsidiaries in London. This was the ultimate culmination of all the measures since the 1927 Cinematograph Film Act that had been designed to involve American finance in British films. The US companies hoped they had found a new seam of commercially-viable movies, but none thought too deeply about what they were buying into. There was no deep pool of directorial talent to be drawn on, even though television was about to produce such interesting new faces as John Boorman and Ken Russell; there was no genre of pictures, outside the Hammer films, which had international appeal. Nor had there been any sort of cultural rethink sufficient to justify the confidence American companies were now placing in British filmmakers.

The pop style of *Tom Jones* was a development of Richardson's magpie approach to cinema aesthetics, already evident in *The Loneliness of the Long Distance Runner,* even drawing upon some pantomime elements from the 'Carry On' films. But the cinema Americans were interested in was the antithesis of the Free Cinema mode. Where the early films of Reisz, Schlesinger and Richards had analyzed a class-ridden society, they were now being asked to celebrate classlessness. Where the old cinematic heroes had beaten their heads against the wall in frustration at the limited range of possibilities offered to them, the new culture celebrated limitless potential. Where the Free Cinema films articulated an animus against television and the pressure of mass culture on 'authentic' cultural values, the new mode adopted styles from television advertisements. And where the previous emphasis was on realism, the new approach emphasized fantasy and knowing nods to the audience.

The shift was not wholly imposed from the outside. The two modes fight it out in Schlesinger's *Billy Liar*, where the hero escapes from the constraints of life in an undertaking business by fantasizing himself as variously a soldier, Winston Churchill, a gunman mowing down his family or an aristocrat living with obliging parents whose behaviour is strikingly different from that of the real screeching proletarians. The summons he receives from a free-floating blonde – 'Leave 'em, Billy, they're not worth it. The whole place isn't worth it. You buy a ticket and get on a train. That's all you have to do' – has been read as a summons for a general change in British cinema. But the shift in focus involved in the journey south did not necessarily reposition the directors who had once rediscovered northern grime into a world which they could explore with sympathy and understanding. When Julie Christie, that blonde in *Billy Liar*, appears as the fashion model of the British-financed *Darling* (1965), Schlesinger remains as distant from his central character, a woman who plays with the emotions of many men and destroys her own happiness by her quest for a good time, as he had from Vic or Billy.

What could directors who had drawn stories from the tensions in English society make films about when the sources of finance were no longer interested in 'England', only in spy stories and lineal descendants of James Bond? The dilemma is particularly evident in the films of Joseph Losey, who could create a masterpiece like *The Servant* about the country's class structure, but seemed all at sea with his Bond spoof, *Modesty Blaise* (1966). There simply isn't any dramatic conflict in a story about a purported villain who wears a Beatle cap, drinks from a huge glass with fish in it and gazes out from his island home on the great blue sea as he waits for his pursuers, a pair of handsome would-be lovers who sing songs like 'We could of, we should of, perhaps we can.' It was as if to prove that it wasn't England that had changed that Losey went on to make *Accident* (1967), a powerful triangle drama involving two very different Oxford academics and their exotic pupil, financed from English sources. Lindsay Anderson showed his isolation from the Hollywood rush with *If...* (1968). Set in a public school, it was a passionate call to arms against national institutions that stifled the individual's potential, and Anderson represented the films as a deliberate challenge to the new aesthetics:

> The more what we might call trendy or eccentric or showy technique has tended to become in the last few years, the more I have felt I wanted to try and make films with as much simplicity and as much directness as possible.[7]

It's the flashiness that makes so many of the British films of the mid-1960s almost unwatchable today. Too many of them are visual firework displays without an emotional centre, or a coherent narrative structure. The New Wave films that do work tend to be those built around a single, larger-than-life character, like *Tom Jones* or *Alfie* (1966), in which Michael Caine plays a cockney Don Juan who 'don't believe in making anyone unhappy, not if you don't have to do it' but is forever breaking the hearts of young girls, until the sight of one of his middle-aged victims going through an abortion forces him into repentance. The formula can be extended to a pop group, as in Lester's Beatles films, or Boorman's *Catch Us If You Can* (1965) centred on the Dave Clark Five, but it looks more than a little shaky when applied to a more

John Schlesinger makes sure he's in control of *Darling* (1965)

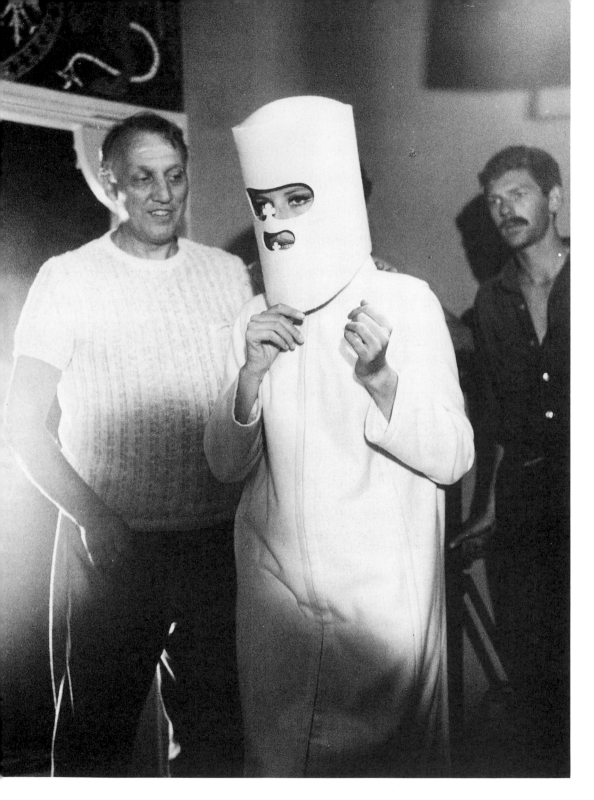

Joseph Losey enjoys himself with Monica Vitti while filming
Modesty Blaise (1966)

complex, not to say maudlin, character like that written by Shelagh Delaney for Albert Finney in *Charlie Bubbles* (1967).

Under their new paymasters, filmmakers were no longer interested in the sort of inner tensions that work at the heart of the more intense and exciting British films. Largely as a result, they had lost the ability to construct complex and resonant narratives. There is a formlessness to the films of the period, which becomes most apparent in such big films as Richardson's *The Charge of the Light Brigade* (1968), which culminates in one of the greatest anti-climaxes of cinema history, or *Isadora* (1969), where the dancer's sublimely silly death offers a decisive, but hardly stirring, conclusion to the film's chronological narrative of her stormy loves, ideas about dancing and travels through Europe. As historical re-creation or biography, these films were interesting, as cinema they were nowhere.

This drift towards incoherence can be seen also in the work of Dick Lester, the most 'pop' director of the decade. For all that *The Mouse on the Moon* (1963) is a slight film, its satirical swipes at the unprogressive nature of British institutions and the nation's difficulty in coming to terms with its global insignificance do find their target. The film shows a small state under the benign tutelage of Margaret Rutherford, pitching to compete with the Russians and the Americans in the space race. When this attempt by pseudo-Britain succeeds, the real British look desperately for evidence of their own national achievement in the first moon landing, and find it in the fact that one of the astronauts is wearing a British watch: 'This is a great day for us. Let no one say we are lagging behind.' While some of the same satirical zest is evident in *The Bed Sitting Room* (1969), Lester's chronicle of a post-holocaust world where a stunned Ralph Richardson imagines he is turning into a bedsitter and a doctor tries to keep the old traditions alive by having someone read the BBC News, and the film shows evidence of a superabundant imagination, the narrative is too unfocused for the satirical barbs to hit home, and the result is often tedious to watch.

The Americans came to London and invested large amounts of money in local film production, but put nothing into the creative infrastructure. They rode a wave for a while, thinking they saw a pool of talent that could be exploited and a cultural scene rich in potential stories which, together with the relative cheapness of British film production, would be enough to guarantee success. They poured money into British films without doing anything to ensure the production boom they started would develop roots. And while British filmmakers began to believe in the 'decline of Hollywood' as their guarantee that the increased popularity of their pictures would be permanent, they weren't disposed to tap the Americans on the shoulder and suggest that perhaps they should start thinking about film schools, new talents programmes, script competitions or anything of that sort.

Karel Reisz in the water to direct Vanessa Redgrave in *Isadora* **(1968)**

Spike Milligan and Dick Lester wonder whether there's life after the holocaust in *The Bed Sitting Room* (1969)

Distinctive directors did emerge at the end of the decade. The new talent came exclusively from television, with the exception of Nicolas Roeg, a cameraman who made his directorial début with Donald Cammell on *Performance* (1970), about the weird results of a meeting between a strong-arm gangster and a drop-out pop star. In TV, where films were being produced on a regular basis, ranging from the sort of imaginative documentary shorts produced for Huw Wheldon's *Monitor* programme to feature-length plays, aspiring filmmakers could try out ideas, take advice from their peers and put enough films through the cameras to develop their own ideas on what they wanted to make films about, and how they would go about it. Such opportunities were no longer available within the film industry.

Documentaries were the training ground for John Boorman, who went off to Hollywood after making his feature début with *Catch Us If You Can*. Peter Watkins made his first feature, *Privilege* (1967), for an American company, after his astonishing depiction of what would happen if a nuclear bomb fell on Kent, *The War Game* (1965), had been banned by the BBC. Another TV graduate was Ken Loach, whose UA-financed *Kes* (1969), about a deprived schoolboy who finds some meaning to his life by befriending a kestrel, is a remarkable indicator of how far a Hollywood studio could be persuaded to go in looking for sellable films after the pop bubble had collapsed. Another significant filmmaker who came out of television was Ken Russell, who continued working on his imaginative TV interpretations of the lives of such composers as Elgar, Delius and Richard Strauss while making his first, uneven, forays into cinema with *French Dressing* (1963) and *Billion Dollar Brain* (1965). He went on to assert his first mature, outrageous, filmmaking style with a D. H. Lawrence adaptation, *Women in Love* (1969), *The Music Lovers* (1970), covering the life of Tchaikovsky, and *The Devils,* an extraordinary collage made up of images of ecstasy, violence and cruelty.

Ken Russell took the removal of restraint and stiff-upper-lip repression that American finance had encouraged and turned it into a distinctive aesthetic style. His films were popular enough to ensure that he could attract US cash well into the 1970s. Elsewhere, however, Britain's imitation of Hollywood was proving to be built on ground more insecure than the area around the San Andreas fault. Penelope Houston had pointed out the dangers early on, in the pages of *Sight and Sound*:

> This is picture-by-picture finance, depending on such chancy things as the tastes of producers and directors, or a type of story in vogue at the moment (a spy boom brings filmmakers to Europe; a Western boom could drive them home).[8]

But there was nothing for filmmakers to do but plunge on, grab every chance that came their way and hope for the best. No easy way could be seen to re-establish British finance for production.

Ken Russell in rocky landscape for *The Devils* **(1970)**

Things weren't going well for the American studios, either at home or in the UK, and they became increasingly desperate, hunting around for the winning formula some had lost and others never found. Universal was the worst case, making 13 British pictures at a cost of $30 million, not one of which was a substantial hit. And, as the ideas became harder to find, film budgets spiralled upwards. It cost United Artists a substantial $6.5 million to make *The Charge of the Light Brigade*. Two years later, when MGM had the not-so-bright idea of remaking *Goodbye Mr Chips* as a musical, and UA tried to bring back the British war film with *The Battle of Britain* (1970), the bill for each picture was something like $12 million.

The films weren't doing business, the unprofitable US studios were being gobbled up by large conglomerates and 'rationalized', changes in US fiscal policy implemented in 1967 to help in funding the Vietnam war now discouraged investment by US companies abroad, and the American unions had initiated a campaign in 1968 to 'combat foreign production by American producers.' Some sort of retrenchment in US financing of British films was inevitable, especially given that American directors were now making films like *Bonnie and Clyde* (1967), *The Graduate* (1967), *Easy Rider* (1969), or *Butch Cassidy and the Sundance Kid* (1969), with the sort of freshness and sense of a connection to aspects of contemporary life which mattered to audiences, and these embarrassed British films off the screen. Fox jumped ship after *Modesty Blaise* in 1966. Paramount closed down its London office in 1968, declaring that 'we now feel that by coordinating and controlling our production activities in Hollywood we can effectively control a programme that will continue to draw from a talent pool all around the world.'[9] The following year Universal closed up shop and MGM shuttered its Borehamwood Studios, disgracefully leaving Fred Zinneman to look after the bills for a cancelled production of André Malraux's *Man's Fate*. The director spent two years in the courts before the American company agreed to honour its commitments.

None of this meant that American companies were no longer interested in financing British filmmakers or even British ideas, but they were no longer committed to doing so, and didn't expect to be sufficiently involved to justify keeping offices in London. Paramount, in fact, planned a British directors company, bringing together the talents of Reisz, Clayton, Schlesinger and Peter Yates, but dropped the idea when most of these directors emigrated to the US anyway. Even as American investment slumped from £100 million annually at its peak to around £30 million at the beginning of the 1970s, the US companies were still doing a lot more for the British film industry than the British seemed able to do for themselves.

But if there wasn't much British money around for film investment, there were also clear signs of dwindling creative energy. The decline of Hammer, the only British company to have benefited from the influx of American cash, was accelerated by the abandonment of its Bray Studios in 1968. The company's films were increasingly expensive, but less and less commercially successful. And although Bryan Forbes made a stab at backing British filmmakers as head of production for EMI, the company that had taken over ABPC in 1969, announcing 14 projects within months of taking over his new post, the line-up did not give the impression that he was in touch with any new sources of cinematic excitement. The most coherent films to emerge from Elstree during this time were both set in the Edwardian era, Losey's glorious *The Go-Between* (1970) and *The Railway Children* (1970), with the latter aiming at that much-lamented but largely-departed family audience. Of the contemporary subjects, *And Soon The Darkness* (1970) was a determinedly routine chiller, while *Mr Forbush and the Penguins* (1971), in which John Hurt alternatively woos Hayley Mills or talks to Antarctic penguins, is simply awful. Meanwhile Nat Cohen, who had brought his Anglo-Amalgamated company under the EMI umbrella, brought to the company the slick thriller, *Get Carter* (1971), directed by Mike Hodges, another TV graduate. Cohen, it seemed, was much more in touch with the mood of audiences than Forbes and, when the latter resigned on 25 March, 1971, he took over EMI's production programme.

'I think if I had been allowed to go on, there would still be a British film industry,'[10] Forbes said in the late 1980s. He was probably deceiving himself. It was not only that the industry needed propping up, but the whole film culture had to be rebuilt, and Forbes had clearly not grasped the scale of what needed to be done. The creative ferment set going at the beginning of the decade had petered out, as directors like Reisz and Richardson lost their sense of direction. The writers whose work they had drawn upon had never become part of the filmmaking community. While directors like Ken Russell and Nic Roeg carried on along their own idiosyncratic paths, and many of the directors who had flourished in the 1960s packed their bags for the trip to LA, there were no indications that those left behind had begun to face up to the economic realities of British film production, or what would have to be done to patch up the damage done to the craft of filmmaking, more particularly screenwriting, during the dead times of the 1950s and into the 1960s.

Descending Spiral

Had it not been for the influx of American capital during the 1960s, British filmmakers might have thought harder at the time about ways to restructure their industry. They could have attempted to negotiate some sort of financial collaboration with the cash-rich TV companies, worked at bringing flexibility to their dealings with the cinema circuits, or pushed for more generous agreements with the ACTT and other film unions that would encourage low-budget films. The process of adjustment, when it came, was all the harder because people had become so used to cosy times, even while the domestic base for British film production had been retracting. Directors who had grown used to thinking big now looked exclusively to Hollywood and had little commitment to the infrastructure of a British production industry. The TV companies couldn't see that there was much of a British filmmaking industry left to do business with, and the ACTT, evidently believing that either the government or the Americans would come to the rescue if they held on long enough, decided to stand by the agreements it had negotiated during the boom time.

The film industry of the 1970s lacked a middle term between the big-budget picture and the film made mostly on goodwill. The big films were still being made by the Americans at local studios. Frequently, as with Kubrick's *A Clockwork Orange* (1971), Hitchcock's *Frenzy* (1972) or Richard Attenborough's *Young Winston* (1972), the stories were English. But Nic Roeg went to Australia to make *Walkabout* (1970) and Venice for *Don't Look Now* (1973), while Ken Russell's *Savage Messiah* (1972) and *Mahler* (1974), although shot in the UK, focused on European characters.

The rest of British film production, however, was impoverished. Many directors launched their careers at the beginning of the decade with shoestring productions, made a promising film or two, then faded from the scene. Barney Platt-Mills, for example, persuaded a merchant bank and some rich friends to put up the £18,500 he needed to finance *Bronco Bullfrog* (1970), his portrait of youthful disenchantment, but was only able to make one more film on the same basis. Neither Stephen Frears, whose *Gumshoe* (1971) is a competent thriller pastiche, nor Robin Hardy who directed the cultish tale of a cop trapped by followers of a pagan cult, *The Wicker Man* (1973), made another feature in the decade. The sort of determination that enabled directors to get together cash from wherever they could find it, and make films for almost nothing, then seems to fade for a while until Ron Peck comes through with *Nighthawks*

(1978), about a cruising schoolteacher, and Derek Jarman, production designer on *The Devils*, brings the styles of his Super 8 mm filmmaking to feature length with his homoerotic *Sebastiane* (1976) and *Jubilee* (1978), a collage of punk gathered into a dystopic vision of England under the second Queen Elizabeth. So unencouraging was the climate for young directors in Britain at this time that Michael Balcon remarked in 1977: 'You don't need talent to get work these days; you need a miracle.'

There was still the residue of a commercial filmmaking industry, but hardly any scope for ambitious or original ideas. EMI, at least, made an effort, putting money into Ken Loach's *Family Life* (1972), about a teenage girl's battles with her family, and the first film from the Monty Python team that was more than just a string of their favourite sketches, *Monty Python and the Holy Grail* (1975). Python did something different on the large screen, but it was difficult to see the point to the other *émigrés* from the small screen, such assorted sitcoms and drama series as *Dad's Army* (1971), *On the Buses* (1971), *The Alf Garnett Saga* (1972), *Man about the House* (1974), *Are You Being Served?* (1977), *Sweeney!* (1976), *The Likely Lads* (1976) and *Porridge* (1979). To confirm that the creative initiative had decisively passed to the new medium, and also demonstrate how fast backwards film craft had moved in 40 years, Rank financed remakes of *The Thirty-Nine Steps* (1978) and *The Lady Vanishes* (1979). Rank had taken over the 'Carry On' series from Anglo-Amalgamated in 1966 and continued it into the 1970s with diminishing returns, until *Carry on Emmanuelle* (1978) demonstrated that nudge-nudge, wink-wink was no longer enough.

The increasingly difficult situation facing new entrants to the industry was investigated by the Lloyd Committee, set up by the Labour government's arts minister in 1965. It reported two years later, recommending the formation of a film school which would provide the sort of training no longer available within the industry. The National Film School (which became the National Film and Television School in 1981) based itself at an old studio complex in Beaconsfield, 20 miles outside London, and received its first students in the autumn of 1971. These included hopeful young writers, directors, cameramen, editors, composers and others. Meanwhile, the BFI Production Board, which had operated since 1964 as the Experimental Film Fund and financed early short films by the likes of Ken Russell, Jack Gold, Stephen Frears and Ridley Scott, now began to make low-budget features. Headed by Mamoun Hassan, the board brought in such remarkable films as Mike Leigh's *Bleak Moments* (1971); Peter Smith's *Private Enterprise* (1974), a study of the struggles of an Asian entrepreneur in the Midlands; Kevin Brownlow's *Winstanley* (1975) about an idealistic community in 17th century England, and the autobiographical *Bill Douglas Trilogy* (1972–8).

Such developments could have only a limited impact as long as there were

129

Fresh faces from TV – three members of the Monty Python team pose on the set of *Jabberwocky* (1977)

Bill Douglas's childhood recaptured in *My Ain Folk* **(1973)**

no real openings in the industry for new directors. There were few places for them to turn. Smith and Leigh moved into television drama, Brownlow directed his attentions to film history and the restoration of classic silent films, and Douglas eked out a living from unemployment benefit and occasional odd jobs. There was a desperate need for new initiatives to create an area of medium-budget production for these directors to move into.

The solution had to lie in a rapprochement between television and the film industry, but the TV companies were largely uninterested. There were odd initiatives such as LWT's financing of the Peter Hall-directed *Akenfield* (1974), which went into the cinemas after its first TV showing, and the filmmaking subsidiaries of the larger ITV companies such as Thames or Southern TV sometimes made an occasional feature. But there were few arguments available for producers hoping to establish greater collaboration between the two media. In Europe most of the top directors worked in cinema, which was sufficient encouragement for the TV companies to buy into features. That simply wasn't the case in the UK, where television drama was of a sufficient quality to attract high-calibre directors, and TV executives could therefore argue that the British film industry was alive and well and living in television. The film industry, by contrast, was associated with inflated budgets and unimaginative aesthetics. Also, the CEA was unwilling to consider relaxing its five-year ban so that television companies could secure prompt access to any features they had financed.

A desire to encourage TV funding of features was among the principles of the New Deal, an imaginative plan by Simon Perry and Richard Craven to bring down the cost of mainstream feature films and improve the prospects of raising finance. Perry and Craven, who had founded the Association of Independent Producers (AIP) pressure group in 1976, would ask major artists, directors and producers to take smaller fees in return for participation in a film's eventual profits. Also, by setting up a programme of films, they hoped that the New Deal would show a sufficient spread of risk to act as a magnet for finance. The idea was scuppered by opposition from the trade unions, as was any other proposal that depended on a distinction being made between visiting productions from the US and films financed from local sources.

'Conditions are worse here than in any of the 23 years I have been over here'[1] remarked the expatriate American producer-writer Carl Foreman in 1975, the year in which tax changes that had driven away many resident aliens began to bite seriously into studio revenues. Proposals for remedying the situation proliferated. The ACTT revived a 1941 proposal for nationalizing the industry, although this was later modified in favour of a call for various forms of state aid. A committee set up by the Prime Minister, Harold Wilson, delivered a report in 1976 reviving the idea of a British Film Authority. Although this had been put forward by every independent report on the film industry since the 1936 Moyne Committee, it was always difficult to discover quite how it could solve the industry's problems.

But the most sustained attack on government lethargy towards the film industry came from the AIP. The association argued that Eady money should be distributed selectively so as to encourage indigenous films of quality, rather than handed out to producers of so-called British films in proportion to their success at the box office. The proposal, although opposed by producers concerned about further discouraging American production in the UK, might have been implemented in a Films Bill had the Labour government not fallen in 1979. What the AIP did manage to achieve was removal of the secrecy about the amounts of Eady money paid out for particular films. When it had been shown how large a proportion of the available money was allocated to regular earners such as the 'James Bond' or 'Superman' films, a ceiling was established on the amount that could be paid out, thus ensuring there was more in the pot for distribution to lesser performers. The AIP also proposed that the NFFC should play a more active role in getting films made, and be less restricted in what proportion of a film's budget it could invest. Their campaigning led to the appointment of former BFI production chief Mamoun Hassan to head the corporation.

The institutional and legislative changes proposed by the AIP were sensible attempts to improve the climate for financing film production. More dubious were the association's ideas about what sort of films their members wanted to make. These centred on nationalism, and seemed to confuse earlier arguments that contradicted each other. With his declaration that 'I think it really is the duty of the director, the writer and the producer to turn their attention to those things in our society which are vital and to explore them in the cinema just as the American industry does,'[2] Craven could have been endorsing Lindsay Anderson's idea of cinema as an agent of social and political criticism. But the paper published to launch AIP's 1984 campaign, for example, echoed a position first put forward by the FBI in the mid-1920s:

> Film is uniquely able to project the British way of life and reflect British values and culture abroad. Such exposure, by helping to maintain awareness and appreciation of Britain among her trading partners and political allies vitally enhances the nation's global image.[3]

The AIP seemed to be waving a flag in the hope that somebody would come to rescue them and, at no point, did one feel that there was, behind the rhetoric, much in the way of serious thought, or any significant body of ideas struggling to gain expression.

The AIP's position was simple pragmatism. How else do you appeal to a national government except in terms of a national cultural identity? But it was also based on the assumption that, because filmmakers cannot make interesting films about people and societies they do not understand, they should only make films about native subjects. That this is nonsense can be shown from the number of interesting films made by foreigners about America, such as Schlesinger's *Midnight Cowboy* (1969) or Milos Forman's *Taking Off* (1971), not to mention interesting pictures made by Americans about Britain and, for that matter, dull films about Britain made by Englishmen. The AIP's position also suggested that British films had to be very much *about* Britain, but the great pictures use culture-specific material to explore universal themes. As director Alan Parker remarked in 1983, 'We should be making good films, good stories, set in Britain. The culture, the milieu, the society, should filter through the films and not, as is so often the case, be their raison d'être.'[4]

In suggesting that directors like Schlesinger, Reisz and Boorman, who had gone to Hollywood, were betraying not only their country but, in some significant sense, themselves, the nationalist argument was unnecessarily divisive. 'I don't believe that any of us feel that we are betraying anything by making larger-scale "international" productions'[6] riposted Karel Reisz to those who complained about his making pictures like *The Gambler* (1974). 'I find things here pretty unimaginative on the whole and I resent people being rather hostile to me about my American films,' complained John Schlesinger ten years later. The AIP's attitude came across as an attempt to prescribe the proper subjects for a British filmmaker to deal with, and was unnecessarily suspicious of imagination and fantasy.

The sort of absurdity that this way of thinking generated was made clear to the international press when critic Alexander Walker took director Nic Roeg publicly to task at the 1985 Cannes Film Festival for bringing to the event a British film, *Insignificance*, which dealt with four American culture heroes gathered in a New York hotel room. The fact that the play was written by a British director, and that the iconic significance of Joe DiMaggio, Marilyn Monroe, Albert Einstein and Joe McCarthy transcended their national origins, meant nothing to Walker, who would presumably have preferred the play centred around Ian Botham, Diana Dors, Peter Medawar and Aneurin Bevan. This black mark against Roeg's sense of national responsibility did not, however, protect the British consul from attack a few days later when he made a mildly derogatory remark about the aforementioned film. At a dinner attended largely by functionaries of the British industry, David Gladstone's sentiments were overheard by veteran producer Betty Box, who took the luckless diplomat roundly to task for being so remiss in his duties to speak up for the nation's filmmakers.

Having built its position around a nationalist case, the AIP was forced into a hole in which it seemed to be arguing, against all the economic realities, that a national industry could survive on the basis of domestic revenues. However, no amount of tinkering with Eady money was ever going to make British production self-financing. The association would have made a much more convincing case for government intervention if this has been presented as a first step towards bringing the British film industry into closer collaboration with fellow members of the European Economic Community, which the UK had joined in 1973. The notion of a European cinema, nurtured by Korda in the 1930s, had been killed off by the rise of Hitler and the coming of the Second World War. Protected by a national aid scheme, then insulated from reality by American finance, British producers had done little to develop relationships with their continental counterparts. Although coproduction treaties had been signed with France and Italy in the mid-1960s, such films as Losey's Franco-British-Italian *The Assassination of Trotsky* (1972) or the Franco-Italian *Lady Caroline Lamb* (1972) were half-hearted, desultory affairs. Project-by-project coproduction would never be the answer. Only when British filmmakers collaborated on an ongoing basis with their European partners, as the French did with the Germans and Italians, could quality films result. The 'Little Englander' attitudes of the AIP made it impossible for the organization to embrace the prospect of European collaboration with any degree of equanimity.

A willingness to accept that filmmakers had to work within the international marketplace might have enabled the AIP to engage more productively with Barry Spikings, production head at EMI, whom they turned into a demon along with ACC's Lew Grade. Spikings and his one-time partner Michael Deeley had developed an approach to film financing based on the recognition that, given the cost of financing significant movies and the smallness of the British box office, it was essential to make films that could be sold in the US. Running the production programme at British Lion from 1972, they only made films where they had a deal with a US distributor to cover half the cost, and sufficient presales to other international distributors to significantly reduce the rest of their risk. In this way they were able to set up films like Roeg's *Don't Look Now* (1972) and *The Man Who Fell to Earth* (1975), consolidate their relationships with American distributors and sufficiently impress the board at EMI to lead to a merger of the two companies.

What alienated AIP from the policy adopted by Spikings and, for a time, Deeley, was the increasing concentration on wholly American films, and seeming refusal to see British filmmakers as a possible source of international pictures. The profits made from such 1978 films as *Convoy, The Driver, The Deer Hunter* and *Warlords of Atlantis* may have pleased the accountants at EMI, but did nothing to rebuild British filmmaking. Spikings might riposte that he just wasn't being offered sufficiently strong projects by native producers but then, since he didn't back new talent and nobody else was doing so on a serious level, how were British filmmakers ever going to start making sellable films? Spikings, it could be argued, was simply taking the easy option.

It was Deeley's financial rectitude that ensured that first British Lion, then

135

EMI, made high-quality projects. After Bernard Delfont had persuaded the EMI board to join with his brother, Lew Grade, in setting up an American distribution company, Associated Film Distributors (AFD), not only did Deeley depart from the company, but other healthy constraints on Spiking's freedom of movement were removed. AFD was, to some extent a revival, of Rank's bid in the 1940s to control the American release of his films in the US, but the plan was executed without the caution shown on that earlier foray. Deeley, who had just arranged a favourable deal with Orion for EMI's films, thought the planned company a stupid idea. EMI's policy had been to handpick films, and resist the sort of pressure to produce that inevitably leads to bad decisions. AFD was not only going to cost $40 million to set going but, once up and running, would require from EMI and ACC a sufficient number of high-quality films to sustain a release schedule that could compete with those of the American majors.

AFD was Grade's final folly in a sortie on the international film business during which he never once showed any understanding of the difference between cinema and television. Having once been an artists' agent, he believed in the pulling power of stars, as was evident in the populist programmes he commissioned for his ATV company, from *Saturday Night at the Palladium* to drama series featuring the likes of Roger Moore and Shirley MacLaine. His deals with artists had occasionally led to investment in features but after the success of *The Return of the Pink Panther* (1974), which coincided with the increased interest of US television companies in feature-length films rather than series, 'Lew' turned his attention seriously towards movies.

Grade borrowed from Spikings and Deeley the recognition that there were distributors round the world hungry for American-style product, and set up a posse of sales agents to strong-arm them into taking packages of his films, mixing in pictures they wanted with the remaining dross. He also made use of the expertise acquired from selling shows such as *The Saint, The Persuaders* and *Thunderbirds* into America. But although he could presell his films to the US TV networks, he could never make them work in cinemas, which is where the profit would have come from.

The problem, of course, lay with the movies rather than the distributors. Believing it was stars who made successful films he gathered together, for example, Roger Moore, David Niven, Stefanie Powers, Claudia Cardinale, Telly Savalas and Elliot Gould – none of them real movie stars – for *Escape to Athena* (1979). But he knew nothing about dramatic structure, or the need for a film to have substance if it is to have the sort of emotional impact that spreads favourable word-of-mouth. Most of the stories came from pulp paperbacks, like *The Cassandra Crossing* (1976), about an American commander who develops a secret chemical device for use in germ warfare, *Capricorn One* (1977), about a reporter who discovers that the first manned

Goodbye AFD – looking after the model for *Raise the Titanic!* (1980)

space-flight to Mars is a hoax, or *Raise the Titantic!* (1980), about an attempt to recover rare minerals from a famous wreck.

AFD became operational in March 1979, long before either EMI or ACC had shown they could sustain a flow of saleable films, and the new company's existence encouraged both Spikings and Grade into a wild spending spree. It's not surprising that what they bought were duds. They were in a hurry, and there was no one at the other end to advise them not to go ahead. Grade's biggest folly was the $36 million *Raise the Titanic!*, but his mistakes were little more egregious than those of his partners. EMI spent $18 million on *Can't Stop the Music* (1980), which aimed to capitalize on the popularity of a group who had faded from the limelight some time before the picture's release, and an even larger amount on *Honky Tonk Freeway* (1981), a film which started off as just a little movie about the eccentricities of smalltown America and ended up a big flop. Along the way ACC picked up such quality projects as *Sophie's Choice* (1982) and *On Golden Pond* (1981), but by the time it came to release them, AFD had been crushed beneath its debts, and the remaining lineup had been handed over to Universal. Grade was not to remain long at the head of ACC, being toppled by the Australian entrepreneur, Robert Holmes a'Court, in 1982.

Grade's proclivity for hokum and Spikings' willingness to shoot himself in the foot made both these would-be moguls easy targets for attack by AIP, but the films that emerged from Rank's renewed involvement in indigenous production did little to strengthen the argument for AIP's nationalism. The unadventurous lineup included David Essex on a motorbike in *Silver Dream Racer* (1980), inappropriately produced when the youth scene was evolving into punk. Among the company's more interesting investments were the Western, *Eagle's Wing* (1978), and Roeg's *Bad Timing* (1981), a slightly vacuous meditation on sex and death of which Rank's chief booker George Pinches was to remark that it was 'a sick film by sick people for sick audiences'. Rank released the film with as much confidence and bravado as the company had previously shown towards such great films as *The Red Shoes* and *This Sporting Life*. In 1981 the Rank Organization went to the Cannes Film Festival to announce that it would spend £16,000,000 on films over the coming twelve months. Two weeks later it cancelled its production plans and declared that 'filmmaking was just not profitable enough'[6].

The failures at Rank, EMI and ACC revealed the absence of executives who understood both the creative and the financial aspects of the business, and had some sort of vision to connect their own policies to the tastes and desires of the contemporary audience. Recognizing the industry's needs for leadership, the Association of Independent Producers was named that way even though its rolls numbered more directors, writers and hangers-on than producers. The revival of British filmmaking, it assumed, would come about through the

Goodbye AFD – devastation on the *Honky Tonk Freeway* (1981)

emergence of a group of 'creative' producers who could take on all the functions previously absorbed within the walls of a studio. They would raise the cash necessary to enable projects to be made, develop scripts with writers, have sure instincts when it came to assigning a particular project to a director and gathering together the rest of the production team, understand sufficient of the nuts and bolts of production to see a film smoothly through all the stages of production, and then ensure it was effectively distributed worldwide.

The nearest the film industry came to finding such a paragon was David Puttnam. A former advertising executive and photographers' agent, he had sufficient energy, charm and persistence to raise the money for his projects, and was also driven by a desire to make films which had something to say about contemporary society. These drives gave some sort of coherence to his output, while his craving for success ensured that he gave a wide berth to parochial subjects. His soft radicalism, respect for old-fashioned storytelling and conscientious attention to detail ensure that, while he's never yet made a really exciting film, he also never made an especially bad one. Amongst British filmmakers that's a considerable achievement.

Puttnam's desire to put his own impress on the films he made drew him towards stories he could relate to personally, from the 'first love' story of *Melody* (1971), to the rock 'n' roll dreams of *That'll be the Day* (1973) and the sour exposé of the underbelly of 1960s glamour in *Stardust* (1974). But it was a combustible relationship with Ken Russell on *Mahler* (1974) that fixed his resolve to work with new, relatively malleable directors who would see him as a partner, not merely as a money-man. He drew on the considerable talents of two directors from commercials, Alan Parker for the kids' gangster musical *Bugsy Malone* (1976), and Ridley Scott for *The Duellists* (1977), before pushing to topline status such directors as Adrian Lyne, Bill Forsyth, Brian Gilbert, Hugh Hudson, Roland Joffé and Michael Caton-Jones. Puttnam's tragedy is that, by helping these directors to international recognition, it becomes extremely difficult to work with any of them a second time. The director no longer feels the need for a strongly interventionist producer, and Puttnam finds it easier to look for another compliant first-time director. By never growing up with his children, Puttnam is cut off from the chance to develop himself to creative maturity. In the late 1980s he sought a way out of this dilemma by working with experienced directors from eastern Europe, such as István Szabó and Jirí Menzel, who looked to him for guidance towards major international exposure, and it remains to be seen how fruitful this sort of collaboration will be.

Don Boyd was often compared to Puttnam in the late 1970s, evidence of a shared talent for self-publicity. Boyd, however lacked the same degree of focus. A graduate of the London Film School, he started by directing his own films, and continued to see himself as a director even while working as a

David Puttnam with *Chariots of Fire* financier Dodi Fayed

producer. Without Puttnam's need to impress his personality on projects, he wanted to be seen as the director's friend, and tended to let directors do their own thing in a way that Puttnam could not have contemplated. Also, by setting up a programme of films, he wasn't able to give individual pictures the necessary level of attention. Although both Alan Clarke's powerful remake of his banned TV film, *Scum* (1979), and Derek Jarman's imaginative interpretation of *The Tempest* (1979) came through Boyd's company, it was difficult to find a common thread that would link these films to each other or to such romances as *Sweet William* (1979) and *Hussy* (1979). In short, the Boyd touch was difficult to discern.

Both Boyd and Puttnam encouraged the press to build them up as potential saviours of the British film industry. Jeremy Thomas, although willing to endorse AIP's campaigns, was largely uninterested in the Britishness of British films. The only one of the three to have significant contacts with the film industry, with family connections to the 'Carry Ons' and the 'Doctor' films, his interest was exclusively in films of artistic ambition. With a desire to direct himself (to date unrealized), he sought relationships with the world's most interesting directors and, while these might sometimes be British, like Nic Roeg or Stephen Frears, they were just as likely to be the London-based Pole Jerzy Skolimowski, the Japanese Nagisa Oshima or the Italian Bernardo Bertolucci. Once Bertolucci had brought him a garland of Oscars for *The Last Emperor* (1987), he was established as one of the world's leading independent producers, able to make projects wherever he wanted, with whomsoever he wanted.

By the end of the 1980s, Puttnam and Thomas had both gathered a similar degree of power in the international marketplace. At the beginning of that decade, however, both had a special interest in reviving British film finance. They had established themselves as producers of quality pictures at a time when the general condition of the industry seemed bleak, but both came a cropper when they became too dependent upon American finance. Thomas had a nightmarish battle with MGM after the company refused to give a release to Roeg's offbeat *Eureka* (1982), which it had fully financed. And Puttnam had several unhappy experiences working in Hollywood for Casablanca Filmworks, where he made films such as Michael Apted's *Agatha* (1978) and Adrian Lyne's *Foxes* (1979). In 1981 he came back to England, hoping that London might become an alternative centre for international film production. For a time things were to work out better than anyone could have hoped during the bleak times of the 1970s.

The Light Brigade

Throughout the 1970s directors had been maturing to a level at which they might hope to direct feature films. Those like Bill Douglas, Chris Petit or Peter Greenaway who had made distinctive films for the BFI Production Board could find no place to work within television. And while graduates from the National Film School might develop their craft skills on pop promos, commercials, TV plays or documentaries, there were some who stood out as feature-directors in waiting. Among them were Michael Radford, who directed two powerful documentaries for TV as well as the feature-length film *The White Bird Passes;* Julien Temple, whose *The Great Rock 'n' Roll Swindle* (1979) and subsequent music videos suggested he had his finger somewhere along the pulse of contemporary youth, and Bill Forsyth, who was only a short time at the NFS but went on to establish his credentials with the micro-budgeted *That Sinking Feeling* (1979). Also, the success of Alan Parker and Ridley Scott encouraged many other, less motivated, commercials directors to put themselves forward as potential helmers of feature films, and there were television directors keen to follow the likes of Michael Apted and John MacKenzie into the cinemas.

Mamoun Hassan's NFFC provided an outlet for only a small part of this frustrated potential. He backed film editor Franco Rosso's film about racial conflict in South London, *Babylon* (1980); Christ Petit's demonstration that his BFI road movie *Radio On* (1979) had been a one-off, the muddled detective thriller *An Unsuitable Job for a Woman* (1981); and Bill Forsyth's second film, the lovable *Gregory's Girl* (1980). He also persuaded a chastened Barry Spikings at Thorn EMI to come in with the NFFC on David Gladwell's adaptation of Doris Lessing's *Memoirs of a Survivor* (1981) and Lindsay Anderson's savage attack on British life, institutions and values, *Britannia Hospital* (1982).

While all Hassan's films were distinctive and interesting, only *Gregory's Girl* was sufficiently successful to give the sense that a British filmmaking revival was in prospect. But optimism was boosted towards the end of 1982 when Channel 4, the TV network set up to provide distinctive forms of programming, and develop the potential of independent producers, unveiled its first package of low-budget films. Jeremy Isaacs, the network's boss, had previously chaired the BFI Production Board and was committed to backing Britain's more artistic film directors, tapping into the new directorial talents fostered by the NFS and securing the publicity of cinema screenings for at least some of the network's drama output. While many of the channel's films were middlebrow items of interest only as TV drama, pictures like *Angel* (1982), a thriller from Irish novelist-turned-director Neil Jordan, Peter Greenaway's *The Draughtsman's Contract* (1982), an intellectual detective story set amongst the bewigged cynics of seventeenth century English rural society, and Michael Radford's juxtaposition of Scottish repression against Italian vitality in *Another Time, Another Place* (1982), all created a new sense of excitement. Since the channel was committed to making 20 films a year, few doubted that films on this level would just keep coming, and such continuity of production would boost the quality of British filmmaking.

But the film that most symbolized hopes for a renaissance in British filmmaking was *Chariots of Fire* (1981), David Puttnam's calculated attempt to show that a picture originated in Britain, and dealing with British characters, could have an international audience. On most levels, this film about two outsiders, a Scot and a Jew, who ran for their country in the 1924 Olympics, was rather ordinary. Nevertheless, it played skilfully on the audience's emotions and offered an old-fashioned, morally satisfying conclusion. It was also promoted and distributed with great skill, and won Academy Awards. Further, the film chimed in with the craving for some sort of national revival, the theme of Margaret Thatcher's election campaign two year's previously and, when Britain went to war against Argentina in 1982, the film came to be seen by some as the Conservative party's rallying cry. The unfortunate result was that Puttnam's campaign for a national cinema came to be seen as an argument for a nationalist one.

How irrelevant the film's Britishness was to its international success was evident from the parallel success of *Time Bandits* (1981) in the American market. Produced by HandMade films, a company set up by the financier Denis O'Brien and ex-Beatle George Harrison to exploit the talents of the Monty Python team, Terry Gilliam's film is an inventive fantasy about a schoolboy who travels through time for meetings with Napoleon, Robin Hood and various other historical characters in the company of a band of dwarves.

The ping-pong debate, encouraged by *Chariots of Fire*, about what sort of view of Britain the nation's films should present, meant that the invitation to fantasy offered by *Time Bandits* was largely ignored. *Chariots* put a roseate tint over its bittersweet view of British institutions, with loving shots of Cambridge and presentations of Gilbert and Sullivan's music theatre, but the films that followed, with their acerbic attacks on Britain, too often became sunk in their own gloom. *The Ploughman's Lunch* (1983), a portrait of hypocrisy centred on London's media world, is sourly ready to adopt the old clichés about the emotional inhibitions that characterize the English male. *No Surrender* (1985), in which a group of aged Protestants and Roman Catholics, dolled up in fancy dress, are accidentally brought together in a Liverpool country club for a New Year's Eve celebration, becomes a journey through

A new view of England — Janet Suzman and Anthony Higgins in
***The Draughtsman's Contract* (1982)**

bedlam hung up on its own despair about the state of British life; while *Defence of the Realm* (1985) is so preoccupied with its revelations about what's involved in running Britain's nuclear state that it never becomes interested in the people trapped in the secret society it exposes. Only *My Beautiful Launderette* (1985), with its portrait of what happens to the son of a sickly idealist when his cynical uncle entrusts him with the running of a small business, seems genuinely interested in its characters – a fascist drop-out, a woman hooked on adultery, a frustrated girl trying to get out of the trap of an Oriental family – and able to create excitement around ideas on race, sex and class.

What was indicated by the concurrent success of *Time Bandits*, *Chariots of Fire* and Richard Attenborough's portrait of the Indian leader, *Gandhi* (1982), was the hunger of the US market for films aimed at an older age group than the American majors currently seemed able to satisfy. Thanks to the surfeit of cinema screens resulting from the development of new multiplex cinemas across the US, and the development of new specialized distribution companies, it was easier than before for British films to secure screenings and show whether they could draw an audience. The financial prospect for these films was also improved by the opening of a new market through paycable services such as Showtime and Home Box Office, and the development of home video.

The feeling that the new media developments would eventually spread from the US to Europe and that, as satellites were launched into the sky, and cables burrowed underground, there would be a phenomenal expansion in the demand for feature films, encouraged financiers to look sympathetically at new film financing ventures. Those who built film libraries today, it was argued, would eventually find themselves sitting on milch cows, raking in the money from reselling films to distributors from Taiwan to Tierra del Fuego. Financiers were also encouraged by the Inland Revenue's decision in 1979 to allow film to be treated as plant for capital allowance purposes, thus entitling film investors to considerable tax breaks.

The contours of a new film production industry rapidly emerged. Out of the large number of small production companies formed to make pop videos or programmes for Channel 4, there were some with a genuine interest in making features. Some of these were no more than a woman, a telephone and an idea, but a few had considerable production experience in other areas and were well-organized to take advantage of the new opportunities. Some companies were formed as subsidiaries of major groups such as the Virgin Records empire, the Moving Picture Company video facilities operation or Central TV, which spawned Zenith Productions, and these outfits had their own money to invest in features. There were also new sources of film finance, such as Acorn Films and United Media Finance, which had tapped the readiness of some institutional sources to back film and television production.

The largest of the new film financing entities was Goldcrest Films and

Richard Attenborough shows he can manage crowds in *Gandhi* **(1982)**

Television, which grew out of a company set up by the Canadian merchant banker Jake Eberts in 1976 to put development money into British features. His startup cash came from Pearson Longman, a division of the Pearson group to which Eberts pitched the argument that the company should position itself to take a lead in exploiting the opportunities presented by cable and satellite television. He pointed out that companies like EMI and ACC failed to exploit the nation's 'outstanding resources in talented people in all facets of filmmaking'[1] and presented a persuasive case that movies did not have to be as high-risk as people supposed. This involved not only reviving the British Lion model developed by Spikings and Deeley which protected downside risk through presales to American distributors and other offshore outlets, but also investing in a balanced portfolio of different films, from major international movies to pictures made primarily for television. He compared movies favourably to oil: 'After all, you never get a completely dry hole, it is always slightly moist.'

Eberts raised £7,450,000, his first major tranche of capital, in 1980 and drew in backing from Pearson and other sources thanks to the success of his early ventures. Eberts had no money in the production of *Chariots of Fire*, having judged the script 'a real downer', and the film was financed by Arab and American sources, but Goldcrest's £19,500 investment in the script was repaid thirty times over. And the company's first big film, *Gandhi*, went on to garner multiple Oscars and attract large audiences worldwide. Even the low-budget films, such as *The Ploughman's Lunch* or *Experience Preferred, but Not Essential*, which rode in on the early publicity for Channel 4's filmmaking activities, attracted considerable attention.

It was some time before Thorn EMI Screen Entertainment (TESE), the new division of Thorn EMI formed under Gary Dartnall in 1982, made an attempt to emulate Goldcrest's success with British talent. The company's focus was on acquiring product from international suppliers to distribute through its international home video distribution. Dartnall pitched TESE to American producers as an international marketing organization which could offer independents a better return outside North America on their product than they could secure from a US major. This led to such unexciting projects as *Wild Geese II* (1985) and *Holcroft Covenant* (1985), whose makers seemingly worked from the assumption that the contemporary cinema audience lived in constant fear of Rudolf Hess being released from Spandau Prison, or a Fourth Reich being established.

To secure British productions, television executive Verity Lambert was commissioned to make five or six films annually. Her lack of experience in feature films and the constant pressure she was under from the sales department led to a programme of little distinction. Bill Forsyth's *Comfort and Joy* (1984), although tougher than his film for Goldcrest and Puttnam, *Local Hero* (1983), was also muddled, and *Morons from Outer Space* (1985), the comic two-

Cowriter Mel Smith adrift in *Morons from Outer Space* **(1985)**

handler in which Mel Smith and Gryff Rhys Jones spent most of the film apart, was an incompetent attempt to spoof US sci-fi films. *Dreamchild* (1985) was imaginative but couldn't justify its £3,500,000 budget and, although *Clockwise* (1985) was a genuinely funny comedy starring John Cleese as an obsessive clock-watcher, it failed to do good business in the US.

Both Goldcrest and TESE were committed to a middlebrow area of filmmaking. Lambert's declared interest in romance, optimism, comedy and entertainment was, it could be argued, a reasonable riposte to the number of British scripts pervaded with class guilt and heavy messages, but it also resulted in too many projects without much sense of excitement or urgency. And while Goldcrest did expand into the fringes of melodrama with *Cal* (1985), about doomed love amidst the Irish troubles, and *Another Country* (1984), as well as taking on the Cambodian Holocaust in *The Killing Fields* (1984), it was difficult for the company to throw off the sense that its notion of good filmmaking was more tepid than full-blooded. Partly responsible for this impression was Puttnam's 'First Love' series, which revived from *Melody* the idea of asking young (and not-so-young) writers to chronicle their early romances. The slight, often whimsical, films that resulted were publicized as Goldcrest's research and development area but, although the 'First Loves' might differentiate competent directors from the other sort, they didn't generate new ideas for movies, nor did they do much to stimulate the imaginations of those who made them.

Nothing that emerged from either of these companies ever seemed particularly daring, imaginative or stirring. Similarly, after the first wave of enthusiasm for the films from Channel 4 had died down, it was clear that its drama director, David Rose, was more interested in television drama than cinema. British filmmakers were working in too narrow an aesthetic band, defined largely by television and at no point making any connection to the cinema culture that had last flourished in the late 1940s. Thus, while the trailer for *Chariots of Fire* sought to place the film in a tradition that included *The Third Man* and *Brief Encounter*, the New British Cinema that emerged never reached anywhere near the emotional voltage achieved by those films. This reflected partly the deficiencies of screenwriters who didn't have the understanding of their craft displayed by Noël Coward or Graham Greene, not to mention directors who couldn't match David Lean or Carol Reed for experience or achievement, as well as a filmmaking industry that just wasn't interested in stories of any emotional complexity.

The only company that worked from a deep knowledge of cinema history, and attempted to break away from TV modes, was Palace Pictures, a video and cinema distributor which had formed an association with Neil Jordan after seeing his first feature, *Angel*. Palace entrusted Jordan with their début production, *The Company of Wolves* (1984), an imaginative series of tales about wolves that chart a girl's sexual awakening. Jordan, the most consistently interesting of the directors to emerge at this time, went on to make *Mona Lisa* (1986), about a naïve ex-con's romance with a black hooker and journey into a dark criminal underworld, but hit a bummer with *High Spirits* (1989). Palace continued to explore cinematic genres with the musical *Absolute Beginners* (1986), the romantic fantasy *Siesta* (1987), the teen-pic *Shag* (1987), the horror *Dream Demon* (1988) and the melodramatic *Scandal* (1989), but its ambitions were consistently hamstrung by bad scripts.

While Palace financed films on a project-by-project basis, Goldcrest built its capital fund up to £35,000,000 with the aim of taking a higher risk profile on projects by selling off a smaller proportion of rights in pursuit of a larger percentage of potential profits. And as Pearson pushed for its subsidiary to become a major audiovisual company, involved in television, video publishing and paycable developments, Eberts' 'boutique' approach to film production, whereby he kept control of finance and contracts, limited overheads and had no major role to play in the production of the company's films, came increasingly under threat. The workload on Eberts became horrendous. 'He began to hate,' said Puttnam, 'what he had developed.' At the end of 1983, Eberts left the company, yielding his place at the head of the company to James Lee, the man who had done much of the pushing for the Pearson group.

Where Eberts was a realist who was frightened of losing money, Lee was a romantic, who saw Goldcrest becoming a major film company that would win through by playing for high stakes. Eberts' blueprint for Goldcrest, designed to exploit the untapped potential of British producers and directors while also proving that film could be a reasonably safe investment, could be considered conservative and unambitious, but that was only because the films he had been responsible for worked in the marketplace. Lee's overriding concern was to make Goldcrest a public company within three years of his takeover, and to establish the company as a major force on the international production scene. To achieve that he was willing to play for high stakes. He became blind to the economic realities of the film market-place and just what it was that had made Goldcrest function successfully under the previous régime.

Changes in that market-place partly explain the policies Lee introduced at Goldcrest. Not only were US paycable companies no longer paying out the sort of sums for low-budget films that had justified Goldcrest's investment in pictures aimed at the Channel 4 end of the market, an area TESE had always considered uncommercial, but the American studios had now got wise to the market for the sort of intelligent, up-market film entertainment that Goldcrest was making, and had begun to compete with films like *Out of Africa* (1985). Goldcrest, Lee concluded, could no longer see itself as an outsider working a gap in the market, it now had to play the Hollywood game in the Hollywood way. Similar pressures drove HandMade from such low-cost comedy as its pig movie, *A Private Function* (1984) to the big-budget hokum of *Shanghai Surprise* (1986), which starred Madonna and Sean Penn, but HandMade never overstretched itself as Goldcrest was to do.

Goldcrest's new ambitions were immediately apparent in Lee's preparedness to increase the company's overheads. Whereas Eberts had always liaised directly with producers, Lee appointed a production head, Sandy Lieberson, who had been Puttnam's partner at the beginning of his career and had more recently run the London branch of the LA-based Ladd company. All the other divisions of the company were expanded and Goldcrest moved from relatively cheap offices in Holland Park to an expensive building in Wardour Street, the traditional heart of the British film community. Goldcrest, Lee seemed to be saying, had arrived. However this increased expenditure was not matched by an increase in output. In fact, Lee withdrew the company from John Boorman's Amazon adventure, *The Emerald Forest* (1985), a film budgeted at a reasonable $14,000,000, with significant presale deals that would have generated some cashflow. And, apart from Puttnam's increasingly expensive experiments with new talent, Goldcrest stopped making low and medium-budget films. It was fifteen months before any other pictures went before the cameras and, when 'Action' was finally called, the company quickly found itself sinking into deep trouble.

At the root of the crisis that developed as Goldcrest went into production on *Revolution, The Mission* and *Absolute Beginners* was the problem of control. Under Eberts, the deal was that producers delivered projects on budget and on time. Under Lee, the lines of responsibility were much more hazy. By setting itself up in competition to Hollywood for projects and talent, the company had given the impression to Hugh Hudson and Roland Joffé, who could have used their Oscar-winning débuts to secure work in LA, that Goldcrest needed them more than they needed Goldcrest. And so the British company had to trade with creative freedom, giving all three directors, none of whom had shown any ability to write a script or put together a coherent film without help from a strong producer, a free board on which to scratch their creative vision. Nobody seemed to be in control and the same problems affected all three films. The scripts were never right, the production teams weren't strong enough to control the films' directors, and the proper financial controls weren't put in place. All three projects were expensive, and Goldcrest's capital was barely sufficient to carry all three, especially since *Revolution* and *Absolute Beginners* started to go seriously over-budget, even though neither was sufficiently covered by completion bond insurance. 'There was nothing,' Eberts was later to remark. 'It was literally an open cheque book.'

Similar control problems afflicted Gary Dartnall's ability to secure a strong series of international films for TESE. 'As the demand for product increases,' he remarked in 1984, 'then the talent becomes more and more scarce. It will

Pig Panic – Michael Palin and Maggie Smith battle with their porcine guest in
A Private Function **(1984)**

go to the company that can give them the greatest return from the product they create.' The deals that Dartnall made with David Begelman were so favourable to the American producer that the company's subsequent owners described them as 'unprecedented in the annals of film history.' TESE was seen as a soft touch and its strategy for securing playable films was not working.

Dartnall decided that Lambert's policies weren't bringing him the best British productions and he set up a series of very generous deals with independent producers. The chosen filmmakers would receive a contribution to their overheads and money with which to develop projects. They would report directly to the head of the company, whose responsibilities included many matters more pressing than reading scripts. Free from financial responsibility, the hope was, they would go on to produce striking commercial films.

Corporate critis hit TESE before these deals had become fully operational, but they could never have worked out. The scale of the enterprise Dartnall was managing made it impossible for him to become actively involved in the projects his producers developed, even had he the experience and judgement necessary. The company's need for product to feed its international film and video distribution network meant it was biased towards giving the go-ahead to projects before they were ready. Outside the marketing and sales personnel, whose judgements were of dubious value, there was no agency to challenge the producers on a creative level, pushing them to make better, more provocative, challenging and commercial pictures.

The existence of Goldcrest and TESE encouraged British filmmakers, offering assurance that they had a future. But while the British film industry needed big companies – to give it coherence, to train up new talent, to experiment with new ideas – neither Goldcrest nor TESE had the spirit to take on these responsibilities, nor to impose themselves on the productions they backed. What happened to Goldcrest demonstrated that the advantages of size could be easily outweighed by the problems growth created. A big company must keep on producing, to cover its overheads and to justify the expectations of its backers. But there is no fixed place in the market for British films. Also, outside a well-regulated environment, when films get made because a company needs product, no one waits around to make sure the script is right and all the elements are in place.

The real problem was that no one any longer knew what a production company should do, especially when those in charge were not ruthless moguls but gentle, intelligent men and women. As producer Simon Perry expressed the problem:

> I don't know how to have a relationship with a head of production. Is he a producer, a coproducer or what? If he is powerful, then what am I doing? If he is impotent or incompetent, then I have no respect for them in any case?

The ideology of the AIP had emphasized the power of the producer to dominate the production process; three decades of critical ideology had elevated the status of the director, but too few British producers or directors had the necessary level of competence. The result was anarchy, then devastation. Just as Goldcrest was unable to contain Hugh Hudson on the Devon moors, or Julien Temple within the walls of Shepperton Studios, so Virgin, a cofinancier of Temple's *Absolute Beginners*, had been unable to control the costs of *1984*, which Perry produced for release during the year of the title. As a result of these cost escalations, and the poor response to Ken Russell's *Gothic* (1986), Virgin withdrew from production, and confined itself to putting up promises of cash in return for distribution rights. Goldcrest limped on until it was sold off at a bargain-basement price to the Brent Walker property and leisure group. TESE was acquired by Menahem Golan and Yoram Globus of Cannon Films, who financed two low-budget pictures, *Business as Usual* (1987) and *The Kitchen Toto* (1987), before they were forced by poor returns for their Hollywood production slate to sell up to the Italian Giancarlo Parretti, whose Pathé company then employed Sandy Lieberson as its British production head.

Following the Goldcrest and TESE débâcles, the initiative moved to smaller companies. Palace continued what it had been doing, although now with its sights more firmly set on success in the US. Working Title, set up by Tim Bevan and Sarah Radclyffe, built on the surprise success of *My Beautiful Laundrette* to make a range of productions, from the sex romp *Personal Services* (1987) to the powerfully-written story of a girl's struggle to win the love of a mother committed to the anti-apartheid cause in South Africa, *A World Apart* (1987). HandMade Films divided its programme between American projects and low-budget British pictures like the comedy, *Withnail & I* (1986). Initial Pictures followed the doomed true-life story of two punk icons, *Sid and Nancy* (1986), with a banal *Alfie* for the 1980s, *The Rachel Papers* (1989). And a number of other producers were able to spin out a deal with the NFFC or Channel 4 into an occasional film.

The energy put into some of these pictures suggested that the model of a film industry as small pockets of energy and inspiration might work better, and make more effective use of the available resources, than a large corporation like Goldcrest or TESE. Small companies can chunter along making low-budget pictures or programmes for TV, and turn to bigger projects when a script is ready and the market right. They don't have the advantage of size with which to pitch for capital, but they can move to exploit tax breaks, international coproduction possibilities or any other source of funding that becomes available, as efficiently as a larger outfit. And there are independent completion guarantors, sales agents and lawyers to carry out the functions that a company like Goldcrest or TESE would keep in-house. The problem with the small production company is that it cannot easily sustain the effort of will to prevent the need

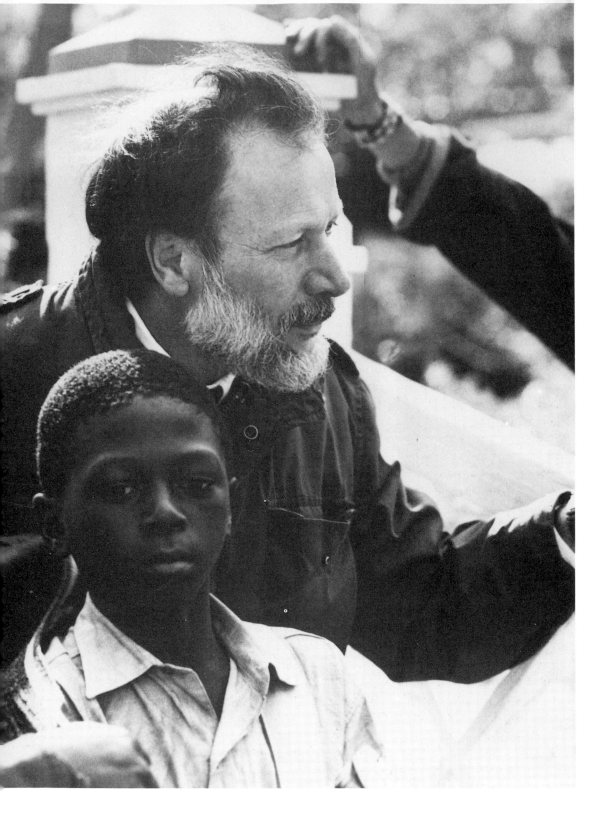

Chris Menges films a South African story in *A World Apart* **(1988)**

for cash from unbalancing the creative aspects of the project. It may do deals that involve putting the wrong sort of pressure on the filmmaker, or dissipating elements in the project that made it exciting in the first place. The pressure to get a deal in place often leads to wishful thinking and bad judgement.

The climate for raising film finance was very hard in the late 1980s. There were no longer any tax breaks available in Britain, and financiers were unlikely now to listen so keenly to talk of a crock of gold at the end of the new media rainbow, when Rupert Murdoch was losing millions on his Sky TV satellite venture and cables were creeping very slowly under the pavements of the nation's cities. Also, British projects were no longer flavour-of-the-month in Hollywood and many of the smaller companies with which British filmmakers had been developing relationships had either gone to the wall or cut back on 'foreign' production. Producers had to spend their energies on getting projects sold, rather than making sure the scripts were right. Fewer films were made, budgets escalated, and every concession possible was made to entice American money. Kowtowing to American finance accounted for the declining performance of those directors whose films had been responsible for the hopes with which the decade had started, from Michael Radford's *White Mischief* (1987), which made no attempt to explore the thriller potential of its plot about the murder of a young wife's lover in colonial Africa, to Neil Jordan's muddled *High Spirits* (1988). American performers popped up in the unlikeliest places; like Bridget Fonda as the plucky Amanda Rice-Davies in *Scandal* (1989). Many projects had a Brit-American angle, such as *Chicago Joe and the Showgirl* (1990), about an American officer serving in Britain during the Second World War, or *Memphis Belle* (1990), about an American bomber crew operating out of the UK.

The drive for commercial success encouraged filmmakers making low-budget films to develop ideas with more commercial potential than those made in the early 1980s. *Paperhouse* (1989) tells of a sick and unhappy girl who finds that what she draws in her waking hours finds its way into her dreams. *How to Get Ahead in Advertising* (1989) follows the misadventures of an advertising executive who develops a boil on his neck that represents the worst part of his nature. *For Queen and Country* (1989) shows a black Falklands vet dealing with the racism he confronts on his return to life on a London council estate, and *Paris by Night* (1989) unravels the dilemmas confronting an ambitious woman MEP who murders a man who is blackmailing her while she attends a conference in Paris. But there's no such thing as a good idea for a movie, only a good movie and, in every case, these films were let down by their writers' poor understanding of the screenwriter's craft. They didn't know how to move, intrigue and amuse the audience, using the language of film to touch the deeper part of the psyche. Good intentions were fully on display, but too little verve, energy, flair.

Part of this declining vigour reflected the lack of any idea about what British films should be doing. When Goldcrest and Channel 4 had been actively commissioning features, their existence and the differences between them stimulated some sort of debate. Were Goldcrest's films nostalgic and excessively nationalistic? Was Channel 4 ignoring all the interesting British filmmakers, like Bill Douglas (whose *Comrades* (1986) turned out to be a masterful, if somewhat amorphous, account of the campaigns mounted by the Tolpuddle Martyrs in nineteenth-century Dorset and their subsequent careers in Australia), or Terence Davies (whose *Distant Voices, Still Lives* (1988) was the only completely assured film of the late 1980s)? Were the channel's films movies or just souped-up television? In neither case was the debate on a very high level, but it did help to focus the attentions of filmmakers on what they were doing. By the end of the 1980s, Goldcrest was no longer interested in British movies and Channel 4 had largely withdrawn from low-budget features. Of the two figures who had led the earlier discussion, Jeremy Isaacs of Channel 4 was now a TV personality running an opera house and Puttnam a producer more interested in making major European films than again rebuilding the British film industry. Nobody had moved into the vacuum left by these figures, and the remaining sources of finance were too fragmented, too lacking in vision of what they were about, to generate the former levels of energy. Meanwhile, the drain of directing talent started by Puttnam during his short period as head of production at Columbia Pictures, when he lured such protégés as Pat O'Connor, Bill Forsyth and Brian Gilbert to Hollywood, continued into 1989 when Neil Jordan and Stephen Frears made their first American films. At the beginning of the 1990s, it was difficult to know where the energy might come from to put British filmmaking back together again.

The Goldcrest Films

In the late 1930s, Michael Balcon concluded from his experiences as head of production for Gaumont-British that the domestic film industry should concentrate on low-budget films aimed primarily at the British market. In 1982, David Puttnam made a remark that seemed to support the same conclusion:

> Ridley Scott is an extraordinarily gifted director. He has a vision I would give anything for. However, *Angel* is a far superior film to *Blade Runner*. It just works better in pure filmic terms.

Puttnam interpreted the respective achievements of Neil Jordan and Scott in relation to the budget level at which each was working: £600,000 for *Angel* against £15,000,000 for *Blade Runner*: he felt that the large-scale filmmaker was forced to satisfy audience expectations in conventional ways, whereas the director with the smaller budget could surprise and astonish. In fact, things would seem to be the other way around. Jordan's picture is a competent piece of narrative filmmaking, while Scott's relies too much on the set direction and camerawork to carry its convoluted tale. Much the same thing could be said of the contrast between the three flops Goldcrest made in 1985 and one film which, although not a spectacular box office performer, nevertheless attracted critical kudos and covered its costs.

Whereas two of the big films were in the hands of Oscar-garlanded producer–director teams, the group that came together to make *Dance with a Stranger* did not encourage any particular expectations. Shelagh Delaney hadn't written a feature script since *A Taste of Honey* and *Charlie Bubbles* back in the 1960s; it would be the first feature film for its producer Roger Randall-Cutler, and director Mike Newell had only one significant previous credit, the television film *Bad Blood* (1981). But what Randall-Cutler did have was a strong idea as to why the story of Ruth Ellis, the last woman to be hanged in England, was worth making. He saw that, by focusing on the forces that drew Ellis to her loser lover, David Blakely, from the other side of the social divide, he could make a passionate and resonant film which touched upon numerous issues relating to England of the late 1950s without getting bogged down in them, as British filmmakers tend to do. The focus was to remain firm while the film evolved, and it influenced every decision that was made.

Delaney was initially reluctant to accept Randall-Cutler's commission, but his determined approach brought her round. When she said that she didn't want to write about real people, he pleaded that the film would be a fictional account of a love affair, with the facts of the case functioning only as a springboard for imaginative interpretation. He was firm about the aim of the film, but not prescriptive about the need to include certain pieces of evidence, or even about what period of the relationship should be covered.

Randall-Cutler talked to two directors about the project before committing to Newell. Michael Radford, who had just finished *Another Time, Another Place*, wanted to focus the issues raised by the case through a trial scene, but neither Delaney nor Randall-Cutler were interested in this approach. Alan Clarke ruled himself out by trying to fit the film into a political analysis of Britain's class system. Newell, by contrast, was at one with writer and producer in seeing the film as the tale of people caught in a dead end of extreme emotions with which they were unable to cope. He accepted the direction in which the screenplay was going, even if he didn't like the then-current version.

Writer and director worked together, overhauling the script and feeling their way towards a revised draft that would give the story a sense of tragic inevitability. Through their discussions, Newell and Delaney transformed the story of a passionate romance that went sour into one about a desperate relationship that always carried within it the seeds of its end. Scenes were re-ordered to emphasize the inexorable logic of the respective characters' actions and their social positions. Characters and scenes were cut back to concentrate the film's narrative on what was happening between the protagonists. Newell and Delaney also looked at individual scenes to find ways of increasing both their emotional significance and their visual force.

The debate between Newell and Delaney was never a simple conflict between the literary ambitions of a writer and the visual sensitivities of a director. Under the pressure of the fact that the film was going to be made, and within a shared objective, writer and director chipped away at the script in order to get to the heart of their story. The result is a film in which every scene between Ellis and Blakely is charged with high-powered emotion, where every action fits a pattern of solitude leading to combustive coupling, followed by explosions of increasing force that make the finale dénouement inevitable, bleak and stirring.

Newell has said that the period of collaboration with Delaney was as detailed as the process of directing the film. Pieces of factual information about the characters and period were thrown into the ring as possible influences on the structure of the script and the film's visual style. 'We were getting,' Newell remarked, 'right into the subject and not in a dull theoretical way, but in terms of very potent areas of people's lives – the part where their fantasies lay.' The process of scripting was a continuous dialogue between the realities of the story they were telling and the universal story they wanted to put on the screen. Newell recalls:

What I said to myself was that there should not be a single action in the story that was not motivated in the most complex kind of way that you could devise – social, character, emotional, medical. Either it was going to emerge that there was a story that had the absolutely essential quality of universality or there wasn't. You were going to prove it one way or the other.'

There was a moment in the evolution of *Dance with a Stranger*, just three weeks before shooting was due to begin, when producer and director realized the script still had not achieved its potential. With Delaney they set about a new structural rewrite, effectively synthesizing all the previous drafts. Until then, Newell argues, the creative team had just been coasting:

Nobody wants to cause themselves the kind of trouble that making a film involves. It is sheer pain for weeks and months. You try to avoid it – be intelligent, be savvy. The final agony is finding out what it is and how you are going to make it. Until the last draft, you know you have cheated and that you cannot cheat, or you will have a terrible time both on the set and in the editing room.

Newell's words contain the key to Puttnam's riddle. While some low-budget films are corrupted by the producer's conviction that a 'cheap' film cannot fail to make its money back, it is generally felt that, at the level of pictures like *Angel* and *Dance with a Stranger*, only through ensuring the script is as good as possible will the film find an audience. The same compulsion doesn't operate on a larger film where the enormous quantity of time and money available seems to justify the assumption that a script's faults can be corrected during production. And, if things don't work out, then the special effects, the crowds of extras, the star names, the expensive director – or something – will compensate for any deficiencies in the overall design. On the three big films made by Goldcrest, the moment of truth to which Newell refers seems never to have arrived.

Goldcrest knew from the beginning that it had a problem with the script of *Revolution*. An internal report presented to Lieberson in the summer of 1984 observed that the script had a strong documentary feel but very little dramatic potential. There was no opportunity for the audience to become involved in the characters or thrill to the resonant images; there was considerable room for visual excess that would divert attention from the narrative. The fighting scenes were repetitive. 'This will be an expensive film' Amanda Schiff concluded, 'and it needs more steel in its structure to justify the expense.' The report was distributed around the Goldcrest offices but, instead of leading to decisive action, its argument was swept under the carpet in a piece of amazing wishful thinking: 'We all recognized,' Lee was later to remark, 'that the screenplay was inadequate, but it seemed to be terribly visual and appropriate to Hudson's strengths.'

During production of a long and complex picture the script should be the one solid bulwark, but Hudson and the film's star Al Pacino were improvising scenes at night before each day's shooting. Meanwhile, Goldcrest desperately handed out money to sundry screenwriters in the hope they could rescue something from the mess. It was no way to make a movie. And in failing to ensure the film started with a good script, Goldcrest had weakened its position in dealing with the filmmakers. As he commuted between his expensive offices in Wardour Street and the playing fields of Devon, Lee realized he was powerless. 'Hugh,' he later recalled, 'made no secret of the fact that our interests were not his interests. He was out there to make a great film; we were the suckers who had put up the money.'

Whatever Hudson actually said to Lee, the situation was one that could have been anticipated. Hudson's long experience in commercials had acquainted him with a style of filmmaking that involves enormous expenditure to considerable, if facile, visual effect. His ability to create resonant images had never been matched by a commensurate facility with characterization, dialogue and narrative structure. Instead of playing to his strengths, Goldcrest needed to compensate for his weaknesses. That it failed to do.

Goldcrest trusted producer Irwin Winkler to keep the production under control, but he had not been the stronger member of the Chartoff–Winkler team responsible for the *Rocky* films. His solo productions, such as *New York, New York* (1977) and *The Right Stuff* (1983), were rambling, if sometimes brilliant, works. None of this can have been unknown to Lieberson who had been working for the Ladd Company when *The Right Stuff* was made under its banner. But, with Winkler often absent from the set, executive producer Chris Burt was left with the unequal task of keeping *Revolution* under control. 'I realized too late,' said Lee, 'that we were dealing with a new style of producer. Winkler sees his role as making a great picture by keeping everybody happy, but not in bringing the film in on budget.'

Nor could anyone be all that surprised when *Revolution* came in at a budget of around £18,000,000. It was a large-scale picture with the costumes, wigs, make-up, antique rifles, buckles, shoes, horses and wagons made just 'right' for hundreds of extras representing the armies of the American Revolution. The Norfolk town of King's Lynn had to be dressed to look like New York. Access to the Dartmoor location chosen for the major battle scene was so difficult that it took a whole morning for cast, crew and extras to reach it. Under such circumstances, it was useless for Goldcrest's executives to start trying to rein things in weeks after production had begun. Information about the serious cost overruns would be referred first to production executive Garth Thomas. He would report the matter to Lieberson who would then ask Lee to liaise with Winkler. 'An alarming amount of time,' Lee remarked, 'had elapsed. Often there was nothing I could do.'

The resulting film is a series of tableaux showing a father and son drawn, reluctantly at first, into the battle to rid the United States of Britain's presence. The opening sequence is thrilling as an enraged rabble topples the statue of King George. Hudson's battle scenes are stunning pieces of composition, choreography and atmosphere. But the moments of drama between these large-scale scenes are depicted in such broad sweeps as to reduce the whole experience to bathos. A young girl repudiates her aristocratic family to follow the revolution and shows her disdain for a British fop by sticking her wig-pin into his leg. Tom Dobb, the film's central character, is content to toady to his masters until they appoint him a pseudo-fox for their hounds and cruelly beat his son's feet. A film which works with epic themes must be rooted in a deep appreciation of human motivation, but the script and Hudson's direction deal only in caricature and stereotype. There are many powerful images in *Revolution* but most of the audience missed them amidst the incoherent narrative.

If Goldcrest's new view of itself as a production company meant anything at all, it should have been able to do something about its youth musical, *Absolute Beginners*. The director was a feature débutant and the producers, Palace, had made only one feature before, which theoretically put the financiers in a strong position when it came to influencing the production. Since the film was being shot in London and its environs, none of the distance problems that arose on either of the other two films should have occurred. Also, Goldcrest's executives had been actively involved in developing the script. Yet, the screenplay remained a mess, and this was the Goldcrest film that went over its original budget by the highest percentage (although still the cheapest).

Julien Temple used the high esteem in which he was held – he was the reason why Goldcrest and Virgin were making the picture – to control the evolution of the project. Those who challenged him or failed to deliver easy solutions were dumped, like wise counsellors from an increasingly corrupt court. Back in 1982 the script had been entrusted to Don Macpherson, the journalist who had originally proposed making a film from the Colin McInnes book. He was a novice screenwriter, who believed they should stick close to the book's picaresque structure. This approach went down well with Temple, who felt that a strong narrative might turn a film designed to shock the British film establishment into just another cheap imitation of an American idea, or a naturalistic account of British youth culture. Temple knew just what he was against.

It was Richard Burridge, who had been at the NFS with Temple and had considerably more screenwriting experience than Macpherson, who proposed turning the film into a musical. This made a neat connection with Temple's pop promo work, but also seems to have reinforced Temple's sense that the only way to see how the script worked would be by letting him make the film. The Burridge–Temple relationship deteriorated steadily. The writer came up

163

Al Pacino and son make their getaway in *Revolution* (1986)

with sparkling inventions which he thought would answer Temple's requests, but found he could neither satisfy him nor ascertain what he was doing wrong. Burridge felt that Temple was disinterested in the project. Macpherson and Temple began to sense that Burridge was out of sympathy with the project. Eventually he left the production.

The next scriptwriter, Chris Wicking, broke away radically from Burridge's drafts and made substantial changes to the script's structure. Although coolly received at Temple's HQ, the new script was rifled for scenes and dialogue that could be incorporated into a new hybrid draft, which became known as the Burridge–Wicking version. Goldcrest and Orion committed themselves to the film on the basis of this text, which was enough, for Temple at least, to put upon it a seal of approval. Wiser judgement was available. After speaking enthusiastically of the 'wonderful, energetic and exciting youth-oriented musical,' Orion's Kerry Boyle went on to explain that the film failed to use every scene to effect. Goldcrest's executives were also anxious about the film's length.

But shooting went ahead, with these problems only half-resolved – a failure that was to undermine the producer – director relationship during filming. Temple reacted very negatively when the producer, Stephen Woolley, demanded that some scenes be cut from the film. 'Julien doesn't,' Woolley later recalled, 'seem to work under pressure in terms of rationalizing things. Everything is important to him, whereas we all know that some things are more important than others.' Temple, by contrast, remarked 'Steve kept on telling me to cut things. It didn't make any sense to me because we had worked on the script.' With Goldcrest by now in crisis and crowds of extras standing around on the set all day waiting for the weather to improve, it is not surprising that filming became a nightmare for everyone involved.

When a halt was called, several scenes had still not been shot. Jake Eberts, newly installed at the company he founded, was appalled by the degree of overspend on the film, the reports he received of producer and director brawling on the set, and what he saw of the picture. 'It was so frighteningly awful, so non-existent that I literally felt a chill going down my back.' Eberts called in veteran producer Alan Marshall, who had produced *Another Country* for the company, to take over the picture, report on what could be salvaged and complete it as quickly and cheaply as possible.

Absolute Beginners is a film of ideas rather than a film about people. It is epic and entertaining, rather than emotional and engaging. The film achieves its objective of depicting a vibrant world where young gays, blacks, trad jazz fans and followers of the Modern Jazz Quartet jostle and compete, but the lead character is not strong enough to carry the picaresque storyline. And although his girlfriend Suzette's talents elevate her from the empty, fornicating vessel of McInnes's book, she remains an uninteresting and unrealized character.

165

There is no hint of what draws Colin toward her unless it be her looks or skill as a dancer. We see a lot of Suzette dancing or thrilling an assembly of fashion correspondents, but Temple's film fudges the crucial moments of intimacy.

Temple and Hudson both ignored their responsibility to work through to a script that could provide the basis for the passionate and visually stirring film that each intended. But the fault was not entirely theirs. They were poorly served by a company that gave the go-ahead to their films when they were not yet ready to be made, and by producers who weren't strong enough to ensure the completion of a film that realized the project's original potential. That the problem lay in the attitudes adopted by Goldcrest Mark 2 is demonstrated by the nature of *The Mission*, coproduced by David Puttnam with an Italian, Fernando Ghia, who had been hustling the project around Hollywood for most of the 1970s. The film did not go over-budget like the others – although its eventual cost was much higher than that originally anticipated by Goldcrest – nor was it such a disaster at the US box office, but it suffered from many of the same faults as the other Goldcrest pictures.

Again it was a big film, with a budget sufficient for enormous ranks of extras and expensive locations in South America. One day's shooting, for example, involved the burning of a complete village constructed in the Amazon jungle. Another required Spanish foot soldiers armed with crossbows, mail-clad horses ridden by knights in armour, half-naked Indians, crew and mules to be carried 1000 miles from the distant province of Salta by helicopter and small craft to the waterfalls on the Argentine border with Brazil and Paraguay. Perhaps the film need not have cost £17,300,000, but it was always going to be a big undertaking.

The team involved in *The Mission* was of a different order to that on the other two Goldcrest films. Director Roland Joffé and Puttnam had worked together successfully on *The Killing Fields*, their film about the relationship between an American journalist and the associate he leaves behind in Cambodia to endure the Pol Pot régime. Screenwriter Robert Bolt, who had been working on the script on and off for over ten years, had previously written such epics as *Lawrence of Arabia* (1962) and *A Man for All Seasons* (1966). Although Bolt had suffered a stroke, Goldcrest's James Lee had no doubts this time about the script's potential; he confidently declared it the best he had ever read.

Puttnam and Joffé placed a lot of emphasis on bringing together for *The Mission* the same crew as had worked on the previous film. But the assembled filmmakers were so buoyed up by their earlier success that they forgot the pitfalls they had nearly fallen into on the earlier picture and the mistakes they might so easily have made. And, having proven himself with his first film, Joffé was less willing to listen than hitherto. As one of his associates remarked after the event:

> Roland is increasingly surrounded by people who say yes when they mean maybe and maybe when they mean no. They hold him in some kind of awe and think he is a great artist. Increasingly there is the danger of him coming into a situation where no one says 'hang on mate'.

Even on *The Killing Fields*, the film had been started before the script was anywhere near the length of the intended film, with the result that the film had to be edited down from a much longer roughcut, and the concluding passages of the film seem confused as a result. Similar problems recur in *The Mission*, and Bolt doesn't bring to scenes the same degree of emotional energy that Bruce Robinson injected into the earlier script. The film feels like one of those movies carved out of a television mini-series, where every scene makes you aware of the lack of information necessary to empathize with the people on the screen and grasp the significance of their actions. But the main problem derives from Joffé's decision to try and make the audience identify with two characters, a penitent slave trader and a Jesuit priest, as they take their individual routes to confront the armies sent in to break up the Jesuit missions and massacre the converted Indians. As a result, we identify with neither, and a film that ought to be passionate, stirring and moving ends up looking like an expensive history lesson.

The excess of cash that seemed to be available for the makers of the three big Goldcrest films fed lazy creativity. The large budgets were taken as a licence to experiment, but not only did the experiment take place in areas where any screenwriter of the old school could have told the filmmakers they should only venture with extreme sophistication, but in every case an attempt was made to resolve the resulting problems during shooting and editing rather than at script stage. Seemingly the directors imagined that their skills with cameras, actors and lights would cover up the mess. They ended up making films that seem to have no idea what they are trying to say. *Dance with a Stranger* may not be a masterpiece of British cinema, but it is at least a film that knows where it's going.

Conclusion

To the question why British filmmakers have only for brief periods been able to create a steady output of interesting, challenging and commercially successful films, one will usually hear the answer that they rarely had enough money. It's not a silly response. Directors and writers can't be expected to develop strong ideas if they're not reasonably confident that the money will be there to finance them, and certainly the sudden decline of British films at the end of the 1940s could be attributed to a cut-off in the financial flow. But it could also be ascribed to a shift in the national mood, and the failure of the production machine to push directors towards projects that would tap their potential and excite audiences. Equally, it was not a shortage of money that caused the crises of the late 1930s, 1960s and 1980s (even though the drying up of financial resources was their most obvious manifestation), but the absence of commercially viable ideas and evidence that the funds made available had been mismanaged.

The ability of Michael Balcon in the 1920s, and of David Puttnam in the 1970s, to raise money for their projects, at times when that seemed the most difficult thing in the world for other producers to achieve, suggests it is generally possible for producers with energy, imagination, a sound business sense and a clear vision of what they are doing, to find the cash for British movies. Neither producer necessarily looked back on the works made at this time as the best they could achieve, but in each case they laid down in dog-days the basis for more exciting production programmes. Similarly the ability of London Films in the 1930s, Rank in the 1940s and Goldcrest in the 1980s to build up substantial capital resources shows that the natural reluctance of local sources of finance to fund British film companies can be overcome if a strong case is presented, and initial projects are successful.

What so often prevents other producers from setting up their projects is the lack of any very clear vision of what they want to make. Too often producers become stuck in the middle of British filmmaking's essential dilemma. If they take seriously those critics who define British cinema as the antithesis of Hollywood, they're forced to reject those elements in cinema that make it possible to address audiences worldwide and secure a measure of financial success. And if they follow the argument that they should be 'projecting' Britain or 'expressing Britain' that doesn't necessarily mean they're going to appeal to youngsters in Palm Springs or Perth. Or they can ignore all these arguments and declare themselves committed to all-out 'entertainment', and end up making films that don't relate to anything of importance at all.

The revivals in British film production associated with Korda in the 1930s and Puttnam in the 1980s were based on films, *The Private Life of Henry VIII* and *Chariots of Fire*, with resolutely British storylines. Because these films gave a positive validation to 'Britishness' it became possible for other filmmakers to feel confident about their cinematic identity. Significantly, Korda rapidly revealed himself as a European or international filmmaker, and Puttnam, after backing *Local Hero* as his homage to Mackendrick's Scottish comedies, turned increasingly to international subjects – even while continuing to beat the drum for the British film industry.

In all the talk about the Britishness of British films, the discussion always comes back to the relationship between British films and British life, never their connection to a national filmmaking tradition. Since neither Puttnam nor any other filmmaker of the 1980s saw the past of British films as a cultural treasure-house they could draw on, the discussion of what constitutes a 'British' cinema always remained on an abstract plane. This has perpetuated the British filmmakers' inferiority complex, and prevented the emergence of any sort of filmmaking revival in depth. The effect of this cultural amnesia is particularly evident in a film like *Sammy and Rosie Get Laid* (1987). Scripted by Hanif Kureishi for director Stephen Frears, as a follow-up to their *My Beautiful Laundrette*, the film builds its images of murderous policemen, oppressed social workers and rioting blacks into a totally disillusioned image of England. But instead of directing that sensibility into a well-structured, powerful narrative that would coax the audience towards seeing the world for a while as their filmmakers see it, they splatter their anger onto the screen in muddled montages of dramatized images from the TV news. The film is the final consequence of the sleight-of-hand performed by Lindsay Anderson and his contemporaries in dismissing the popular aspects of Britain's cinematic heritage, and arguing for a British cinema that engages with British politics and life, rather than with audiences.

Cinema developed at the beginning of the century to cater for the needs of societies that increasingly lacked any consensual system of belief, where the old bonds that had united communities were breaking down under the pressure of increased urbanization, travel and new communications media. It provided a new forum in which people could enter experiences other than their own, in order to build their own systems of value and belief. Cinema offered people visions of hope that would lift them up, and visions of horror that, when faced, would enable them to cope better with their fears about the future. Through what they saw on the cinema screen, audiences could come to a better understanding of themselves – their fears and inhibitions, their longings and the things they dreaded – and hope to find some meaning in their lives.

CONCLUSION

Television has usurped some of cinema's functions, particularly as a provider of information. But it has also freed cinema to realize more fully its potential. By pushing out the notion of cinema as 'family entertainment', it has enabled filmmakers to explore more deeply into areas of the unconscious that society's moral guardians previously ruled out of bounds. By emphasizing cinema's scale and image quality, it has focused filmmakers' attentions on the medium's ability to touch the deepest emotional layers, the areas of the unconscious where hopes and fears reside. If it had not been for the lack of courage and imagination on the part of the country's cinema owners in the late 1950s, perhaps the British would not have learned to try and live without cinema.

But, as British filmmakers forgot what separated cinema from television, they also lost contact with their national cinematic tradition. They learned to think of British films as either soft and soppy, or sordid and nasty, somehow a schizophrenic cinema. But a definition of cinema as a medium for enabling society to deal with both its hopes *and* its fears can bring together these poles, the cinema of dreams and the cinema of nightmares. In this perspective, British cinema becomes not a sick cinema split irrevocably between the positive and the negative, Ealing and Hammer, Gainsborough and wartime realism, but a healthy cinema where each is the distaff side of the other, and their coexistence is an indicator of a film culture's vitality.

Understanding that cinema is not a medium for conveying messages, but a vehicle for exploring emotions, is the precondition for a vital popular cinema. Not every commercially successful film is a 'good' film, but filmmakers have to respond to what the successful films tell them about the audience's psyche. It's not good enough complaining that the audience doesn't understand or that it's not interested in ideas; films which don't reach out to their public have failed in their mission. British filmmakers who think that putting British life on the screen is enough, even if the result comprises only fictionalized versions of last year's news linked to speeches about the state of the nation, will never be worth anything. Only if filmmakers can listen to the hopes and fears of the people among whom they live will they touch chords that resonate with audiences around the world.

Whether the films are comedies or fantasies, melodrama or horror, the challenge is to create films that deal not only with the bland surface of life, but with its seething unconscious. And once filmmakers have learnt to touch deeper resonances, to be less concerned with the everyday, then they'll feel happier about their position vis-à-vis Europe or America. Instead of feeling insecure or unconfident when dealing with other film cultures, they'll be happy to exchange ideas, share resources, recognize links and collaborate.

British filmmakers often talk about the need to make films that touch universal themes, but too rarely has there been an environment that would stimulate filmmaking on that sort of level. One looks around in vain at the film industry of the early 1990s to find the glimmer of an understanding about how to establish a process that would take every promising story and realize its inner potential, a process that would draw the key participants on a film into a hunt for the kernel of a film at the heart of an interesting idea.

Independent producers apply most of their energy nowadays to stitching together deals; writers are more frightened of what the development process will do to their idea than how it can be improved by the attentions of others, and directors feel they must prove themselves not by realizing the potential of a script but by subverting it in favour of their 'vision'. Nowhere is there any hope of seeing realized the vision with which Jake Eberts once inspired John Boorman of 'a friendly base, a place of sanity where we can work, knowing that our projects will not be snatched away at any moment, knowing that one can work steadily among sympathetic people.'

Most of the energy that writers expend on their projects is simply wasted. There is no focus to what they do, no mechanism to ensure that new ideas grow in the waste of half-good concepts, or that promising ideas become excellent scripts. The problem is partly that the process of getting films made is so slow. It may take ten years or more from the conception of a project to the cash being made available. And in all that time the producer will be rejecting other ideas, turning away writers with other, sometimes better, projects, holding on so that the script upon which he or she has invested so much time and money can finally be bulldozed into production. And the more money they've invested – in repeat option payments to hold on to the rights to a book, or securing rewrites from the novelist whose name may help on the script cover, but who doesn't give a toss about screenwriting – the less easy it is for producers to simply let go, even if they know, in moments of insight, the project just isn't going to work.

And when the cash finally becomes available, that producer doesn't have the energy to adapt the dog-eared screenplay and make sure it really does work, bashing together the heads of writer and director so that, in a final moment of intense effort, they can bring the script to completion. The director will undertake to sort out the problems on the floor, while the writer is probably not much interested since he or she cashed the cheques a long time ago. And the producer must get on with the next project if he or she is to stand any chance of paying off the overdraft before the end of the millenium.

That's not to say there's any lack of interest in training: refining film school courses so that students develop a fine understanding of the nitty-gritty of filmmaking and arranging attachments to film productions so that they learn to do things just as badly as they've been done before. There's even money sometimes made available to give young directors a chance to show what they can do. But one chance only. And that's a shame because filmmaking isn't a matter of the single individual with talent, but a lot of talented individuals having their potential released by a process that's directed towards the making of good films.

But what sort of system would generate interesting and relevant ideas, then transform them into great scripts for great films? Not a system that turns ideas into cold plot summaries which are then hustled around production companies like so many pieces of real estate, but one which treats them as sources of cinematic potential, to be knocked around, even used to spawn larger, braver ideas. Too many contemporary films are premature births, incubated in hype but unable to grow into healthy films that will mean something to an audience.

'The evidence shows,' remarked Michael Balcon in 1977, 'that Britain has been effective only when its filmmakers have operated from a studio or house base. It would be wise, when considering any future model for the industry, to build on this tradition.' It's no surprise that this suggestion didn't attract much notice when the AIP was putting together proposals for reviving the British film industry. It was hard enough then to conceive of getting together the budget for a single film, let alone gathering the cash necessary to lease property, construct buildings and support a weekly payroll of film technicians, plasterers, gardeners, cooks and sundry others.

Studios are irrelevant to contemporary audiovisual production. Where taste and the market for films are always changing, an institution committed to producing a regular output of six, ten or more, films a year is a definite non-starter. But that doesn't mean there aren't aspects of the studio system that couldn't be usefully imitated. What was it, after all, that distinguished the good studios from the bad studios? The difference between, say, Gaumont-British during the 1930s or Gainsborough during the 1940s and Jupp's London Films or Maxwell's BIP, was that the former created environments in which writers were encouraged to work at new ideas and think up interesting stories, try anything because one could see from the script whether or not it had the chance of working or not.

Screenwriting is cheap compared to the process of film production, and writers can be productive even when there isn't the money immediately available to make films. Also, the more opportunity writers have to develop their craft within a stimulating and challenging environment, the better their work is likely to be. And if the scripts are good, so that the director and everybody else feels they've got something substantial to work from, then the greater the chance they'll work to enhance what has been written, rather than tearing it apart.

It's possible to imagine a group of enlightened production companies combining their resources to form script factories that would emulate the working conditions of a studio's script department. They would employ screenwriters willing to work consistently in a stimulating creative environment;

on a salary and likely to miss out on the occasional big deal, but always working at developing first-class scripts. They'd work to producers who weren't just there to say yea or nay to a project but played an active part with everybody else on the team in generating and nurturing ideas. Finished scripts could be auctioned off to one of the associate producers, or even to outsiders, and the next development stage involving director and producer could take place either within the script factory, or outside.

Such script factories would not need to be enclosed enclaves within the filmmaking culture. They could provide a reading and consultancy service for young writers with projects of their own, helping them to develop on to the stage where they might join the factory themselves. They could take on projects submitted from outside for doctoring and further development. The factories would be achieving their aim if they set standards in the craft of screenwriting, so that scripts might again be produced with the complex internal resonances of Graham Greene's *The Third Man* or Noël Coward's *Brief Encounter*. Also, as pockets of energy and enthusiasm within the film industry, they could generate ideas about cinema that would percolate out through the rest of the culture.

The obstacle to the creation of script factories on the model outlined above lies in a system that prefers to pay a few people substantial sums of money to write scripts that aren't very good, but at least carry a name on the cover that might possibly ring a bell with a source of finance. Their interests are not likely to be served by a system that acknowledges no one ever wrote a great script on their own, and that it doesn't matter where the ideas come from as long as the script becomes a film that rings bells with an audience. So many films are bad for all the wrong reasons, because of the writer's vanity, the director's pride or the producer's bad temper and, as long as that's the reality of British filmmaking, there's no hope of building on the brief moments of achievement in the national cinema, or creating a cinema that really speaks to people. And a cinema that doesn't do that isn't worth anything at all.

Appendix:
Dance with a Stranger

In 1955, former nightclub hostess Ruth Ellis went to the gallows for killing David Blakely, a man whose wealthy origins and good looks had seemed to promise her a rise up the social scale. Some 15 months into the relationship, she had lost her job, her peace of mind, her health and hope for the future. All she had left, apart from a son, was the man who had engineered her downfall. When he repudiated her, she killed him. In the eyes of the law that executed her she was wholly guilty, but public opinion suspected that the responsibility lay elsewhere.

In developing *Dance with a Stranger*, producer Roger Randall-Cutler was aware of the way in which class attitudes had prevented the development of an easy relationship between Blakely and Ellis. He was not, however, primarily interested in articulating class questions directly through, for example, a courtroom drama structure. If the story was told convincingly from the inside, he felt the issues would emerge naturally. The question for the filmmakers to explore was the attraction that pulled those people together and why they made such a mess of their lives. From that basic information, audiences could build their own arguments.

The first script that screenwriter Delaney delivered was structured differently from the eventual film but it contained nearly all the building blocks. It was, as Randall-Cutler had hoped, a story about tragic love, where those involved were locked in a chamber of horrors comprising equal portions of jealousy, obsession, hatred, despair, self-pity, self-justification, masochism, sadism and lust for revenge. The dialogue was also sharpened with a maudlin wit that alleviated the generally bleak tone of the tale. When, for example, Blakely asks Ellis to marry him, she comes back at him: 'Why? Are you pregnant?' The screenplay's emotional perception and the conviction in its portrait of the central character grabbed attention.

The first script had demonstrated that there was a film to be made about the Ruth Ellis story, but Randall-Cutler wanted to go to a second draft before finding the money or appointing a director. Michael Radford and Delaney worked together on the second draft, but Radford's desire to include the trial in the script met with fierce opposition from Randall-Cutler. 'The second draft,' he remembered, 'was a backward step. He wanted to make a different film and to write the script himself.' Radford left the project. After equally abortive discussions with Alan Clarke, Randall-Cutler approached Mike Newell on the basis of his film *Bad Blood*. Its account of a paranoiac man who goes on the run with a shotgun in the wilderness of New Zealand had some parallels to *Dance with a Stranger* in its depiction of people without the intellectual or imaginative resources to cope with life's pressures. Newell's grasp of the Ellis–Blakely story as a tale of people caught in a dead end of extreme emotions with which they are unable to cope was in harmony with Randall-Cutler's area of interest.

There were to be two more drafts of the script before the cameras finally rolled on *Dance with a Stranger*. Newell was fascinated by the scale of the story and its mythic references but felt that Delaney's script was too literary. 'There was a subject buried in there with a quality of universality, but what I was reading on the page did not have that dimension to it.' Writer and director worked together, feeling their way towards a structure which would give the story a sense of tragic inevitability.

Newell retraced Randall-Cutler's steps in exploring the story's hold on public consciousness. The speed with which Ellis had passed through the judicial system suggested that society had been taking its revenge on her for living a fast life style, but the response to her execution indicated that the law was out of touch with the public mood, attempting to dam up transformations in social mores that could no longer be held back. A signalman based near Holloway prison had said that the birds stopped singing when she died. Newell remarked:

> Somehow, Ruth Ellis seemed to get right to the back of the national cortex. There was obviously a kind of unspoken national conspiracy to hang this woman. The law was not framed in such a way that she could be acquitted, but then juries were very loth to hang people and would find the most extraordinary non-legal excuses to let them off. In this case, they didn't.

The press write-ups from the period revealed that the Ruth Ellis saga had opened a window into British society that many wanted to keep shut. The sordid violence at its heart ran counter to the British character depicted in films of the 1950s like *Genevieve*. As Newell remarked:

> What I remember is that they were all so charming. The one thing that you could rely on from a Brit was that he had the right accent, you knew exactly where he stood, and he was charming. Even then one was smelling a rat. You knew that we had, perhaps, a greater talent for hypocrisy than any other nation.

Together and separately, Newell and Delaney hunted out titbits of information about London and its people in the mid-1950s. Each new piece of evidence was shared as a possible influence on the structure of the script and the film's visual style. Newell recalled a morning when Delaney arrived with a list of what a nice young woman of 1955 would have in her wardrobe: a tweed suit for travelling, a morning frock, three evening dresses and so on. The result of these researches is evident in the film's use of clothes and make-up to suggest that women were the playthings of men. Their tulle dresses, which rustle and creak, told an inner truth of women as weak creatures who would just flop on the floor unless they were belted and padded up. Ruth is defined by her physical appearance: the Chanel suit on the racetrack, the heavy make-up, the peroxide hair all speak of a woman striving to win her way into the world of a man to whose expectations she panders. Likewise, the manicured nails that rap on the taxi window as she journeys to commit murder tell of her grating frustration.

The history of the relationship between Ruth Ellis and David Blakely always suggested a four-part structure. In the first section, the ground rules for the liaison are established around Ellis's job in the Little Club. In front of the club bar, Ellis is available to Blakely and, despite her attempts at repudiation, he always ends up in her bedroom. When she loses her job because of Blakely's unruly behaviour, Ellis moves in with her alternative boyfriend, Desmond Cussen. Not only does this shift the focus of the film to another, quieter, relationship, but it transforms Blakely into a background presence as he struggles to re-establish control of the woman he lusts after.

The next transition, effected after Cussen sees Blakely and Ellis entering the Hyde Park Hotel, results from the subsequent break-up of the Cussen–Ellis household. Living in digs, Ellis is free to re-establish her liaison with Blakely but she is also pregnant and, therefore, undesirable to her free-floater lover. He, in turn, is under pressure from his friends, the Findlaters, to break this liaison with a common, hysterical woman. Whereas previously it was Blakely who consistently sought out a reluctant Ellis, the hunter has now become the hunted. Ellis and Blakely no longer occupy the same claustrophobic space, in which Blakely can continually impose himself upon her life. As she slides down into despair, she needs him more but finds him less. Finally, following her miscarriage, Blakely cuts himself off totally from his former lover. Increasingly hysterical and distraught, she puts an end to the cause of her agony by shooting him.

The initial rewrites pointed up this structure. In the final version, each scene of the first section shows the relationship following a fixed pattern of separation leading to attempted rejection, tension and the articulation of desire. Blakely's frequent infidelities, which are irrelevant to that pattern, are no longer highlighted as in the third draft script. Also, whereas in the early drafts of the third section, Blakely sometimes stays to sleep with Ellis, for the final version he never seems to remain long enough to satisfy her desire.

There were changes to the order of scenes to emphasize that the evolution of the Ellis–Blakely relationship took place according to the inexorable logic of their respective characters and social positions. For example, a scene where Ellis picnics with Blakely's friends beside the track where he is racing was moved from the middle to the beginning of the narrative. It was also rewritten to contain all the polarities of the film in a quasi-synopsis of the picture's themes. Ellis's excited screeching at the race attracts the sneering scorn of Carole Findlater. Ellis responds to an attempted seduction by Blakely's friend Cliff with an allusion to her lover's potential for violence. The Chanel suit worn by Ellis marks her out as distinctly as her behaviour from Blakely's more socially elevated associates, particularly his potential fiancée, 'a nice-looking, well-brought-up, well-groomed young woman, discreetly pretty, and dressed out of Burberry's and Jaeger with a bit of Hermes thrown in.' Also, the beginning and end of the Ellis–Blakely relationship are marked by the only two scenes of explicit love-making in the film. In Ruth Ellis's brightly lit, pink-adorned bedroom above the Little Club, the couple enjoy cynical sex while getting to know each other. For their final scene together, Blakely comes across the bruised and battered Ellis on the smog-laden streets of the city. He takes his pleasure of her against the dustbins in a side alley.

In early drafts, many scenes illustrated the sexual basis for the Ellis–Blakely relationship. Blakely's taking a bath originally introduces a scene of simple sex. 'They begin to make love. Not heavy frantic humourless passion, but playful, affectionate, pleasurable, rather calm enjoyment in each other's limbs, eyes, mouths, which eventually develops into a complete union of their bodies.' In the film, this scene is a moment of aggression and heightened tension as both lovers reproach each other for their irresponsible attitude to life. Similarly the drive into the country, taken by the two lovers to visit Blakely's family home, becomes a way of pointing up the class difference that dooms the affair of the two lovers, whereas in the third draft, by contrast, it focused mainly on love-making.

This excision of sex had even more effect on the film's portrayal of Ellis's liaison with Cussen, the fastidious and timid older man who is always giving to Ellis, but never asks for anything in return. The development process heightened the contrast between Blakely's brutish treatment of Ellis and Cussen's frustrated longing. In early drafts, Cussen and Ellis go to bed after the Racing Car Drivers' ball. In the film, a forlorn Cussen is left at the front door and his inability to consummate his love is a joke between the doomed lovers at their first bedding. 'Has Desmond slept in this bed?' asks Blakely. 'Come to think of it, he must be the only man in London who hasn't,' is her acrid reply. There is another forlorn scene, in which Ellis and Cussen lie in bed and she sings 'I still believe', the number she associates with Blakely. 'Couldn't you at least forget Blakely when you are in bed with me,' asks the quietly jealous 'other' lover.

It was to be a common criticism of *Dance with a Stranger* that the film failed to show what drew Blakely and Ellis into bed together, what it was they say in each other's eyes. Randall-Cutler says that the sex scenes in the early drafts were only there to attract the attention of the financiers. 'We never,' he said, 'felt the need to see them in bed, romantically entwined.' Newell and Delaney extended that logic into the script. The copulations could be assumed – they were not what was interesting about the relationship. By ending the scenes of nocturnal friction between the lovers at the point before they declare an armistice on the couch, they focused attention back on to the sources of friction and conflict. After Ellis discovers that Blakely has become engaged and rejects him, his arrival culminates not in bedding, but with an expressionist shot of his face reflected in a mirror, with his shadow stretched out on the wall. Another scene in the bedroom ends with Ellis desperately hitting out at this man who is making her life such misery, with the mournful sound of a saxophone wailing in the background.

From the time when she first meets Blakely, Ellis is on an emotional rollercoaster to disaster. The simple coupling at the beginning of the film turns very quickly into pain, anger and neurotic jealousy. Every move in the game turns the ambitious and attractive girl, with a certain entrepreneurial instinct, into a doomed character, rapidly losing her physical allure and her ability to control her destiny. Ellis moves from a position where she is moving up the social ladder to utter degradation, symbolized in the sordid scene of her final copulation with Blakely. Finally, in the scene immediately before the film's climax, she loses even the respect of Desmond Cussen, the man who has only her best interests at heart. Taking advantage of Ellis's drunken and distraught state, Cussen fumbles with her skirt in a moment of uncharacteristic aggression. Finally, Ellis's self-respect has gone.

The same drive to concentrate the film's narrative on what was happening between the three protagonists led, from first draft to final cut of the film, to the excision or reduction of various characters and scenes. It took some time to discover which of Delaney's creations did not add significant extra information about the film's central issue, but the film was gradually pruned back to a core. 'We were relentless,' remarked Randall-Cutler. 'The film wasn't going to let the audience off the hook at any point.'

One woman whose role in the film was drastically reduced over successive drafts was the barmaid, whose cynicism about the Little Club's clients is in stark opposition to Ellis's desperate striving to be loved by all the men around her. In early scripts, she also offered Ellis an alternative social life away from both Blakely and Cussen, as well as providing comfort after an abortion. The script process took out any women who, by presenting an alternative concept of 1950s femininity, would distract attention from Ellis's situation. There were many who lived the fast life like Ellis and didn't suffer her fate, but the question of what distinguished Ruth Ellis from others in her circle did not interest Newell or Delaney. The only scene in the film that focuses on the attitude of other women to Ruth's desperate liaison involves two hostesses chattering in the ladies' lavatory about their current conquests and Ellis's unseemly behaviour. The scene was created to provide a moment of light relief just before the violent scene in the club that leads to the firing of Ellis from her job and puts her life on a downward course. Its presence is, in some ways, inconsistent with the rest of the film's aesthetic, but the scene nevertheless retains its sharp focus simply because of the force of the subsequent moments. 'It is,' concedes Newell, 'absolutely necessary dramatically, but it's a clumsy way of doing it.'

Two major sequences were cut from the film during editing. In all the scripts, following her expulsion from the Little Club, Ellis joins a fashion school. The comic and sometimes pitiable scene of young novices going through their paces was designed to be charming but, when viewed by producer and director, it just seemed to stop the flow of the story. It didn't contribute anything much about Ellis's character and it diminished the significance of what Blakely had done in causing her expulsion from the Little Club, suggesting, for a passing moment, that there might still be a future for her that did not depend on finding a man or, in the context of the film, resolving her relationship with Blakely.

The other scene cut in the final stages was a fight between Blakely and Ellis after his prize Emperor car has exploded at Oulton Park. This was the only scene written solo by Newell. Randall-Cutler says the decision to cut this confrontation was based upon the poor quality of the performances that day, but there may have been reasons why the actors were not able to give of their best. This confrontation had been written by Newell as an opportunity for Blakely to fight back and explain his case. 'Are you satisfied now?' he says. 'If you'd allowed me to concentrate instead of hounding me while I was working on her, this wouldn't have happened. You're a jinx. Well, that's the end of it now. I'll have to sell her.' However, the film had already established Blakely's tendency to blame Ellis for his own failings and become violent when things were not going well. Furthermore, the scene was vestigial, seeming to restart a torrid relationship that had already ended by the dustbins.

The Oulton Park row was scripted to immediately precede Ruth's miscarriage. 'We saw some merit,' said Randall-Cutler, 'in both of them losing their babies.' It was a rather too clever connection for a film which not only has more of an emotional than an intellectual thrust, but is never otherwise even-handed in its treatment of Blakely and Ellis. By cutting the Oulton Park race to four shots of the Emperor's demise, the film establishes a direct connection between that scene and the one in the country pub. Ellis, frantic at not being able to find Blakely to discuss her pregnancy, hunts him down to the pub where he sits with friends and relations, 'toffee-nosed twats who think the sun shines out of your porthole.' Blakely hits her there and, in the following scene, brutally makes love to her in an alley. The Oulton Park race follows. When Ellis miscarries, the viewer still carries the image of Blakely's blows and the

179

sordid love in the smog. Her bleeding is implicitly connected to Blakely's violence against her.

Having clarified the structure of *Dance with a Stranger* and trimmed some of the peripheral characters, Newell and Delaney also began to look at individual scenes to find ways of increasing both their emotional significance and their visual power. By going through each section of the script and asking themselves what every moment would signify to the audience, they ensured that there would be no point in the film which was simply time-filling light relief. It was a matter of juggling the elements that Delaney had created, considering them in relation to the pattern of events that they had already formulated, and reshaping the scenes for maximum impact.

Delaney had, for example, always intended to refer to Blakely's engagement. The fiancée stood as a symbol for all the other women in Blakely's life, as well as indicating the impossibility of Ellis's hopes of marriage. It was only after discussion with Newell, however, that she incorporated her fully into the narrative. In the first draft, there is simply a reference at the racetrack to a 'typical example of the kind of girl my mother wants me to marry'. In the third draft, Ellis alludes jokingly to Blakely's engagement: 'I stopped taking you seriously the day I opened *The Times* and saw the announcement of your engagement in the Forthcoming Marriages column.' In the film, a long-shot from Ellis's point of view of the embrace between Blakely and Burberry prepares us for the engagement; the fiancée's presence creates the first look of tension in Ellis's face. Immediately after the racetrack scene, Ellis goes into a florist's to despatch some roses to the affianced man, with a request for the return of her door key. There is then a sharp cut to the arrival of the same flowers on Ellis's bed as the lusting lover returns to her. The sequence is tight, powerful and to the point.

Newell's impact on the script can be specifically located in some of the visual set pieces, which made active what had only been latent in previous texts. A key example is the scene in the smog, where Blakely and Ellis make love for the last time. In previous scripts, one of their meetings did take place in such grime. The weather was used to mark the passage of time, like other references to Easter and Christmas. It also provided an atmospheric indication that the relationship took place in a world where there was little joy or hope. In the film, however, the scene acquires additional resonances, suggesting it is only in this bleak environment that the lovers can still meet. It is linked to the battering Ellis receives from Blakely at the pub and hints that she has taken up as a prostitute to make money. 'She looks at him – unkempt, unshaven, desperate. A fallen angel, he starts gently to pull the scarf from her face and, with the other hand, pushes the hood of the coat she is wearing off her head. He sees that she is wearing a small silver crucifix around her neck.' The talk is of vampires and the mood is one of horror and despair.

A solemn moment for Miranda Richardson and Rupert Everett in
Dance with a Stranger **(1985)**

A similar shift from the explanatory to the visually suggestive takes place in the first scene between Ellis and Blakely after the former's expulsion from the Little Club. The mood is prepared by their meeting in a desolate urban landscape, a dingy and bleak corner of London where Blakely lurks, waiting for Ellis. They return to Cussen's flat for a scene of furtive love-making, which reveals Ellis's callous attitude to her new lover and her inability to control her longing for Blakely. It also allows Blakely to feel his inferiority in relation to Cussen, a sense that all his problems come from not having an apartment to offer the woman he sometimes loves and always lusts after. In previous scripts these were rationalized in uneconomical dialogue. 'How can you live here like this?' he says. 'You're supposed to love me! And you're sleeping with him. How can you? Because he's got his own flat and pays Andy's school fees? Is that the reason, because if it is it makes you nothing more than a tart.' In the film, the jealous lover simply wanders through Desmond's flat. 'David abruptly turns and leaves the room. He openes the door of the hallway. It is Desmond's study. He slams the door. He opens another door. It is Desmond's bedroom.' The 'message' is conveyed in emotionally-stirring images, rather than descriptive words.

This restructuring of scenes to secure visual impact further fictionalized a narrative based upon documented events. A similar sleight of hand allowed Newell and Delaney to transform an abortion into a miscarriage. 'She had everything,' said Randall-Cutler, 'miscarriages, abortions, ectopic pregnancies. We were aware that this was part of her state of mind shortly before the murder, but we had to decide what it was saying to us and try to weave it into the script.' The abortion scene in previous drafts did not, however, make the implicit connection between Ellis's loss of her baby and her decision to kill Blakely. It was a semi-comic moment in which she and a friend flag down a luxurious limousine for a lift to a backstreet abortionist. The suggestion is that abortions are just part of Ellis's regular routine, rather than moments of emotional loss and dismay. As filmed, however, the miscarriage scene is quietly devastating. Following the departure of Cussen and Ellis's expressive remarks about her 'brain jumping out of her head', the camera holds on her moment of pain as she pulls back the sheets and reveals her bloodied state. When she falls below the screen, her son Andy wakes and goes off to get help.

Newly invented in the final script was the metaphorical opening scene. Whereas previous versions had simply conveyed basic information about Ellis's life, the image of cars racing out of control through the streets of Knightsbridge conveys a heightened mood and a craziness that seems likely to end in destruction. Cussen, solidly gripping the wheel of his Ford Zephyr is a man who – as in his dealings with Ellis – plays safe. The others are going all-out for what they can get. The metaphor is suggested by Blakely's faltering ambitions as a racing car driver and the scene links up neatly to another, more expository, scene by the racetrack where Ellis and Blakely are brought together publicly for the first time.

This analysis of the ways in which Newell and Delaney worked together to make the script of *Dance with a Stranger* more cinematic and powerful is not meant to suggest that Delaney's original invention was deficient. The majority of Newell's interventions were, as director on the set, to realize the force of Delaney's images. Neither Newell nor Delaney, for example, made any changes, at the scripting stage, to the Racing Car Drivers ball where, after a period of separation, Ellis and Blakely are brought back together. But it is Newell's direction that points up the personal agonies of the two characters. Their reunion is comic, as Blakely leads Ellis in a leaden-foot attempt at dancing. She returns to Cussen, her escort for the evening, but the camera shows that she has moved back into the Blakely orbit. As the lights move across the room, we hold on a close-up of her pensive face, with 'Forget Who's To Blame' from the theme tune playing over the soundtrack. As Ellis and Cussen leave, the camera cranes down to Blakely dancing. Now the light is on his face, and he looks away from the girl in his arms towards the recently-departed couple. The gaze suggests that his next destination will be Ellis's flat.

The relationship between Newell and Delaney worked because both had the same goal: to uncover the realities of Ruth Ellis's life and thus to explain her final act of murder. Their analysis, however, was not schematic. 'We never set out,' said Randall-Cutler, 'to explain why she did it. We simply presented the circumstances that precipitated the action, putting in sufficient evidence to substantiate an understanding of those events.' The film's fascination lies in its mysteries, which leave the questions open for the audience. Blakely's attraction to Ellis clearly did not lie in the fact that he was a charming guy who gave her a good time. It is unlikely to have been simply a matter of his performance in bed – she had plenty of other men to satisfy her physical needs. What kept drawing them together? Since Ellis's miscarriage could be traced, however indirectly, to the mental and physical violence unleashed by Blakely, did she blame him for the loss of her child? Since he was clearly lost to her, why didn't she just pick herself up and put the pieces of her life back together? Viewers of the film are offered a way into these dilemmas which, for the characters, were inextricable. The audience is only as wise as what happens on the screen. There is no rhetorical address to the camera in which they expound upon a problem that they see and understand. 'In the movies I like,' Newell remarked, 'the characters are not even aware of the problem, let alone able to address it. The film shows people in the grip of things that they are unable to deal with, but have to suffer anyway.'

In this subjective approach to its material, *Dance with a Stranger* broke away from the social and documentary concerns of much British film and television drama. Unsurprisingly, many film industry executives were unable to grasp the way in which the film worked and unwilling to make the emotional journey that the film offered. One producer objected that it was 'just a story about lovers,' which failed to explain why the trial and execution had such a grip upon the national consciousness. Another producer remarked confidently that the film was 'commercial death,' because of its relentless solemnity. This argument was repudiated by another who pointed out with some disdain that 'the subject matter sets it into an area where you know that even if you get it half right you will get some audience, even if it is a rather mordant titillating thing.'

The multiple levels of reference and allusion that infused the film's account of England in the mid-1950s also seemed to escape many newspaper critics. The film was seen to be dodging the crucial issues by failing to plead the abolitionist cause or follow the Ruth Ellis story into the courtroom. 'Not even Ellis's presumed death-wish at her trial is confronted,' said one, 'nor are the mores of the period where the "hooray" set were happy to copulate with the barmaid-likes of the forlorn Ellis, but never to conjugate. The social division is hinted at but never fully developed.' But every aspect of the relationship between Blakely and Ellis can be interpreted in the light of the one's desire to marry a fallen aristrocrat who might take her up the social scale and the other's inability to find a place within that world from which to pull his mistress into marriage. The alternatives would have been a crude speech explicitly and uncinematically laying out the socio-political issues involved, or epic scenes of class conflict which would have been a digression from the film's internal story.

Some British critics seem to have been over-influenced by their own memories of the Ruth Ellis case, but their analyses were not enough to prevent audiences from discovering the film for themselves. Around the time of the film's opening, a barrage of journalese laid out the facts about capital punishment, class, fashion, music, cars and other interesting areas touched on in the film. The negative critical reaction, unlike that in France and the US where critics were either enthusiastic or adulatory, indicated the gap between Britain's literary-oriented film scribes, and the perception of audiences. The scorn poured on the film by the industry's executives is more significant. Many in positions to influence which films get made had still not made the leap from their understanding of television drama, where they acquired their reputations for spotting projects, to cinema.

Notes

Preface

1 Sue Summers, 'Putting the Budget before the Box Office', *Listener*, 21 August 1986, p. 13
2 Interview with the author, December, 1985

Introduction

1 Michael Powell, *A Life in Movies*, London, 1986, p. 262

1 Beginning Behind

1 Cecil Hepworth, *Came the Dawn*, London, 1951, p. 55
2 ibid., pp. 107–8
3 *Bioscope*, 10 October 1914, p. 241
4 Rachael Low, *The History of British Film (1906–1914)*, p. 209
5 ibid., p. 95
6 Hepworth, op. cit., p. 143
7 ibid., p. 119
8 Low, op. cit. (1906–1914), p. 134
9 *Bioscope*, 26 August 1915, p. 875, quoted Low, op. cit. (1914–1918), p. 122
10 *Kinematograph Weekly*, 24 May, 1917, p. 73, quoted Low, op. cit. (1914–1918), p. 66

2 Transition

1 Hepworth, op. cit., p. 168
2 ibid., p. 168
3 *Bioscope*, 31 October 1928, p. 32, quoted Low, op. cit. (1918–1929), p. 143
4 Brunel, *Nice Work*, London, 1949, p. 106
5 Hepworth, op. cit., p. 141
6 George Pearson, *Flashback*, p. 125
7 Pearson, op. cit., p. 141
8 Publicity material for *Little People*, quoted Low, op. cit. (1918–1929), p. 162
9 Pearson, op. cit., p. 125
10 Paul Rotha, *The Film Till Now*, London, 1950, pp. 81–2
11 *Bioscope*, 24 June 1926, p. 23, quoted Low, op. cit. (1918–1929), p. 298
12 *Kine Weekly*, 14 April 1927, quoted Ryall, *Hitchcock and British Cinema*, London, 1986, p. 24
13 C. M. Brunel, op. cit. p. 102
14 The Film Society's preliminary manifesto quoted Brunel, op. cit., p. 113
15 Michael Balcon, *Michael Balcon Presents...A Lifetime of Films*, p. 27
16 Hugh Castle, *Close Up*, vol. iv, no. 4, April 1929
17 Kenneth Macpherson, *Close Up*, vol. 1, no. 1, July 1927
18 *London Evening News*, 16 November, 1927, quoted Spoto, *The Life of Alfred Hitchcock*, London, 1983, pp. 102–3
19 Will Hays, quoted Margaret Dickinson and Sarah Steet, *Cinema and State*, p. 12
20 Parliamentary Debates (Commons), 29 June 1925, vol. 185, col. 2084, quoted in Dickinson and Street, op. cit., p. 19
21 *Film Renter and Moving Picture News*, 1 January 1927

3 Reaching England

1 *Kinematograph Weekly*, 5 January 1928, p. 38 (quoted in Dickinson and Street, op. cit., p. 35)
2 Brunel, op. cit., pp. 167–168
3 Pearson, op. cit., p. 193
4 Brunel, op. cit., p. 166
5 Rotha, op. cit., p. 110
6 *Bioscope*, 1 January 1930, p. 73
7 John Grierson, *Grierson on the Movies* (ed. Forsyth Hardy), London, 1981, p. 111
8 *The Era*, 11 November 1931, p. 10, quoted *Michael Balcon: The Pursuit of British Cinema*, p. 19
9 Powell, op. cit., p. 236
10 Basil Dean, *Mind's Eye*, London, 1973, p. 193
11 *Film Dope*, no. 11, January 1977, p. 5
12 Powell, op. cit., p. 184
13 Rodney Ackland, *The Celluloid Mistress*, London, 1954, p. 34
14 *Kine Weekly*, 28 August 1930, p. 25, quoted Robert Murphy, 'A Rival to Hollywood', *Screen*, vol. 24, no. 4–5, p. 97
15 Dean, op. cit., p. 135
16 *Kine Weekly*, 29 March 1928, p. 50, quoted Murphy, *Screen*, vol. 24, no. 4–5, p. 97
17 Graham Greene, *The Pleasure Dome*, London, 1972, p. 203
18 *World Film News*, February, 1937 p. 15, 1930, p. 25, quoted Murphy, *Screen*, vol. 24, no. 4–5, p. 103
19 Greene, op. cit., p. 120
20 Kenneth Barrow, *Mr Chips: The Life of Robert Donat*, London, 1986, p. 101
21 Barrow, op. cit., p. 142
22 Dean, op. cit., p. 256
23 Low, op. cit., (1930s), pp. 51–2
24 Balcon, op. cit., p. 101
25 Balcon, op. cit., p. 79

26 Dilys Powell, *The Golden Screen*, p. 13
27 Dilys Powell, op. cit., p. 15
28 *Kine Weekly*, 27 April 1939
29 Greene, op. cit., p. 228
30 Greene, op. cit., p. 39
31 Grierson, op. cit., p. 114
32 Balcon, op. cit., p. 61
33 Jeffrey Richards, *History Today*, March 1983, p. 17
34 Quoted in N. Pronay and D. Spring, *Propaganda, Politics and Film, 1918–45*, London, 1982, p. 122
35 Balcon, op. cit., pp. 41–2
36 See Graham Greene, 'Subjects and Stories', in Charles Davey, *Footnotes to the Film*, London, 1938, pp. 66–7, Quoted Richards *The Age of the Dream Palace*, p. 89
37 Greene, *The Pleasure Dome*, p. 211

4 Dark Conflicts
1 Michael Redgrave, *In My Mind's Eye*, London, 1983, p. 173
2 *Kinematograph Weekly*, 8 January 1942, p. 87, quoted Murphy, op. cit., p. 34
3 Balcon, op. cit., p. 134
4 Dilys Powell, *Films since 1939*, London, 1947, p. 28
5 *Screen* 13, no. 2, (summer 1972), p. 47
6 Monja Danischewsky, *White Russian Red Face*, London, 1966, p. 134
7 Michael Powell, op. cit., p. 241
8 Michael Powell, op. cit., p. 384
9 *Kinematograph Weekly*, 8 January 1942, p. 87
10 Dilys Powell, *The Golden Screen*, p. 54
11 Eric Ambler, *Here Lies Eric Ambler*, London, 1985, p. 226
12 *Tendencies to Monopoly in the Cinematograph Film Industry*, London, 1944, p. 6
13 Balcon, op. cit., p. 154
14 Balcon, op. cit., p. 48
15 Sue Aspinall and Robert Murphy, *Gainsborough Melodrama*, p. 65
16 ibid, p. 64
17 Powell, op. cit., p. 623
18 Powell, op. cit., p. 603
19 Muriel Box, *Odd Woman Out*, London, 1974, p. 196
20 *News Chronicle*, June 1948
21 *Report of the Working Party on Film Production Costs*, London, 1949, p. 7
22 Alan Wood, *Mr Rank*, London, 1952, p. 226
23 Quoted by Pascal-Philippe Volle, *The Rank Financial Disaster of 1949*, unpublished thesis, LSE, 1987, p. 32
24 *New Statesman and Nation*, 12 November 1949

5 Indian Summer
1 *A Pretty British Affair*, broadcast on BBC2, 17 November, 1981
2 *Kinematograph Weekly*, vol. 335, no. 1969, 11 January 1945, p. 31

3 *Daily Mail*, 14 March 1956, quoted by Geoff Brown and Laurence Kardish, *Michael Balcon: The Pursuit of British Cinema*, New York, 1984, p. 40
4 Powell, op. cit., p.160
5 *The Daily Sketch*, 27 November 1953, quoted by Volle, op. cit., p. 55
6 Quoted by Volle, op. cit., p. 32
7 Durgnat, *A Mirror for England*, London, 1970, p. 123
8 Greene, Introduction to *The Third Man and the Fallen Idol*, London, 1974, p. 3
9 *Screen* 13, no. 2 (summer 1972). p. 55
10 *Ealing Comedies*, broadcast BBC1, 8 September 1970
11 *Film* 15, Jan.–Feb. 1958, quoted by Andy Medhurst, *British Film Culture 1956–1964*, unpublished paper for the 1989 BFI Summer School
12 CEA Annual Report, 1960, p. 9
13 The Rank Organisation, Annual Report 1960, p. 29

6 Dirty Words and Pop
1 Lindsay Anderson, 'Get Out and Push!' in *Declaration*, edited by Tom Maschler, London, 1957, p. 157
2 Alexander Walker, *Hollywood England*, London, 1974, p. 84
3 Quoted by Carl Foreman in 'What Film Shall We Make Next?' *International Film Annual*, edited by William Whitebait, no. 2, London, 1958, p. 120
4 Walker, op. cit., p. 149
5 Walker, op. cit., p. 79
6 *A Report on the Supply of Films for Exhibition in Cinemas* (London, 1966) p. 80
7 Elizabeth Sussex, *Lindsay Anderson*, London, 1969, p. 29
8 Penelope Houston, 'England, their England', *Sight and Sound*, 35, 2, spring 1966, p. 56
9 Quoted Walker, op. cit., p. 410
10 *Elstree – Britain's Hollywood*, broadcast on BBC2, 14 April 1989

7 Descending Spiral
1 Walker, *National Heroes*, London 1985, p. 134
2 'New Deal: An Interview with Richard Craven and Simon Perry', *Sight and Sound* 47, no. 3, (autumn 1978), p. 142
3 *Screen International*, 3–10 November, 1984
4 Interview with author, December 1983
5 John Russell Taylor, 'Tomorrow, the World: Some Reflections on the Un-englishness of English Films', *Sight and Sound*, 43, no. 2 (spring 1974), pp. 80–83
6 *Screen International*, 14–21 June 1980, p. 1

8 The Light Brigade
1 Press Release, Tuesday, 26 April 1977

Bibliography

General

ARMES, ROY, *A Critical History of British Cinema*, Secker and Warburg, London, 1978

BARR, CHARLES, (ed.), *All Our Yesterdays*, BFI, London, 1986

CURRAN, JAMES and PORTER, VINCENT, (eds), *British Cinema History*, Weidenfeld and Nicolson, 1983

DICKINSON, MARGARET and STREET, SARAH, *Cinema and State: The Film Industry and the British Government, 1927–84*, BFI, London, 1985

ROBERTSON, JAMES C., *The Hidden Cinema: British Film Censorship in Action*, Routledge and Kegan Paul, London, 1989

Silent Era

CHANNAN, MICHAEL, *The Dream that Kick: The Prehistory and Early Years of Cinema in Britain*, London, Routledge and Kegan Paul, 1980

LOW, RACHAEL and MANVELL, ROGER, *The History of the British Film, 1896–1906*, Allen and Unwin, London, 1949

LOW, RACHAEL, *The History of the British Film, 1906–1914*, Allen and Unwin, London, 1949

LOW, RACHAEL, *The History of the British Film, 1914–1918*, Allen and Unwin, London, 1950

LOW, RACHAEL, *The History of the British Film, 1918–1929*, Allen and Unwin, London, 1971

1930s

KULIK, KAROL, *Alexander Korda – The Man Who Could Work Miracles*, W.H. Allen, London, 1975

LOW, RACHAEL, *Filmmaking in 1930s Britain*, Allen and Unwin, London, 1985

RICHARDS, JEFFREY, *The Age of the Dream Palace: Cinema and Society in Britain 1930–1939*, Routledge, London, 1984

RYALL, TOM, *Alfred Hitchcock and the British Cinema*, Croom Helm, London, 1986

1940s

MURPHY, ROBERT, *Realism and Tinsel*, Routledge and Kegan Paul, London, 1989

TAYLOR, PHILIP M., (ed.), *Britain and the Cinema in the Second World War*, Macmillan, London, 1988

WOOD, ALAN, *Mr Rank: A Study of J. Arthur Rank and British Films, 1906–1914*, Hodder and Stoughton, London, 1952

1950s

BARR, CHARLES, *Ealing Studios*, Cameron and Tayleur, London/David and Charles, Newton Abbott, 1977

DURGNAT, RAYMOND, *A Mirror for England*, Faber and Faber, London, 1970

HILL, JOHN, *Sex, Class and Realism*, BFI, London, 1986

P.E.P., *The British Film Industry*, P.E.P., London, 1952 (supplement 1958)

PIRIE, DAVID, *A Heritage of Horror*, Gordon Fraser, London, 1973

1960s

WALKER, ALEXANDER, *Hollywood, England: The British Film Industry in the Sixties*, Harrap, London, 1974

1970s

WALKER, ALEXANDER, *National Heroes: British Cinema in the Seventies and Eighties*, Harrap, London, 1985

1980s

EBERTS, JAKE and ILOTT, TERRY, *My Indecision is Final*, Faber and Faber, London, 1990

PARK, JAMES, *Learning to Dream*, Faber and Faber, London, 1984

Autobiographies

ACKLAND, RODNEY and GRANT, ELSPETH, *The Celluloid Mistress*, Allen Wingate, London, 1954

BALCON, MICHAEL, *Michael Balcon Presents . . . A Lifetime in Films*, Hutchinson, London, 1969

BRUNEL, ADRIAN, *Nice Work, 1906–1914*, Forbes Robertson, London, 1949

DEAN, BASIL, *Mind's Eye*, Hutchinson, London, 1973

HEPWORTH, CECIL, *Came the Dawn, 1906–1914*, Phoenix House, London, 1951

PEARSON, GEORGE, *Flashback*, Allen and Unwin, London, 1957

POWELL, MICHAEL, *A Lifetime in Films*, Hutchinson, London, 1969

Bibliographies

ARMES, ROY, *A Critical History of British Cinema*, Secker and Warbug, London, 1978

CURRAN, JAMES and PORTER, VINCENT, (eds), *British Cinema History*, Weidenfeld and Nicolson, 1983

Index

ABPC 16, 66, 82, 89, 99, 113, 116, 127
Absolute Beginners 151, 152, 155, 163
Accident 12, 118
Acheson, Dean 91
Ackland, Rodney 47
Acorn Films 146
Agatha 142
Airship Destroyer, The 22
Akenfield 132
Alfie 118
Alliance 26–27
Allied Filmmakers (AFM) 15, 116
Ambler, Eric 76
American companies, links to UK 49,
    50, 135
American domination 26, 40, 91, 115,
    116–7, 121, 124
American stars, importation of, 34–5
And Soon the Darkness 127
Anderson, Lindsay 106, 108, 111, 118,
    143, 169
Angel 144, 150, 159, 161
Anglo-Amalgamated 85, 129, 111, 127
Annakin, Ken 99
Another Country 150, 165
Another Time, Another Place 12, 144
Apted, Michael 142, 143
Archers, The 70–1, 77
Archibald, George 89
Armchair Theatre 104
Asher, Irving 58
Asquith, Anthony 38, 43, 60
Assassination of Trotsky 135
Associated Communications
    Corporation 135–6, 148
Associated Film Distributors (AFD)
    136, 138
Associated Rediffusion 116
Associated Talking Pictures (ATP) 46,
    47, 49
Association of Cinematograph and
    Allied Technicians (ACTT) 128, 132
Association of Independent Producers
    132, 133, 138, 155
Attenborough, Richard 115
Auteur theory, deficiencies of 12–14

Bad Blood 175
Bad Lord Byron 81
Bad Timing 138
Balcon, Michael 34–5, 36, 44, 50, 58,
    59, 61, 62, 67, 69, 76, 78, 97, 104,
    115–6, 129, 159, 168, 172
Baldwin, Stanley 38–40
Balfour, Betty 33
Ball, Sir Joseph 69
Bank Holiday 64
Barker, William George 24
Battle of Britain, The 126
Battle of the River Plate, The 94

Baxter, John 90
Bed Sitting Room, The 121
Beddington, Jack 69
Behind the Mask 96
Belles of Saint Trinians, The 103
Bernstein, Sidney 62
Bertolucci, Bernardo 142
Bevan, Tim 155
BFI Production Board 129, 143
Big Swallow, The 19
Bill Douglas Trilogy 129
Billion Dollar Brain 124
Billy Liar 117
Biro, Lajos 57
Black Narcissus 73
Black November 8, 38
Black, Ted 81
Blackmail 47, 49
Blade Runner 159
Bleak Moments 129
Blue Lamp, The 81, 82, 104
Bolt, Robert 167
'Bond' films 117, 118, 13
Bonnie Prince Charlie 85
Boorman, John 117, 124, 172
Boultings, John and Roy 91, 92, 103
Box, Betty 134
Box, Muriel 76, 81, 86
Box, Sydney 89, 115
Boycott, American 86
Boyd, Don 140
Boyle, Kerry 165
Brandy for the Parson 91
Brave Don't Cry, The 90
Brent Walker 155
Bridge on the River Kwai, The 88
Brief Ecstasy 62
Brief Encounter 12, 75, 77, 150, 173
Brighton Rock 82
Britannia Hospital 108
British and Colonial 22, 23, 143
British and Dominions 49, 58
British Board of Film Censors (BBFC)
    61, 67, 104, 106
British Film Authority 132
British Film Weeks 34
British Instructional Pictures 38
British International Pictures (BIP) 41,
    47, 172
British Lion 85, 87, 90, 115, 135, 148
British National 75
British National Film League 34
British Screen Club 34
Broccoli, Albert 90
Bronco Bullfrog 128
Brook, Peter 113
Brothers in Law 103
Brownlow, Kevin 129, 132
Brunel, Adrian 28, 35, 36, 42, 43
Bryanston 116

Budgets, excessive 55, 85, 126, 162–7
Bugsy Malone 140
Burridge, Richard 163, 165
Business as Usual 155
Butterfly, The 23

Caesar and Cleopatra 85
Cage of Gold 78
Caine, Hall 24
Caine, Michael 118
Cal 150
Calling Bulldog Drummond 92
Calvert, Phyllis 72
Cammell, Donald 124
Can't Stop the Music 138
Cannes Film Festival 134, 138
Canterbury Tale, A 70, 73
Carlton-Browne of the F. O. 103
Carreras, James 111
Carry On Sergeant 103
'Carry On' series 129, 142
Casablanca Filmworks 142
Casandra Crossing, The 136
Catch Us If You Can 118, 124
Catherine the Great 55
Caton-Jones, Michael 140
Cavalcanti, Alberto 70
CEA 132
Censorship 61–2, 104
Central TV 146
Channel 4 143, 146, 151, 155, 158
Charge of the Light Brigade, The 121,
    126
Chariots of Fire 8, 144, 148, 150, 169
Charlie Bubbles 121, 159
Charter Productions 89
Chase films 20, 24
Chicago Joe and the Showgirl 157
Christopher Columbus 86
Cineguild 77
Cinema admissions 66, 75, 87
Cinematograph Act (1927) *see* Quota
Cinematograph Exhibitors Association
    (CEA) 104
Cinematograph Films Council (CFC)
    76, 77
Citadel, The 59, 64
Clair, René 55
Clarendon 22
Clark, Kenneth 69
Clark, Robert 89
Clarke, Alan 142, 160, 174
Clarke T. E. B. 82, 96
Clayton, Jack 106, 126
Clockwork Orange, A 128
Close Up (magazine) 37
Cohen, Nat 127
Cole, George 103
Columbia Pictures 59, 158
Comfort and Joy 148

Comin' Thro' the Rye 30, 34, 99
Company of Wolves 150
Comrades 158
Confidence, lack of 23
Conflict of Wings 90
Corelli, Marie 24, 27
Cosh Boy 94
Courtauld, Stephen 58
Courtenay, Tom 108
Courtneidge, Cicely 44, 52
Coward, Noël 12, 35, 159
Craven, Richard 132, 133
Crichton, Charles 97
Cricks and Martin 22
Criminal, The 111
Cronin, A. J. 59
Cultural amnesia 169
Curse of Frankenstein 92
Cutts, Graham 34, 35

Dam Busters, The 94
Damned, The 111
Dance with a Stranger 159–61, 167, 174–84
Danischewsky, Monja 70, 78
Darling 118
Dartnall, Gary 152, 154
Davies, Terence 158
Davis, John 89, 91, 113, 116, 118
Dead of Night 73
Dean, Basil 46, 47, 58
Dearden, Basil 47, 99, 115
Deeley, Michael 135, 136
Defence of the Realm 146
Delaney, Shelagh 121, 159–61, 174–84
Delfont, Bernard 136
Desert Victory 69
Devils, The 113, 124, 129
Dickinson, Thorold 47, 61, 77, 97
Distant Voices, Still Lives 158
Dixon of Dock Green (TV series) 104
Doctor in the House 103
'Doctor' films 142
Documentary movement 60, 69, 70
Don't Look Now 113, 135
Donat, Robert 52, 57, 59
Douglas, Bill 129, 132, 143, 158
Dr No 115, 117
Draughtsman's Contract, The 12, 144
Dream Demon 151
Dreamchild 150
Duellists, The 140
Dunkirk 94
Durgnat, Raymond 91

Eady Levy 90, 133, 134
Eagle Lion Films 76
Eagle's Wing 138
Ealing Studios 35, 67, 69, 76, 79, 81, 85, 88, 94, 96, 99
Eberts, Jake 148, 151, 152, 165
Edge of the World 42
Edison 18, 22
Elvey, Maurice 25
Emerald Forest, The 152
EMI 127, 129, 135–6, 138, 148
Entertainer, The 113
Escapade 94
Escape 47
Escape to Athena 136
Eureka 142
European cooperation 37, 135
Evergreen 44

Experience Preferred, but Not Essential 148
Experimental Film Fund 129
Exports to US 28, 49, 58, 75–6, 146

Fallen Idol, The 12, 85, 88
Family Life 129
Famous Player–Lasky 26, 27
Father Brown 88
Federation of British Industries (FBI) 38, 133
Fields, Gracie 44, 47
Film Industry Defence Organisation (FIDO) 104
Film Society, The 36
Finance, shortage of 19, 41, 168
Fire 20
Fires were Started 69
First a Girl 44
First Love films 150, 152
First of the Few, The 67
Fish Called Wanda, A 12
Fitzgerald, Scott 59
Flames of Passion, The 34
For Queen and Country 157
Forbes, Bryan 115, 127
Ford, John 96
Foreman Went to France, The 68
Foreman, Carl 132
Forever England 52
Formby, George 46, 47, 58, 68, 103
Forsyth, Bill 140, 143, 148, 157
49th Parallel 67, 75
Four Feathers, The 55
Four Just Men, The 64
Fox Farm 30
Foxes 142
Frears, Stephen 128, 129, 142, 158
Free Cinema 106, 115, 117
French Dressing 124
Frenzy 128
Friday the Thirteenth 44
Frieda 78
From Russia With Love 117
Front Page Story 96

Gainsborough 35. 41. 59, 72, 78–81, 85, 86
Gandhi 146, 148
Gater Committee on Film Production Costs 86
Gaumont-British 35, 41, 44, 50, 58, 75, 159, 172
General Film Distributors 75
Genevieve 99, 175
Gentle Sex, The 71
Get Carter 127
Ghia, Fernando 166
Ghost Goes West, The 55
Gideon's Day 96
Gilbert, Brian 140, 158
Gilliatt, Sidney 46, 59, 81
Girl Must Live, A 60
Giudice, Filippo del 77, 89
Gladstone, David 134
Gladwell, Michael 143
Gold, Jack 129
Goldcrest Films 8, 10, 16, 17, 148, 150, 151, 158, 159–67, 168
Goldfinger 117
Goldwyn, Samuel 22
Gone to Earth 88

Good Companions, The 44
Good Time Girl 81
Goodbye Mr Chips 59, 60
Goodbye Mr Chips (remake) 126
Goose Steps Out, The 68
Gothic 155
Government intervention, call for 133
GPO Film Unit 69, 70
Grade, Lew 135, 138
Granger, Stewart 72
Great Expectations 75
Great Rock 'n' Roll Swindle 143
Green Man, The 103
Greenaway, Peter 143, 144
Greene, Graham 12, 50, 57, 60, 61, 62, 89, 91, 150
Gregory's Girl 143
Grierson, John 60, 69, 90
Group 3 90–1
Guest, Val 46
Gumshoe 128

Hagen, Julius 42
Haggar, William 20, 23
Hamer, Robert 66, 88–9, 97
Hammer Films 92, 111, 113, 126
HandMade Films 144, 151, 155
Happy Breed, This 75
Hard Day's Night, A 117
Hardy, Robin 128
Harrison, George 144
Hassan, Mamoun 129, 133, 143
Hatter's Castle 72
Hawkins, Jack 96
Hay, Will 58, 68
Hecht, Ben 59
Henry VIII 24
Hepworth, Cecil 18, 20, 22, 25, 26, 28, 30, 33
High Spirits 151, 157
Hitchcock, Alfred 12, 17, 27, 35–6, 37, 42–3, 52, 55, 59, 60
Hobson, Valerie 57
Hodges, Mike 127
Holcroft Covenant 148
Holiday Camp 81
Holt, Seth 111
Home Box Office 146
Honky Tonk Freeway 138
Houston, Penelope 124
How to Get Ahead in Advertising 157
Howard, Leslie 28
Hudson, Hugh 140, 152, 155, 161–3, 166
Hue and Cry 82
Hulbert, Jack 44
Hussy 142

I Know Where I'm Going 73
I'm All Right Jack 103
Ice Cold In Alex 94
Ideal 26, 41
Ideal Husband, An 85
If... 118
Ill Met by Moonlight 88
In Which We Serve 71, 75, 77
Independent Producers 77–8, 85, 87
Inferiority, British filmmakers' sense of 15–16, 37, 60, 169
Initial Pictures 155
Insignificance 134
Intervention, government 25
Isadora 121

Isherwood, Christopher 46
It Always Rains on Sunday 78
It's Love Again 44

Jamaica Inn 60, 72
Jarman, Derek 129, 142
Jennings, Humphrey 70, 71, 108
Jew Süss 50
Joffé, Roland 140, 152, 166, 167
Jones, Griff Rhys 150
Jordan, Neil 144, 150–1, 158, 159
Jubilee 129
Judgement Deferred 91
Jupp, Ralph Tennyson 23

Kes 124
Kid for Two Farthings, A 88
Kidnappers, The 96
Killing Fields, The 150, 167, 169
Kind Hearts and Coronets 76, 88, 97, 108
Kind of Loving, A 108
Kinemacolor 22
King Solomon's Mines 52
Kingsley, David 115
Kitchen Toto, The 155
Knight Without Armour 55
Korda, Alexander 8, 42, 50, 55, 57, 67, 82, 85, 87, 105, 135, 169
Kureishi, Hanif 169

Lady Audley's Secret 27
Lady Caroline Lamb 135
Lady Hamilton 68
Lady Vanishes, The 59, 60, 64
Lady Vanishes, The (remake) 129
Ladykillers, The 99
Lambert, Gavin 94
Lambert, Verity 148, 154
Laughton, Charles 50
Launder and Gilliatt 99
Launder, Frank 46, 81
Lavender Hill Mob, The 82
Lawrence of Arabia 88, 115, 166
Leacock, Philip 94–6
League of Gentlemen, The 92
Lean, David 12, 66, 73, 77, 88, 92, 150
Lee, James 151, 152, 161, 162, 166
Legislation, calls for 38
Leigh, Vivien 57, 69, 85, 97
Lejeune, C. A. 57
Lester, Richard 116, 121
Let George Do It 68
Lieberson, Sandy 152, 155, 161, 162
Life and Death of Colonel Blimp, The 68, 77, 85
Life of Charles Peace 20
Lion Has Wings, The 67
Listen to Britain 71
Literary adaptation 24–5
Little People, The 33
Lloyd Committee 129
Loach, Ken 124, 129
Local Hero 148, 169
Lockwood, Margaret 64, 72
Lodger, The 35–6
Loew, Marcus 34
London Film Company 23, 172
London Film School 140
London Films 17, 57, 82–3, 91, 168
Loneliness of the Long Distance Runner 108, 117
Look Back in Anger 106
Losey, Joseph 111, 118, 127

Love on the Dole 62, 67
Low, Rachael 24
Lucky Jim 97, 103
Lumière Brothers 18
LWT 132
Lyne, Adrian 140

Macdonald, David 42
Mackendrick, Alexander 66, 88–9, 97–8, 116, 169
MacKenzie, John 143
Macpherson, Don 163
Madeleine 75
Maggie, The 97
Mahler 128, 140
Major Barbara 85
Man in Grey, The 72
Man in the White Suit, The 97
Man is News, This 42
Man of Two Worlds 77
Man Who Could Work Miracles 55
Man Who Fell to Earth, The 135
Man Who Knew Too Much, The 36, 52
Man Without Desire, The 28
Man's Fate 126
Mandy 97
Mankiewicz, Herman 59
Manvell, Roger 71
Market, small size 27, 40
Marks, Leo 113
Marshall, Alan 165
Mary Jane's Mishap 19
Mason, James 72
Matthews, Jessie 44
Maxwell, John 41, 42, 47, 50, 58
Mayer, Louis B. 16, 59
Me and Marlborough 52
Meet Mr Lucifer 104
Méliès, Georges 22, 23
Melody 140, 150
Memoirs of a Survivor 143
Memphis Belle 157
Menzel, Jiri 140
MGM 58, 59, 82, 90, 99, 126, 142
Millions Like Us 71
Minerva Films 28
Ministry of Information (MOI) 67
Mission, The 152, 166–7
Modesty Blaise 118, 126
Monitor (TV series) 124
Monopolies Commission Report 115
Monopoly, growth of 75, 77, 113–5
Montagu, Ivor 36
Monty Python and the Holy Grail 129
Morons from Outer Space 148
Motion Picture Patents Company (MPPC) 22
Mouse on the Moon, The 121
Moving Picture Company 146
Moyne Committee 132
Mr Forbush and the Penguins 127
Murder 47
Murdoch, Rupert 157
Music Lovers, The 124
My Beautiful Laundrette 146, 155, 169
Mycroft, Walter 47

Nanny, The 111
National character 12, 14
National Film Finance Corporation (NNFC) 89–90. 133. 143. 155
National Film School (NFS) 129, 143

Nationalism 47, 61, 71, 138, 144, 168–9
Nationalization, call for 132
Nell Gwynn 50
Net, The 92
New Deal 132
New Media optimism 146
New World Studios 59
Newell, Guy 30
Newell, Mike 159–61, 174–84
Newman, Solly 49
Night Mail 60
Night Must Fall 113
Night Train to Munich 68
Nighthawks 128
Nine Men 70
No Surrender 144
Non-commercial approach 30–33, 168
North Sea 69
Novello, Ivor 35
Number 17 43

O'Brien, Denis 144
O'Connor, Pat 158
O.H.M.S. 52
Odd Man Out 77
Odette 94
Oliver Twist 75
Olivier, Laurence 57, 69, 113
On Golden Pond 138
On the Night of the Fire 62
One of Our Aircraft is Missing 71
Orion 136, 165
Ornstein, George 117
Osborne, John 113
Ostrer Brothers 47, 52
Ostrer, Isidore 41, 58
Ostrer, Maurice 41, 72
Our Little Errand Boy 20
Overproduction 58

Pacino, Al 162
Palace Pictures 150, 163
Palache Report 76
Paperhouse 157
Paramount 49, 126
Paris by Night 157
Parker, Alan 134, 140, 143
Parretti, Giancarlo 155
Pascal, Gabriel 85
Passionate Friends, The 75
Passionate Summer 96
Passport to Pimlico 82
Pathé, Charles 23
Pathé-Frères 19, 22–3
Paul, Robert William 18, 19, 23
Pearson Longman 148, 158
Pearson, George 30–31, 42
Peck, Ron 128
Peeping Tom 111
Perfect Strangers 57, 82
Performance 124
Perils of Modern Motoring, The 20
Perry, Simon 132, 154
Personal Services 155
Pertwee, Michael 46
Petit, Chris 143
Phantom of the Opera 38
Piccadilly 42
Pimpernel Smith 68
Pinches, George 138
Pink String and Sealing Wax 73
Pinter, Harold 12

INDEX

Plaschkes, Otto 10
Platt-Mills, Barney 128
Pleasure Garden, The 37
Ploughman's Lunch, The 144, 148
Powell and Pressburger 88–9
Powell, Dilys 43, 46, 60, 69, 71, 72
Powell, Michael 12, 17, 42, 70–1, 73, 77, 85, 89, 111
Pressburger, Emeric 12, 70–1, 73
Priestley, J. B. 44, 61
Private Enterprise 129
Private Function, A 152
Private Life of Henry VIII 50, 52, 169
Privilege 124
Provincial Cinematograph Theatres 23
Prudential Assurance Company 57
Psycho 111
Puttnam, David 8, 11, 111, 144, 150, 158, 159, 166, 168
Pygmalion 85

Q Planes 59
Quatermass films 92, 104
Quota 16, 40, 41, 49, 58, 117
Quota Quickies 41–3, 58

Rachel Papers, The 155
Rachel's Sin 23
Radford, Michael 143, 157, 160, 174
Radio On 143
Radlyffe, Sarah 155
Railway Children, The 127
Raise the Titanic! 138
Randall-Cutler, Roger 159–61, 174–84
Rank Organization 16, 75–8, 96, 104–5, 113, 129, 136, 138, 168
Rank, J. Arthur 75, 81, 82, 85, 86–7, 89, 97
Rat, The 35
Reach for the Sky 94
Rebecca 59
Red Shoes, The 12, 73, 77, 86, 138
Redgrave, Michael 66
Reed, Carol 12, 47, 66, 88–9, 91, 150
Reeves, Michael 113
Reiss, John 10
Reisz, Karel 106, 113, 117, 126, 127, 134
Relph, Michael 97, 115
Rembrandt 55, 57
Rescued by Rover 20
Reservist Before the War and After the War, A 20
Restrictive practices, American 28
Return of the Pink Panther, The 136
Reveille 33
Revolution 152, 161–3
Rich and Strange 47
Richard III (1911) 24
Richard III (1955) 105
Richard, Cliff 116
Richardson, Tony 106, 113, 116, 127
RKO 49, 90
Robinson, Bruce 169
Roeg, Nic 113, 124, 127, 134, 142
Rome Express 46, 50
Romulus Productions 89, 106
Rookery Nook 44
Room at the Top 106
Rose, David 150
Rose, William 99
Rosso, Franco 143
Rotha, Paul 34, 43

Russell, Ken 113, 117, 124, 127, 129

Sailors Three 68
Sammy and Rosie Get Laid 169
Sammy Going South 116
Samuelson, G. B. 26, 28, 33
San Demetrio London 70
Sanders of the River 55
Sapphire 104
Saraband for Dead Lovers 73
Saturday Night and Sunday Morning 108, 113
Savage Messiah, The 128
Saville, Victor 34, 59, 61
Scandal 151, 157
Schach, Max 57
Schlesinger, John 117, 126, 134
School for Scoundrels 88
Scott, Ridley 129, 140, 143, 159
Screenwriting 25, 46, 47, 52, 57, 171–3
Script factories, proposal for 172–3
Scum 129
Seance on a Wet Afternoon 116
Sebastiane 129
Secret People 97
Sellers, Peter 103
Selznick, David O. 59, 91
Selznick, Lewis 23
Servant, The 111, 118
Service for Ladies 42
Seven Arts 116
Seven Days to Noon 91–2
Shag 151
Shanghai Surprise 152
Shaw, George Bernard 61, 85
Shearer, Moira 73
Ship that Died of Shame, The 92
Ships with Wings 69
Shipyard 60
Shooting Stars 38
Showtime 146
Sid and Nancy 155
Siesta 151
Silver Dream Racer 138
Simon and Laura 104
Sing as we Go 44
Sink the Bismark 94
Sixty Glorious Years 50
Sky TV 157
Sleeping Tiger, The 111
Small Back Room, The 88
Smallest Show on Earth, The 99
Smith, G. A. 22, 23
Smith, Mel 150
Smith, Peter 129, 132
Soldier's Return, The 20
Somlo, Joseph 89
Sophie's Choice 138
Sound Barrier, The 92
Sound, arrival of 43
Southern TV 132
Spanish Gardener, The 12, 96
Spiegel, Sam 90
Spikings, Barry 135, 138, 143
Splinters 43
Spy in Black, The 59
Squibs Wins the Calcutta Sweep 33
St John, Earl 89
Stardust 140
Stars Look Down, The 64
Stevenson, Robert 59
Stoll 26–27, 28
Studios, Cricklewood 27

Studios, Denham 55, 57, 75, 87
Studios, Pinewood 75, 89
Studios, Shepperton 82
Studios, Twickenham 42
Summer Holiday 116
Summers, Sue 8
Sweet William 142
Szabo, Istvan 140

Target for Tonight 69, 75
Taste of Fear 111
Taste of Honey, A 159
Tawny Pipit 78
Tax breaks 146, 157
Television 104–5, 108, 128, 132, 143, 170
Tempest, The 142
Temple, Julien 143, 155, 163–6
Temptation Harbour 82
Thames TV 132
That Sinking Feeling 143
That'll be the Day 140
The Go-Between 127
Theatre, dominance of 47
There Ain't No Justice 64
They Drive by Night 62
They Flew Alone 72
They Met in the Dark 72
Things to Come 55
Third Man, The 91, 150, 173
39 Steps, The 12, 52
Thirty-Nine Steps, The (remake) 129
This Happy Breed 77
This Sporting Life 108, 138
Thomas, Jeremy 142
Thorn EMI Screen Entertainment (TESE) 8, 10, 16, 148, 150, 152, 154, 155
Tigon 113
Time Bandits 144
Titfield Thunderbolt, The 96
To Paris with Love 88
Tom Jones 117, 118
Too Many Crooks 103
Top Secret 103
Train of Events 82
Trevelyan, John 106
Trouble in Store 103
Tunnel, The 50
Twentieth Century–Fox 49, 50, 59, 90, 126
29 Acacia Avenue 76
Two Cities 77
Two Little Waifs 20
Tyrrell, Lord 61

Ultus, the Man from the Dead 30
United Artists 76, 116–7, 126
United Media Finance 146
Universal 76, 126
Unsuitable Job for a Woman 143
Urban, Charles 22

Veidt, Conrad 50
Victim 104
Victoria the Great 50
Violent Playground 94
Virgin Vision 146, 155
Vortex, The 35
Vote for Huggett 81

Walkabout 128
Walker, Alexander 134
Wallace, Edgar 27

War Game, The 124
Warner Bros. 49, 58, 90
Warner, Jack 81
Watkins, Peter 124
Watt, Harry 69
Way to the Stars, The 66
Wells, H. G. 27, 55, 61
Welsh–Pearson 30, 33
Went the Day Well? 70
Wessex 77
When the Devil Drives 22
When We are Married 72
Whisky Galore 97
White Bird Passes, The 143
White Corridors 96
White Mischief 157
Whitebait, William 94
Whom the Gods Love 58
Wicked Lady, The 12, 72, 73, 81

Wicker Man, The 128
Wicking, Chris 165
Wilcox, Herbet, 34–5, 40, 43, 50, 58, 72
Wild Geese II 148
Williamson, James 18, 19, 20, 23
Wilson, Harold 132
Winkler, Irwin 162
Winnington, Richard 86
Winslow Boy, The 85
Winstanley 129
Wisdom, Norman 103
Witchfinder General, The 113
Withnail & I 155
Woman Tempted, The 41
Woman to Woman 34
Women in Love 124
Wooden Horse, The 94
Woodfall 113

Woolf, C. M. 36
Woolley, Stephen 165
Words for Battle 71
Working Title 155
World Apart, A 155
World War One 26
World War Two 66–73, 135

X the Unknown 92

Yank at Oxford, A 59
Yates, Peter 126
Young Mr Pitt, The 69
Young Ones, The 116
Young Winston 128
Yule, Lady 75

Zenith Productions 146
Zinneman 126
Zukor, Adoph 24